THE COUNTRY LAWYER

THE COUNTRY LAWYER

Essays in Democracy

By

F. Lyman Windolph

Foreword by

Owen J. Roberts

UNIVERSITY OF PENNSYLVANIA PRESS

Philadelphia

1938

Second Printing, March 1939

Manufactured in the United States of America by the Lancaster Press, Inc., Lancaster, Pa.

London
Humphrey Milford
Oxford University Press

For permission to reprint certain chapters in this volume acknowledgment is made to *The Atlantic Monthly; The Forum; The Annals of the American Academy of Political and Social Science;* and *The Review.*

FOREWORD

EACH of the following essays, irrespective of its setting as one of the series, is of intrinsic interest. Those which describe the country lawyer's experiences are marked by ease and naturalness; those which present the author's views on legal and political questions are clear in method and forceful in statement; the remaining three have all the literary grace of the occasional essay at its best.

The collection is appropriately entitled *The Country Lawyer*. Its perusal well may engender in the metropolitan lawyer a sense of values lost by immersion in the more intense and narrowing activities of a city practice. If demonstration were needed that the country lawyer's way of life is the good way, here is the proof. The essays progressively present different aspects of this way of life, and form a satisfying and convincing composite picture.

The country lawyer's intimate contacts with all sorts and conditions of men in the vicissitudes of life, great and small, afford him a knowledge of human nature, ordinarily denied to his professional brother of the metropolis; and the close relation he maintains with all the human instruments of justice—fellow lawyers, judges, and jurors—is alien to the practice in a great city.

These form the raw material from which the country lawyer constructs his philosophy of life. To them is added leisure for reflection and synthesis; leisure, also, for the amenities of culture. In the successive chapters the author gives us not only the raw material, but offers the fruits of his use of it in thoughtful and challenging conclusions on matters professional, political, personal, and literary.

Thus he illustrates and portrays in its fullness the good life of the country lawyer, as he has lived it. The book should persuade ambitious youth that the country lawyer's rôle holds out possibilities of a rich and useful and happy career. Moreover, there is implicit the truth, which it is to be hoped the author will some time elaborate, that the country lawyer enjoys an unrivaled opportunity for service, and not merely as guide, counselor, and friend to his neighbors individually, but also as a civic leader in bettering the social and political conditions in his own community.

OWEN J. ROBERTS

Kimberton, Pa.,
July 25, 1938

CONTENTS

I

THE COUNTRY LAWYER

I CAME to the bar more than twenty-five years ago in the small American city near which I was born and in which I was brought up and educated. It had then a population of less than fifty thousand, but it was the center of a rich agricultural county so bounded by hills and by a great river as to form a naturally distinct geographical and political unit. The county had been settled half a century before the Revolution, and had existed as a separate judicial district for almost a century. In its courts James Buchanan, Thaddeus Stevens, and a score of other great lawyers had practised, and at the time of my admission to practice there were members of its bar who not only remembered the giants of other days but who had shared in and were able to transmit a legal tradition which stretched unbroken to 1729. In this community I have passed the whole of my professional life. In the course of it I have perforce written deeds and wills, organized corporations and issued bonds, settled estates and searched titles, and tried every sort of civil action from replevin to divorce and every sort of criminal case from assault and battery to murder. I have, in short, for better or worse lived the life of what the profession knows as a country lawyer.

Now the true test of the country lawyer is not the size or importance of the community in which he does his work, but rather the sort of work which he does and the sort of people for whom he does it. Some years ago I met a member of the bar of New York who was employed by a society engaged solely in the apprehension and prosecution of men who had married and deserted Jewish women. From year's end to year's end he traveled from place to place trying desertion cases, and I venture to say that he knew more at first hand about the comparative law of desertion throughout the United

States than any authority living. Such a man is obviously not a country lawyer, no matter where he may practise. On the other hand I remember with pleasure a conversation which I had not long ago with an old man who had practised for almost half a century in a remote county, whose largest town has less than three thousand inhabitants. In the course of our conversation he referred to himself as a country lawyer, and a moment afterward, in making some reference to me, made it clear that he regarded me as exactly the opposite. I think, however, that he was mistaken. If a lawyer performs every sort of legal service for every sort of client—the poor and the lowly as well as the rich and the well born—he is, within my definition at least, a country lawyer, and no arbitrary distinction based on density of population or the like can make him anything else.

Every sort of legal service for every sort of client—the very phrase brings to my mind a succession of pictures, some of them amusing, some of them tinged with sadness and tragedy, and some of them altogether gracious and lovely. There are memories, such as must come to every lawyer, of the routine of consultations and settlements, of trials by jury and hearings before magistrates, of wills made *in extremis*, and secret sorrows and disgraces unknown to the world at large. There are likewise memories—no less clear, but less directly connected with the law—of long drives to sales, a legal brother beside me in a buggy hired at a livery stable, and of cheerful talk about men and books as our horse jogged through the quiet countryside; of the sales themselves, with half a township as witnesses if not as bidders, the voice of the auctioneer rising and falling, and his chosen clerk keeping a record of purchases and making change with miraculous efficiency;[1] of road views, where a

[1] At a sale of personal property in the country, the clerk will sometimes, between noon and sundown, record the sale of eight hundred items, posting his entries as he goes, and will collect the total of the successful bids in cash without a discrepancy of so much as a penny. This is, however, an exceptionally hard afternoon's work.

keg of beer was as essential a part of the proceedings as the presence of the viewers themselves; and of a score of other aspects and incidents of rural civilization, some of which have passed away never to return, during the term of my own practice.

Of these recollections there is none which gives me greater pleasure than that of the country surveyor at work. Ordinarily there is no reason why a lawyer should be present at the making of a survey, but on one or two occasions some real or anticipated dispute about the meaning or effect of a deed has made it desirable that I should actually see the lines run on the ground. Now all our land titles are founded upon grants from the original proprietor, and just as, in Eastern mythology, the world rests upon the back of an elephant which in turn stands upon a turtle, so the proprietor obtained his title from King Charles II. It is as much a piece of impertinence to ask the source of the King's title as to inquire what the turtle stands on. Of course not every piece of land may actually be traced to the original proprietor, on account of lost deeds or the like, but many of them may. I am familiar with one tract, oddly enough a small one, whose present description is precisely the same as that contained in the first grant.

The running of boundary lines necessarily depends upon the location of landmarks, and the true worth of a country surveyor depends much less upon his skill with a transit than upon the accuracy of his information—necessarily acquired either by personal experience or by tradition—as to where these landmarks are to be found. The deeds refer to them only in general terms—"beginning at a white oak, a corner of lands of John Doe," thence by a certain course so many perches to "a stone," thence to "an iron pin," or to "a black oak," and so on. With such a description, a city-bred surveyor, however expert he may be, is as helpless in the setting of a disputed fence as a lawyer. I have stood on a wooded hillside looking for a stone—such a stone as might seem to serve as a monument—but seeing only white oaks (disturbingly numerous) and feeling only a sense of the futility of learning. Confronted by such a problem, the country surveyor lays aside for a moment the calling in which he is perhaps compelled to earn the greater part of his livelihood, and, not without a proper consciousness of the burden of responsibility resting upon him, comes grandly into his own. The question involved is rather of fact than of law, and its solution depends upon knowledge possessed by him alone. Surely there is nothing finer than the air with which, ignoring suggestions, he strides—it would be a slander to say jumps—into a bramble bush and scratches out, not his eyes, but the very stone which was pointed out to him by his grandfather, also a surveyor, half a century before.

On the witness stand in a courtroom he is a far less satisfying figure than on his native hills, because, all things being equal, erudition is always less satisfying than knowledge. In the country his worth and skill are self-demonstrating—the event itself speaks. But before a judge and jury he must justify himself and his profession in words, and he feels that in order to do so he must be given an opportunity by the lawyer who calls him as a witness to explain the variations in the magnetic compass. This is a mysterious subject, whose relation to the actual practice of surveying may, for all I know, be slight or none, but every country surveyor expects to have his qualifications as an expert tested in court by being interrogated about it. The question is no sooner on the lips of counsel than the answer is ready. In the year 1700 the magnetic compass pointed five degrees to the west of the true geographical north. Between 1700 and 1800 it moved four degrees to the eastward and so on. I doubt whether any respectable number of jurors have been much enlightened by the recital, but a disappointed witness sometimes means in the end a disappointed client, and five minutes devoted to the eccentricities of the compass are not too big a price to pay in order to put a witness at his ease.

It has been said that the trial of cases is the culmination of the lawyer's art. In the matter of dramatic intensity and interest, murder cases, as much in the country as elsewhere, are in a class by themselves. It is true that before country judges the point at issue is, as a rule—whether wisely or not—tried much more strictly than in the big cities and that witnesses are more rarely permitted to unfold in their testimony the entire stories of their lives. In my own county I am satisfied that the trial of Thaw, for example, would not have lasted at the most more than three days. It is likewise true that juries in murder cases are secured much more rapidly in the country than in cities. The original theory of trial by jury was that an accused person ought to be tried by a jury selected from his vicinage or neighborhood, because the jurors, being his neighbors, would be likely on that account to know something about him at first hand. Some tradition of this theory has persisted in the country, so that an intimate and detailed examination of prospective jurors with a view to uncovering some possible bias is not ordinarily permitted. Indeed—and apart from any theory—it would be impossible in many rural jurisdictions to secure twelve citizens who, if the defendant was a native of their county, did not know him or at least know something about him.

But making due allowance for the incidental differences in practice which tend to make a murder trial in the country less sensational than elsewhere, the essentials of legal solemnity and human interest necessarily remain. In my state the formal arraignment of the accused has been abolished in all cases except trials for murder and there is a strangeness, as of another age, in hearing the clerk ask the prisoner how he will be tried and in hearing the prisoner, usually prompted by his counsel, reply, "By God and my country." Then, too, the selection of a jury, though never a question be asked by the attorneys on either side, presents to the prisoner and his counsel a series of decisions on which life and death literally depend, and each of which seems more momentous than the last until only the twelfth juror remains to be chosen. The prospective juryman, on his name being called, presents himself at the entrance to the jury box. The clerk, standing facing him, asks the three time-honored questions—whether he has such conscientious scruples as would prevent him from rendering a verdict of guilty of murder in the first degree, the penalty being death, if the evidence should warrant the same; [2] whether he has formed such an opinion as would prevent him from rendering a verdict in accordance with the evidence; and whether he can be perfectly impartial between the Commonwealth and the prisoner. If the answers of the juror do not disqualify him, the clerk then says, "Juror, look upon the prisoner. Prisoner, look upon the juror. How say you, challenged or not challenged?" If the prisoner's attorney knows his business and has had reasonably good luck, a few, though perhaps a very few, of his original twenty peremptory challenges remain. There is a tense moment during which he consults his jury list or engages in a whispered colloquy with his client. If the juror comes from the regular panel, counsel for the defense probably knows something about him, but if there has been a special venire, as usually happens before the twelfth juror has been selected in a murder case, there is nothing to do except to judge by appearances and be governed accordingly. Old practitioners will tell you that in such cases butchers, carpenters, and all those who habitually handle edged tools are to be avoided. However kindly they

[2] As the result of a comparatively recent statute, the jury, if it finds the defendant guilty of murder in the first degree, must determine whether the penalty shall be death or imprisonment for life, and the clerk now says, "the penalty for which may be death," instead of "the penalty being death."

may be personally, they will bring in verdicts of murder in the first degree more readily than other men. The juror looks about him, uncertain whether to walk into the jury box or to return to his seat. Though the other eleven jurors would vote to acquit, this man may persuade them to find a verdict of guilty. On the other hand, his voice alone may save the defendant. Everything seems to depend upon him. "Pass the juror," says counsel for the accused. The judge looks up quickly and clears his throat. There is a long sigh from the spectators. The trial is ready to begin.

If the trial of cases is, for those who participate in it, a universal experience wherever the jury system is in force, there are other activities of the country lawyer which have no parallel in the practice of his brothers in the large cities. There is, for instance, the work of conveyancing—an art which is inextricably connected in my mind with a local custom known as "the first of April rush." It is said that the date was determined in the first place by the fact that tobacco—which for time out of mind has been one of our principal crops—was invariably paid for in the spring; but be that as it may, the custom itself resulted from the existence of a state of society sufficiently simple to permit a farmer to transact the whole of his annual worldly business, other than farming, between the morning and evening of a single day. From one April to another he lived entirely upon credit, paying no bills and expecting none to be paid. On the first of every April, rain or shine, he went to the county seat, and having established himself at a hotel, called upon his banker and withdrew enough money to meet his needs. Sometimes, indeed, he withdrew his entire balance in order to assure himself that it had been safely kept, and, because of the crowd within, counted it sitting on the curb in front of the bank. When his financial arrangements had been completed, he set about meeting his debtors and creditors, seeking them at the offices of their lawyers and being sought by them at his lawyer's office, paying only in cash and receiving payment in like manner. When evening fell he was in the enviable condition of the Miller of the Dee—all his accounts were closed. He returned his funds to the bank, which had obligingly remained open to receive them, and went home for one year.

This is "the first of April rush," as it was when I came to the bar and as it had been for upward of a century before. It is not exactly so now—the use of checks is much greater than formerly and the crowds on the streets are smaller. Village banks and stores have taken over a considerable part of the business. There are fewer entire families in attendance and fewer hangers-on. To a large extent, however, the principle of an annual settlement day remains. It began with the farmer but it did not end there. In a city of sixty thousand inhabitants, nine leases out of every ten run from April to April. All mortgages, except by special agreement, are made payable on April first. Not only are the conveyances of all farms fixed for that day, but of a large proportion of properties in the city as well.

The result is bedlam indescribable. There are titles to search, leases, deeds, and mortgages to prepare and have executed, liens to be satisfied, and settlements to attend. Let no sophisticated metropolitan practitioner talk to me in this connection about the obligations of efficiency. Nothing is harder to change than a custom, and against this particular custom the veriest efficiency expert would break himself in vain. Of course, the requisite legal papers may be prepared in advance, but there is no way to compel a seller to sign and deliver a deed until the buyer is ready to pay over the purchase price, and no way to compel a buyer to pay the stipulated price until he is in funds and the seller is able to deliver possession. I have never been able to complete more than six or at the most eight settlements in a day, and yet on a certain twenty-fifth of March a number of years ago I was confronted with one hundred and eight settlements supposedly to be made on the first of April by myself and a single assistant. In such a situation there is nothing to do except to get to the office as early as one can in the morning, stay there as long as one can stay awake, and hope for the best. The great day will pass, what remains undone will be finished somehow in the days that follow, and peace will come with the spring.

And yet, when the tumult and the shouting have died and the buyers and sellers have departed, not all the incidents of the April season are vexing or unpleasant ones. I remember in particular an old man, a farmer, who for many years made me his annual visit on the first of April. He had a small amount of money invested in mortgages, and invariably there was some change in his investments about which he wished to consult me, or at least the necessity for a trip to the courthouse in order to enter a receipt for principal paid on account. On a certain first of April I saw him early in the morning, sitting as usual in the reception room of my office, but I knew of no business of his requiring my attention that year and I was too busy to speak to him at length. He waited patiently for me all morning, and though I have no doubt that he went for dinner during the noon hour, he must have returned to his place immediately afterward, because I noticed him there from time to time during the course of the afternoon. Evening had fallen and the crowds had melted away before I had an opportunity to invite him into my private office for an interview. When we had shaken hands and seated ourselves, I asked him to tell me what business had brought him to the city. I shall never know whether he had come to value our annual conferences for their own sake and was unwilling to admit even to himself that a time had come when there was a less valid reason for them than formerly, or whether in the simplicity of his heart he credited me with a greater store of wisdom than I possess, but he answered only that he was considering buying a new plough, and that he wanted to know what I thought about it.

Now I am unfortunately blessed with no knowledge whatever about farming, but we had, nevertheless, an unhurried talk for perhaps ten minutes about farming in general and ploughs in particular. In the end we decided to buy the plough. I went to the outer door with my friend and said good-bye to him there, intending to return to my desk. The stenographers had left for the day and the office was empty. Suddenly I realized that I was very tired and that it was time to stop work. I got my hat, locked the door, and walked out into the April twilight with wet eyes.

> Four ducks on a pond,
> A grass-bank beyond,
> A blue sky of spring,
> White clouds on the wing:
> What a little thing
> To remember for years—
> To remember with tears.

I will not say that one who is not touched and humbled by such an incident as this is a bad man, but I think that he will never be entirely happy or successful as a country lawyer. A measure of compensation for small fees and for the lack of great causes is to be found in that sense of legal totality which comes from a general practice. There is a picture—surely familiar to every lawyer who studied for his profession in the office of a preceptor—which shows the law as a gigantic tree, its roots buried in the common earth and its top reaching to the heavens. From its trunk grow the alternating branches of property and persons, of contracts and torts, of crimes, remedies, and government. The subject of equity is reduced to a small limb and bankruptcy to an even smaller one, while injunctions appear as a twig no thicker than the stem of a leaf.

I like to think that at one time or another I have perched on almost every limb of that tree.

But the chief compensation of the country lawyer is the richness of his share in the heritage which belongs of right to all the members of the three learned professions. Doubtless in the old sense there are no longer any learned professions. The architect, the engineer, the journalist, the scientist, and a hundred others have, indeed, fed as well upon learning as the physician, the lawyer, and the divine, but the old magic authority of learning—the old faith that education necessarily, or at least presumably, brings wisdom and goodness to its possessor—is as dead as that benefit of clergy which once served, with whatever injustice, to express it. And yet, because the great experiences of men are still births and deaths, their great concerns health, liberty, and happiness, and their great aim salvation, the three learned professions remain as obviously as ever in a place apart. After all, learning was never more than one of their incidental distinctions. Now as always their true distinction lies less in their achievements than in their purposes and in the resulting intimacy and beauty of those human relationships which occur so frequently in the life of the country lawyer. Whether or not his training has made him learned, his experience ought to make him wise and good.

It is not true that only God can make a tree. The Devil could make a tree if he tried, but only God can make men and women. With all of them we stand in jeopardy, and by some of them, it seems to me, He saves us every hour.

II
KING STREET

Ibam forte Via Sacra, sicut meus est mos,
Nescio quid meditans nugarum. . . .
Horace, *Sat.* I. 9.

KING STREET is the main street of the city in which I live. The city lies today, as when Kipling's Red Jacket visited it, in "a kindly, softly country there, back of Philadelphia"—so far back, indeed, that it has been from its foundation the center of an independent community and has recently celebrated the two-hundredth anniversary of its elevation to the dignity of a county seat. History will tell you that it was once the largest inland city in the United States, and that when the frightened Continental Congress fled westward after the battle of Brandywine it became for a few hours the capital of the United States, but these glories—if glories they were—have long since departed. Though every census has recorded its steady growth, it is a small city now.

Since I was born in the county over which it presides, I may call it my own city by an unimpeachable title which, however, suffers somewhat in dignity because of the fact that three of my four grandparents were born elsewhere. Anything less than title by birth is, as we reckon such matters, no title at all. Not long ago, in the heat of a political campaign, we were earnestly exhorted not to let "outsiders" tell us how to run our city, though of the two denizens—I will not be so unkind as to say aliens—thus held up to public suspicion one had lived among us for more than a quarter of a century and the other for at least half of that period.

So it comes about that my ancestral memories are perhaps less vivid and authentic than they would be if more of my progenitors had been to the manor born. I may not, for instance, speak of historical matters with the authority of my tobacconist, who conducts his business on the very site on which his great-great-great-grandfather established it in 1770. Though I attended the college that Benjamin Franklin helped to found, I can throw no light on the solution of the once mooted question whether he was personally present when the corner stone was laid. I remember the stagecoaches lumbering into King Street over the old stone bridge across the Conestoga River, but not the Conestoga wagons in the days of the Oregon Trail. I was born in the house once occupied by Baron Stiegel on the farms which he named Elizabeth, after his wife, but no echo comes to me of the salutes he caused to be fired from a neighboring hill (called Cannon Hill to this day) to welcome him home at the end of his journeys.

One of the Baron's neighbors, by the way, was a manufacturer of iron and a mighty hunter as well. One day, enraged at his failure in the chase and being deep in his cups, he drove his pack of foxhounds into the fire of one of his furnaces and burned them alive. The last to go through the door of the furnace was his favorite white bitch. She fawned upon him and cried piteously, begging to be spared, but he forced her remorselessly into the flames. Men say that on winter nights she still gives tongue, and that as often as she does so it is the doom of her cruel master to rise from his grave and follow her over the frozen hills of our northern townships. I too have heard strange sounds on winter nights, but I cannot certainly affirm that they came from the throat of the white bitch.

Let our legends be what they will. I am less concerned to recount hearsay than, like Mark Antony, "to speak what I do know." In order to do so I must confine myself to the last decade of the old century and the first of the new one —in which I grew up, went to school and college, and studied law—and to the years since then, in which I have been continuously engaged in the practice of my profession.

About three months after my graduation from college I began to study law, or, as our rules of court express it, to "serve a regular clerkship in the office of a practising attorney." It is almost impossible to assert that this is a bad way to study law, since, for want of a different one, it is the way in which all the lawyers of America received their legal education up to comparatively recent times. On the contrary, given the atmosphere of an old-fashioned law office, a preceptor with the time and ability to transmit to his student the fruits of his own experience, and a student not too easily discouraged by the absence of the stimulus that comes from competition and discussion with other students, I think it is an excellent way to study law. It has passed away utterly in the large cities and is passing away in my own city as well, because the circumstances which made it possible have in large measure ceased to exist. The fee to be paid by a student for his tuition was in my day, and still is, fixed by tradition at two hundred dollars, one half payable upon registration and the other half upon admission to the bar. As Thaddeus Stevens, whose office was popular with law students, is said to have remarked: "Some pay; some don't." I paid the whole of my fee a year or two after I had begun practice. No one ever asked me for the money.

A student in a law office has no rights that anyone is bound to respect. In times long past he was expected to sweep out the office and to attend to the stove in the winter, but I had no such tasks to perform. I searched titles, wrote deeds and mortgages, copied wills and other legal papers, and spent much time in court listening to the leaders of the bar of that day, the most famous of whom was an ex-attorney-general of Pennsylvania, whose former partner, then a member of the state Supreme Court, was afterwards its Chief Justice. In addition I learned to know a number of local characters directly or indirectly connected with the administration of justice.

There was a woman—for whom, as it now seems to me, something might have been done—who suffered from the delusion that she had a case which was just about to come up and who sat in court from the beginning to the end of every session waiting for her case to be called. There was a freckled colored man named Sam, a bootblack, who went the rounds of the law offices every morning, plying his trade and retailing the gossip of the day. There was an eccentric lawyer of morose appearance but consistently convivial habits, a strange mixture of Dr. Johnson and Boswell—given like the former to sudden and startling ejaculations, and like the latter to the making of minute written records of casual conversations. I once heard him begin an argument in the Orphans' Court about the distribution of the estate of a man named Grimes by remarking in a resonant voice, "If Your Honor please, old Grimes is dead." For all his eccentricities, he was a careful and competent lawyer, scrupulously exact in the transaction of his professional business, and as methodical in his personal habits as one of his predecessors at the bar—whom I never knew, but of whom I have often heard—who was accustomed to shave every other day, and who attended divine service only on those alternate Sundays when the calendar brought the rite of shaving into proper conjunction with the rites of the church.

The simplest and most rudimentary act of a lawyer is to hang up a sign and sit down to wait for his first client. Every lawyer who has done so—and who has exercised the self-denial, endured the disappointments and been rewarded by the satisfactions which ordinarily belong to that experience—will come to feel toward the practice which he afterwards acquires something of the sense of wonder with which Darius

Clayhanger in Arnold Bennett's massive novel of that name regarded the business of his printing establishment.

> Darius's pride in the achievement of his business was simply indescribable. . . . How had he done it? He did not know. Certainly he did not credit himself with brilliant faculties. He knew he was not brilliant; he knew that once or twice he had had luck. . . . To Darius there was no business quite like his own. He admitted that there were businesses much bigger but they lacked the miraculous quality that his own had. They were not sacred. His was, genuinely. Once, in his triumphant and vain early manhood he had had a fancy for bull-dogs; he had bred bull-dogs; and one day he had sacrificed that great delight at the call of his business; and now no one could guess that he knew the difference between a setter and a mastiff!

The Greeks said truly that you become a carpenter by doing carpenter's work. In like manner you become a trial lawyer by trying cases. It is almost in the spirit of Darius Clayhanger that I think of the trial of my first case before a court and jury.

The case arose from a dispute in connection with the sale of a crop of tobacco. The ostensible plaintiff was the owner of the farm on which the tobacco had been grown, but the real party in interest was his son, a young man of about my own age who had cared for the tobacco without help from anyone and whose entire compensation for a year's work on his father's farm was represented by the price which the tobacco would bring. A few days in advance of the trial I went over the case carefully with all of our witnesses. At the conclusion of my examination the father said, "You are a young man. Do you think you are fit to try this case alone?" I answered that I thought I was, and waited for what seemed to me the inevitable additional question as to how many other cases I had tried. He said nothing further, however, and we went to trial.

The contract between the seller and buyer had provided that the tobacco was to be of merchantable quality and the defense was that it did not conform to this description. I am inclined to think that the experienced and busy lawyer who represented the defendant had not prepared his case with very great care. At all events he put on the stand among other witnesses a tobacco buyer who had seen the tobacco on its way to delivery at the defendant's warehouse, and asked him what the quality of the tobacco was. "Well," answered the witness, "it was not the kind of tobacco I was buying." The presiding judge turned in his chair. "That is not the question," he said, "was it merchantable?" The witness hesitated. "Yes," he answered at length, "I think it was merchantable." If I had been more experienced I would have known that for all practical purposes the case was over at that point. I did not know it, but I had enough sense not to cross-examine the witness.

A day or two after the verdict had been rendered I chanced to meet one of the jurors, a retired blacksmith who had worked for many years in the blacksmith shop at the bridge across the Conestoga. I had known him all my life and as a matter of course we shook hands. I expected that he would congratulate me at once on the skill and address with which I had handled the tobacco case. Instead he talked for some minutes about indifferent matters. Finally he said, "That was a very easy case you had. Anybody could have won that case, and it did not take us long to decide it." Across the lapse of more than a quarter of a century I can see that he was quite right, but at the time it seemed to me that he was sadly lacking in appreciation. My client was more generous. On the day on which the verdict was paid I settled my accounts with him and received from him the fee to which I was entitled. "I was a little afraid about you at first," he said, "but you did all right." As soon as he had left me, I went into the tobacco shop on King Street and with a part of the fee bought a pipe on which I had had my eye for a long time. It is still the best pipe I have and I would not part with it for a good deal.

The *dramatis personae* of a small community are infinitely various. In addition, they acquire a semi-official standing and a local universality of influence which have no counterparts in a really large city, except perhaps in the lives of the notorious figures of its underworld. The reason lies in the very nature of provincial civilization. A lawyer or a musician living, for example, in London or New York may, if he chooses, so order his affairs as to spend all of his leisure hours in the company of those interested in the work in which he is engaged or engaged in similar work of their own, but the resident of a small city can of necessity make no such selection of his acquaintances. For better or worse, he must reckon with the whole of a small environment rather than with a selected portion of a large one. He must, in short, accept the common lot of social interdependence, and, as Mr. Chesterton has somewhere pointed out, live a broad life at the inevitable risk of living a shallow one.

Breadth and depth are, after all, relative terms. When used in a figurative sense they are inaccurate as well. Our most influential citizen during the early years of my practice was the minister of one of our local churches—a small, frail man without physical distinction of any sort—who was probably unheard of outside the limits of the city in which he lived and worked. I remember having heard my mother say that in her youth she thought him a little mad because of the perfect simplicity with which he bowed to everyone he met, whether he knew the person or not. He was not a modern man. I think he lived and died happy, but he would have been happier still if he had been born in the great days of the thirteenth century. He was the only person I have ever known who spoke naturally in the language of Saint Francis' "Canticle to the Sun."

The truth is that I did not really know him. I saw him hundreds of times, but I have no recollection of having ever addressed him except once, and then only by making a written inquiry as to a date shown in the baptismal records of his parish. He answered me in longhand by the next post, thanking me at the outset for my "good letter" and giving me the information requested. As a matter of fact, my letter was in no way different from any other formally worded inquiry. Doubtless he did not stop to reason about the matter, but I think nevertheless that he did not call it good merely as the result of a literary habit. It was a letter from a man, and therefore his instinct was to regard it as a good letter. At bottom he cared more about people than about ideas.

He cared more about charity than about efficiency. I am sure that he gave his support to all the organized efforts for social welfare that were made in his day—to the ministerial associations, the community-service associations, and the law-and-order societies. He would no more have thought of opposing the work of such organizations than of opposing the work of the fire department. It is better to damage property with water than to let fires burn, and it is better for society to put prostitutes in jail than to have them walking the streets. But in his heart he had no interest in abstract conceptions like society. He knew a good many prostitutes, although I am not sure that he realized the business in which they were engaged. If he had realized it, I do not know what he would have done. It might have been something as irrelevant as to stoop down and with his finger write on the ground.

If the members of provincial society are more dependent than others in their personal relationships, they are far more independent than others in their attitude toward the law and the problems with which the law is concerned. A whole chapter of legal history is suggested in the contrast. The times have passed when drunkenness was regarded as an aggravation of a crime committed, and when every citizen boasted of his right to bear arms. In these instances we have all turned about face—drunkenness, though we have sought by statute to prevent it altogether, may now be pleaded everywhere as a defense to crime, and the trend of modern legislation is to forbid the bearing of arms without a license from the police. There are, however, other connections in which the older tradition of independence and responsibility persists. A man may still lawfully strike in his own defense, eject trespassers from his real estate, retake his stolen goods, and abate nuisances, but it is only in the country that such rights amount to anything in practice—it is only in the country that one may still watch the erection of a "spite fence" or observe the discomfiture of a telephone company whose employees come to set a pole in a prepared hole and find the hole occupied by a heroic, sturdy old lady who refuses to budge.

The spite fence with which I am most familiar is not really a fence at all. It was constructed by a client of mine who had no actual spite in her heart, but who acted, as she thought, defensively; and it is in its way a masterpiece of ingenuity. The client in question, an unmarried woman of middle age, lived alone in a small house which had belonged to her parents and in which she had been brought up. She spent most of her leisure time in the kitchen, which opened to the south on a small and pleasant garden. When, in course of time, the property on the south changed hands and her new neighbor, who was a barber, began to construct a window looking directly into her garden and kitchen, she was outraged beyond measure. Her sense of outrage lay principally in a feeling that she was being imposed upon because she was a woman, and that if she had had "a man in the house" no one would have dared to disturb her privacy. I purposely said nothing to her about obstructing the window, telling her simply that her neighbor was entirely within his rights, that he probably felt a need for additional light and air, and that there was no reason to suppose that he wanted to spy upon her.

A week or two passed; the offending window was completed and proved unendurable. She arrived in her own mind at the idea of shutting it and called to her aid a sympathetic plumber, who was both an architect and an artificer. Together they sank in concrete two pipes, to the tops of which they screwed a steel plate exactly the size of the window. The window was on the property line and the plate shut it as effectively as a lid shuts a box.

Within a few days I received a call from the barber, who, as I suspect, had previously consulted his own attorney and had been advised that he was without a legal remedy. It was summer, and he complained that the steel plate cast heat into his house in such a way as to make life unendurable for himself and family. I explained to him that I regretted his inconvenience, but that there was nothing I could do to help him. At parting he said, "You tell that woman to take that plate down or I will paint my house red, white, and blue, in stripes." This threat was duly transmitted to his antagonist, but she remained inflexible. It was the barber's last move. He never carried out his patriotic idea about the painting. Years have passed and I do not know whether or not he has moved away. I do know, however, that the plate remains triumphantly in place.

Much has been written recently about life in villages and small cities in the United States, and the composite picture presented is, to say the least, an unpleasant one. I think it might well be argued that this picture is false. If a philosopher were to make a list of the things men in the abstract would say were best worth living for—friendship, leisure, beauty, quiet—it is certainly not in the big cities that he would find them. There is, moreover, a certain charm in small communities—in the definiteness and finality of their social categories, in the simplicity of their human relationships, most of all in the genuineness of the interest which their members feel toward one another—which springs perhaps from the qualities of those very defects which have been so much in the public eye. It has been said that there are two words for everything, the word that swells and the word that belittles. Perhaps the swelling words in this particular connection are those which have remained unwritten.

But I am not a philosopher, and I have no wish to do anything so dreary as to engage in a debate on the relative merits of rural and urban civilization. Still less do I wish to set up the proposition that life in small cities is stupid, narrow, and ugly, and then to rebut it, as one rebuts the proposition that all crows are black by producing one white crow. There are, God knows, enough evil things in every community, big or little, to give pause to the most ardent local patriot about to cast the first stone. I mean to do no more than to bear testimony to some of the characteristics of life in the small city with which I happen to be best acquainted. The testimony is true. I cannot speak for Main Street, but King Street is at all events a real street in a real city.

If you're off to Philadelphia this morning,
And wish to prove the truth of what I say,
I pledge my word you'll find the pleasant land behind
Unaltered since Red Jacket rode that way.
Still the pine woods scent the noon; still the catbird sings his tune;
Still autumn sets the maple forest blazing.
Still the grapevine through the dusk flings her soul-compelling musk;
Still the fire-flies in the corn make night amazing!
    They are there, there, there with Earth immortal,
    (Citizens, I give you friendly warning)
    The things that truly last when men and times have passed,
    They are all in Pennsylvania this morning.

III
COUNTRY JUSTICE

THERE is no need to quote authorities in order to convince the people of the United States that disregard of law constitutes one of the major problems with which the present generation is confronted, and that any intelligent inquiry as to how our laws may be better enforced necessarily involves a consideration of how the procedure of our criminal courts may be reformed.

That a reformation of this procedure is badly needed seems, indeed, to have been taken for granted by nearly everyone who has discussed the subject during the course of the last decade. The reforms suggested (or actually adopted in certain states) have been many and various. They include allowance of a conviction without proof of the defendant's guilt beyond a reasonable doubt, abolition of the rule forbidding comment on his failure to testify in his own behalf, a reduction in the number of the jury and abolition of the requirement of a unanimous verdict. Some of these innovations are comparatively unimportant, but in the aggregate they express a profound and growing distrust in trial by jury as a means of administering justice in criminal cases.

Now trial by jury is the most characteristic contribution which our race has made to the practical science of jurisprudence. On that account, if for no other reason, it ought not to be lightly discarded. It was in its origin essentially a rural instrumentality, and the interesting suggestion has been made on a number of occasions—notably by Dean Pound in the course of an address to the Judicial Section of the American Bar Association—that its present disrepute results very largely from the unsuccessful attempt to adapt it to the needs of an increasingly urban civilization. If this is so, it may be worth while to record the comments of a country lawyer on the trial procedure of courts in the large cities. Many of the matters usually included in the term "procedure" are so universal and rigid as to be incapable of being changed except by constitutional amendment. Others, however, are entirely local and flexible, and are governed by rules of court, which may be altered at pleasure, or merely by the customary practices of the courts in which they occur. If trial by jury works better today in the country than in the cities, perhaps it does so less in the nature of the case than because, for reasons not in themselves compelling, it is administered in the country more nearly than elsewhere in accordance with its own genius and traditions. Perhaps, in short, there has been too much adaptation instead of too little, and the trouble is not so much with the instrument as with the way in which the instrument has been used.

What most surprises a country lawyer about the trial of cases in large cities may be summed up in a single sentence. In most instances the practice followed seems extraordinarily wasteful of time. This comment is the more surprising because efficiency is on the whole preached with more fervor and practised with more consistency in the large cities than anywhere else. Indeed in every connection except the trial of cases the city lawyer sets a record of promptness which the country lawyer cannot hope to equal.

In the course of a general country practice I have been employed at various times to prepare mortgages intended to secure issues of corporate bonds. A mortgage of this sort is an elaborate legal document whose average length is perhaps thirty thousand words. If I were instructed tomorrow to prepare one, there would be descriptions to secure, forms to consult, and various alternate provisions, both as to the terms of the bonds and as to the remedies of the bondholders in case of default, to consider and pass upon. A large amount of typewriting would have to be done. After the copy had been given to the printer there would be proof to read and corrections to make. At the very least it would take me a week to have such a mortgage ready for execution, though there are law firms in New York which would undertake to do the same work in twenty-four hours. And yet a country judge and two country lawyers can dispose of a murder case in a number of days no greater than the number of weeks which would be required to dispose of it in any one of a dozen metropolitan jurisdictions.

I once made this point in the course of an after-dinner speech in the presence of one of the leading trial lawyers at the New York bar. In the course of his own speech, which followed mine, he said, "My friend doesn't know what practice in the country really is. He ought to move to [the middle-western state in which the speaker had begun his own practice]. *Out there they will try a case for four days for a fee of ten dollars.*" The remark struck me as significant because of its unconscious disregard of the point really involved. The speaker instinctively felt that it was a foolish thing to try a case for four days for a fee of ten dollars, though presumably not a foolish thing to try a case for forty days for a fee of, say, a thousand dollars a day. And yet it is to be observed that I had spoken—and that I am now writing—not about money but about time. Great gifts receive and deserve to receive a great reward. The testimony is unanimous, however, that four days is a long time in which to try a case in the country.

But indeed I do not mean to argue that the jury system is good because it is prompt, though promptness is conceded to be one of its outstanding merits even by those who are opposed to the system as a whole. I mean rather that where the jury system is not administered promptly it is not administered characteristically and therefore is not administered well. Moreover, I am not referring to delay in bringing cases to trial. The problem of the congested court calendar is one peculiar to the big cities, and much good work has been done in recent years in the effort to solve it. I am referring to delay occurring in the actual trial of cases and arising from causes which have no necessary connection with the differences between conditions in the country and in the cities.

Some of these causes were illustrated in the trial of George Remus for the murder of his wife, which took place in Cincinnati during the concluding months of the year 1927. The illustration is a good one because it would be difficult, if not impossible, to find a murder case in which the issues were less complicated. The killing was admitted and the only defense was insanity, the defendant contending that he had been insane at the time of the killing, but that he was sane at the time of the trial. Hypothetical questions were excluded, seemingly by agreement, and as I read the newspaper reports of the proceedings the testimony of all the alienists examined occupied only one day.

The defendant had killed his wife on October 6, 1927, and was called for trial on November 14 of the same year. (There can be no denial therefore that he was accorded a speedy trial. Not many rural jurisdictions can show an average record of greater promptness, and I doubt whether greater promptness is in general desirable.) On December 20 his case was submitted to the jury, which rendered a verdict of not guilty in nineteen minutes. Including the nineteen minutes, the trial occupied thirty actual days, the time not spent in court between the two dates named being represented by Sundays and one additional day on which the presiding judge (no doubt a loyal alumnus) went to see the Ohio State football team in action.

The first five of these thirty days were spent in selecting a jury. To a country lawyer this seems unreasonably long. Mr. Justice Riddell, Justice of Appeals of Ontario, Canada, in his interesting review of the Sacco-Vanzetti case, says that he never but once saw it take more than half an hour to obtain a jury in a murder case, and that on that one occasion it took forty-eight minutes. I am afraid that justice even in the rural parts of the United States is not quite so rapid as that of the Canadian variety, but it would be hard to convince an American country lawyer that there oan be any good reason for spending more than a day at the most in the selection of a jury in any sort of case.

It appears that in Ohio the prosecution has four peremptory challenges in a murder case and the defense sixteen, though in a number of other states, my own included, each side has twenty. On the other hand, the practice followed in Ohio necessitates the selection of thirteen jurors—the thirteenth sitting as an emergency juror but taking no part in the decision of the case unless one of the other twelve is disqualified. As a matter of fact, however, the length of time required to obtain a jury does not depend to any great extent upon rules such as these, but upon the number and nature of the questions which counsel are permitted to ask prospective jurors. In my own jurisdiction the clerk of the court asks each juror three general questions—whether he has conscientious scruples against capital punishment; whether he has formed an opinion; and whether he can be impartial. I have occasionally heard counsel ask questions of their own—usually as to a possible relationship or intimacy with the accused or with witnesses who were to be called. I have never heard an examination intended to find out a juror's state of mind, in the abstract, toward the antecedents of the defendant or toward such a defense as he was likely to interpose. Moreover, I do not know what is meant by seating jurors tentatively. When we seat them we do so for all purposes, and there is no opportunity to revise the decision arrived at.

In the Remus case the defendant—who had formerly been a member of the bar and who took an active part in his own defense—was permitted to ask prospective jurors whether they would be prejudiced against him because he had (1) served a term in the federal prison at Atlanta, (2) testified before the Wheeler senate investigating committee at Washington, (3) testified in the Warden Sartain case at Atlanta, and (4) been involved in the Jack Daniels distillery case in Indianapolis and St. Louis. A juror in answer to questions like these said, "I do not favor bootleggers." One of the defendant's attorneys thereupon said, "You still have that prejudice against bootleggers, haven't you, Miss Thompson?" and counsel on the other side objected—it appears not because of the scope of the examination but because, as he put it, "Every law-abiding person is supposed to be prejudiced against crime and criminals." A little later on the defendant, acting on his own behalf, asked a juror whether the fact that Mr. Taft, who was one of the counsel for the prosecution, was a son of the Chief Justice of the United States would prejudice the juror in the trial of the case. The juror answered "No" and, turning to Mr. Taft, remarked, "Kind of funny how that is, that examination." A country lawyer thinks it is kind of funny too, but five days of it is too much.

It is too much not because time is of more importance than justice but because, in addition to wasting time, it puts justice in jeopardy. If the questions propounded were not entirely without relevancy, it is fair to assume that those jurors who, like Miss Thompson, did not "favor bootleggers" proved objectionable to the defendant, and that their fellows who lacked that prejudice against crime which, in the philosophy of counsel for the prosecution, every law-abiding person is supposed to have, proved equally objectionable to the prosecution. Presumably, therefore, the ideal juror was someone without any views whatever about the enforcement of the Eighteenth Amendment. As most of us remember, such Americans were not easy to find during the period in which the Amendment was in force. I suggest, moreover, that when found they were not likely to prove desirable jurors. Trial by jury does not presuppose a tribunal composed of twelve persons altogether devoid of ideas or even of prejudices. It does presuppose a tribunal of sufficient intelligence and courage to arrive in spite of prejudice at a just determination of the issues submitted to it.

Both during and after the selection of the jury in the Remus case additional delay arose from extended legal arguments, during at least three of which the jurors were removed from the courtroom. On one of these occasions the defendant had asked a juror whether the fact that he had been disbarred as a practicing attorney in the State of Illinois because of his conviction for violating the Volstead Act would be likely to prejudice the juror against him. Counsel for the prosecution said that they objected to the question because they knew other reasons why the defendant had been disbarred, and the jurors were taken from the room while the court was told what the other reasons were. In the course of the altercation that followed, the defendant said to one of the opposing counsel, "Man, if I had you in the corridor I would wreck you physically." A colleague of the threatened attorney replied, "Get back on your own side of the railing or I will take a crack at you."

It would be hard to show that the jury missed anything in being denied this particular piece of repartee, but it nevertheless seems to a country lawyer that the objection of counsel might well have been ruled on promptly and in the presence of the jurors. Indeed the practice of removing the jury during the discussion of questions of law is, so far as I know, almost unknown in the country. When such a question has arisen in the course of a trial I have sometimes seen the trial judge engage in a whispered colloquy with counsel for both parties before making his ruling. Less frequently I have seen a judge send out for a law book or adjourn a few minutes in advance of the usual hour in order to consult the authorities. The same legal points must certainly come up in one jurisdiction as in another. Most of them may be disposed of in advance of the trial by judgments entered on demurrers or motions to quash the indictment, or after the trial as the result of motions in arrest of judgment or for a new trial. New trials are unquestionably an evil, but I doubt whether an analysis of the reports of the various appellate courts would show that more convictions are reversed in appeals from rural jurisdictions than in appeals from the trial courts of large cities. I doubt in short whether elaborate arguments are more effective than brief ones in reducing errors in the admission and rejection of evidence.

Here again the loss of time involved is to be regarded as symptomatic of an ailment rather than as the ailment itself. A trial by jury is a drama which ought to move with as few interruptions as possible to its appointed close. A jury is an entirely casual body, called together for a single purpose and dismissed as soon as that purpose has been accomplished. It passes chiefly upon human veracity, and it does so not by the application of technical rules but in the light of common sense. A just verdict depends much less upon the learning and ability of the jurors than upon their maintenance of a certain emotional detachment in which the contentions of both parties as presented in the testimony may be considered and compared. Other things being equal, the shortest trial is always the best.

Moreover, the removal of a jury from the courtroom for hours and indeed sometimes for days at a time makes a very bad impression on the jurors themselves. I once exchanged letters about the merits of the jury system with a civil engineer, seemingly a highly intelligent man, who lived in Los Angeles. He complained that he had belonged to a peripatetic jury which had been led in and out of court half a dozen times without having been permitted to find out what the case in which it was sitting was about. His point was not so much that this procedure wasted his time and that of his fellows while the lawyers argued questions which would probably be re-argued in any event, as that the law treated jurors as if they were only quasi-competent—that is, incompetent to hear the whole story whether of fact or law—and he resented what he thought was an unfair reflection on his intelligence.

I am not sure that his attitude in this respect was entirely justifiable, but it serves to demonstrate that if a jury is to do its work well there must be a limit to the number of confusing interruptions to which its members are subjected. There must likewise be a limit to the amount of eloquence to which they are subjected. In the Remus case this eloquence lasted for almost three days. Cases differ so greatly in complexity that it is hazardous to say how much time ought to have been allowed for summations in a given instance, but I believe most country lawyers would agree with the general statement that no case can be closed more effectively than in speeches limited to an hour for each side. If the facts of a particular case make an hour inadequate, the alternatives presented are to leave something unsaid or to submit to jaded jurors instead of to fresh ones the evidence upon which alone their verdict ought to depend. The risk of a miscarriage of justice involved in the adoption of the first of these alternatives seems to me in every way smaller than that involved in the adoption of the second. If this is heresy against the traditions of forensic eloquence, I shall have to take the consequences. I am persuaded, however, that it is not heresy but sound doctrine. When one considers that a lecturer speaking to those who have voluntarily come to listen to him can rarely hold the attention of his audience for more than an hour, it must be obvious that under ordinary circumstances a lawyer cannot expect to hold for a longer period what is, in a sense at least, the involuntary attention of a jury.

But it may be said with truth that if we deduct the time spent in the Remus trial in the selection of a jury and in the closing addresses of counsel, there remain upwards of twenty days which were occupied with the taking of testimony. I have not said that the Remus case was badly tried, but only that it illustrated some of the practices which make justice less rapid and, as I view the matter, less certain in the courts of big cities than elsewhere. Perhaps, indeed, within certain standards of trial procedure it was excellently tried, but I venture to think nevertheless that the examination of the witnesses would have been completed in the country in less than the time which was actually required. This is so because the standard of trial procedure to which the average country judge conforms requires him to rule out as irrelevant much evidence which the average metropolitan judge would admit without question.

In order to test these conclusions it is not without interest to compare the Remus trial with the so-called "witchcraft cases" which were tried a little more than a year afterwards in the small city of York, Pennsylvania. The murdered man was one Nelson Rehmeyer, who lived alone in the country about fifteen miles from York. He was what is known as a "powwow doctor" and possessed among other treasures a book called *The Long Lost Friend*, which is a treatise on witchcraft and other occult practices. (I may say in passing that I am the owner of a copy of this book, and that if it confers upon its possessor a tithe of the virtues and powers which it professes to confer Rehmeyer must be regarded as having been a happy man.) During the latter part of the year 1928 a family named Hess, who also lived in York County, had lost numerous chickens from disease and theft. They concluded that someone had put a "spell" on them and employed another powwow doctor, whose name was Blymyer, to lift the spell. Blymyer stated that in order to do so he would have to have a lock of Rehmeyer's hair and the latter's copy of *The Long Lost Friend.* On the evening of November 27, 1928, Blymyer, Wilbert Hess (a son of the owner of the bewitched chickens) and a boy named Curry went to Rehmeyer's house in order to get the lock of hair and the book, and in the course of a struggle killed him.

Blymyer, Hess, and Curry were indicted for murder, and demanded separate trials, which under the laws of Pennsylvania they had a right to do. The right in question is purely statutory, and I doubt whether it is wisely accorded. At all events three successive trials were required, the first of which began on Monday, January 7, 1929. The time which elapsed between the murder and the trials was therefore a day or two longer than that which elapsed between the killing of Mrs. Remus and the arraignment of her husband. In two of the three cases the defense, as in the Remus case, was insanity. In the third case, the defendant denied having struck the deceased, and contended at least by implication that he had acted throughout under the domination of his two associates.

The three trials lasted exactly six days. In the case against Blymyer, which was tried first, three hours were required to select a jury. There were two closing speeches, each fifty minutes in length. The jury deliberated for two hours and rendered a verdict of guilty of murder in the first degree, with a penalty of imprisonment for life, at 7:30 o'clock on the evening of Wednesday, January 9. The trial of Curry began on the following morning at 9:30 o'clock, and a jury was obtained in one hour and ten minutes. At the conclusion of the testimony, counsel for the defendant addressed the jury for thirty minutes and counsel for the Commonwealth for forty minutes. The jury was out for two hours and fifty minutes, and brought in a verdict of guilty of murder in the first degree, with a penalty of imprisonment for life, at 1:42 p.m. on Friday, January 11. Hess was immediately called for trial. In this case the selection of a jury consumed two hours, the final speech of the defendant's attorney lasted for one hour and ten minutes, and the final speech of the District Attorney lasted for forty minutes. At 7:25 p.m. on Saturday, January 12, the jury, after a deliberation of two hours and fifteen minutes, rendered a verdict of guilty of murder in the second degree, the maximum penalty for which is imprisonment for twenty years.

The "witchcraft cases" would have proved a nine-days wonder to the press and public except for two important circumstances. In the first place—and as already pointed out—they did not last for nine days. In the second place the manner in which they were tried made it impossible for the press to convert them into a wonder of any sort. When the first trial began at least a hundred representatives of metropolitan newspapers were in court, and the public had been informed that a "witchcraft trial" without a precedent in a century was about to be held. The truth was, of course, that the subject of witchcraft was involved only to the extent that it had a bearing on the question of the sanity of the defendants and that the cases were not a whit more interesting or important than rural murder trials ordinarily are. The presiding judge refused to permit telegraphic instruments to be installed in the Court House, refused to be photographed, and excluded photographers from the courtroom. The defendants were represented by experienced trial lawyers. Their cases were presented to the jury in due course, but before the week was out most of the reporters had gone home. One of them afterwards wrote a magazine article commenting bitterly on the reception which he had received and contrasting it with his reception at a historical pageant which had been held in the same city a few months previously.

I must deal here with an objection which will instantly occur to almost every reader. Hunterdon County, New Jersey, is as definitely rural as York County, Pennsylvania, yet the trial of Bruno Richard Hauptmann, which took place at Flemington, Hunterdon County, in January and February of the year 1935 was not only long drawn out, but was conducted in an atmosphere of almost unparalleled sensation and sentiment. If I thought this objection were valid I might perhaps dismiss it by saying that the notoriety of the exception is sufficient proof of the existence of a contrary rule. In my opinion, however, at least a partial answer may be made on the merits.

In the first place the evidence in the Hauptmann case was both circumstantial and complicated. Both the prosecution and the defense were compelled to make use of expert witnesses, and much time was necessarily consumed in the examination and cross-examination of these experts. In addition, a number of adjournments were granted at the request of the defense on account of the absence of persons described as material witnesses.

Nevertheless, the entire trial—including the selection of a jury, the addresses of counsel, the charge of the court and the deliberations preceding the verdict—was completed in thirty-two actual days. In other words, though the issue in the Hauptmann case was beyond comparison more complex and difficult than that in the Remus case, the trial in Flemington occupied only two days more than the earlier trial in Cincinnati.

But in the second place, though Mr. Justice Trenchard, who presided in Flemington, may perhaps be described as a country judge, the lawyers in active charge of the Hauptmann case were not country lawyers. Mr. Sidney B. Whipple, in his recent and authoritative review of the case,[1] concludes that

[1] *The Trial of Bruno Richard Hauptmann*, Doubleday, Doran and Co., 1937.

the blame for the unseemly features of the trial rests squarely on "publicity-seeking lawyers" and principally on Edward J. Reilly of Brooklyn, the chief counsel for the defense. In Mr. Whipple's opinion,

> . . . the position [of Mr. Reilly] is worthy of some comment. His visits with his distinguished client were comparatively few. His "press" (because he was generous in words and promises) was comparatively large. Altogether he struck an incongruous note in the whole proceedings. Florid, expansive, and given to the type of histrionics that impresses the small, urban mind, he could not seem to realize that he was dealing with an entirely different kind of mentality. In Brooklyn he might berate and bully a police witness with impunity, because many a Brooklyn juror would enjoy seeing a policeman's importance deflated. But country folk have more respect for the police, whom they regard as a protective and not unkindly force. They were, in this case, decidedly unimpressed by the clothes, the manner or the arguments of Hauptmann's chief advocate.

I have not read all the testimony in any of the cases to which reference has been made. On that account my opinion as to the merits of the verdicts rendered is entitled to little weight. If I were pressed for an opinion I should have to say that the verdict in the Remus case seems to me to have been without justification and that the verdicts in the Hauptmann case and in two of the three witchcraft cases seem to me to have been abundantly justified. In the instance of Curry, who was only fourteen years of age, I think a conviction of murder in the first degree was probably too severe.[2] With these questions I am, however, not primarily concerned. I am comparing general practices, not particular results. The guilt or innocence of all of the defendants was, in accordance with our

[2] Curry's conviction was reduced by the State Board of Pardons from murder in the first degree to murder in the second degree. An application for his parole was subsequently refused. Hess's minimum sentence will expire in 1939 and he will no doubt be released at that time.

system of jurisprudence, for determination by the juries which tried them. The verdicts speak for themselves. Under any system of jurisprudence innocent men will sometimes be done to death and guilty men will sometimes go free. Moreover, no lawyer can be unmindful of the fact that though all of the verdicts were in accordance with the evidence, they were perhaps quite different from those larger determinations of guilt or innocence in which the law has no part and which, being founded upon knowledge, are without the need of evidence.

So much may be taken for granted. It may likewise be taken for granted that a question exists whether trial by jury in criminal cases ought to be retained. If, however, as seems likely, this question is to be answered in the affirmative, the reforms which are most needed are not to be accomplished by constitutional or statutory changes in the rights of accused persons or in the rules of evidence. They are procedural rather than structural. They depend upon lawyers and judges rather than upon laws and amendments, and upon customs rather than upon formal rules. The country lawyer and the country judge have much to learn from the city lawyer and the city judge, but they have something to teach in return. They speak and act in the authentic tradition of the methods and practices which caused our ancestors to write into the constitutions of the original states their conviction that trial by jury ought to remain as theretofore.

IV
DEFENDING A BAD CAUSE

ON SUNDAY, February 1, 1623, Archbishop Laud recorded in his diary that he had that day stood by the most illustrious Prince Charles Stuart, at dinner. The Prince "was then very merry, and talked occasionally of many things with his attendants. Among other things, he said that if he were necessitated to take any particular profession of life he could not be a lawyer, adding his reason: 'I cannot (saith he) defend a bad, nor yield in a good cause.' "

Twenty-six years afterward, almost to the day, the former Prince, then Charles I, was beheaded at Whitehall, though whether in a good or a bad cause—whether as a glorious martyr or an inglorious tyrant—is a question about which honorable and patriotic Englishmen contested with one another on the field of battle as well as in debate for more than a century after his death, and came at last to peace and a mutual toleration rather than to agreement.

The cause of King Charles has passed, never to be finally decided, into the realm of old, unhappy, far-off things. His theory of the divine right of kings is dead, but his opinion about the practice of law is as representative of the opinions of a large number of intelligent men and women today as it doubtless was when he made his casual statement of it on that Sunday morning three hundred years ago.

I have listened a score of times to informal discussions among laymen about the ethics of the legal profession. Sometimes no more is expressed than a mere personal disinclination to be a lawyer, as on the part of Prince Charles, because of the necessity of urging unconscionable claims and defenses. Sometimes a question is asked like that which Boswell addressed to Dr. Johnson: "But what do you think of supporting a cause which you know to be bad?" Sometimes an apologist argues in the words of Dr. Paley, the English theologian, that "there are falsehoods that are no lies . . . a criminal pleading not guilty; an advocate asserting the justice, or his belief in the justice, of his client's cause . . . no confidence is destroyed, because none is reposed; no promise to speak the truth is violated, because none is given."

I must confess to a dislike for this last piece of casuistry. I object to the reference to advocates immediately after criminals; and I do not relish the implications of the statement that the falsehoods of an advocate are not to be regarded as lies because nobody will believe them. But, whatever form of words may be used, the truth is that many people feel that the successful practice of law, particularly in criminal cases, is incompatible with conduct which is in the highest degree honorable, and with speech and thought which are in the highest degree candid. And the further truth is that this feeling is centered about the supposed duty of a lawyer in what are commonly referred to as "unjust causes."

The accepted legal canons defining that duty have been stated many times, but unfortunately for the most part in books which are to be found only in the hands of lawyers and students of law. My purpose is not so much to restate them as to set down my own observations about the problem of unjust causes. If what I have to say is almost entirely concerned with the defense of accused persons, the reason lies in the fact that criminal practice, as all the world knows, presents the question under consideration in its most acute and debatable form. Like most lawyers in active practice in small cities, I have tried both civil and criminal cases, often with an intimate knowledge of surrounding circumstances and an opportunity for insight into hidden motives that are not possible of attainment in our larger centers of population; but apart from this experience I cannot claim to speak with any special authority either as a lawyer or as a moralist. I am comforted, however, by the conviction that at all events I know as much about the practice of morality as Dr. Paley did about the practice of law.

There are four sources of information from which a lawyer representing a defendant in a criminal prosecution may be said with any degree of accuracy to "know that his client is guilty": (1) the entry of a plea of guilty in open court; (2) personal observation, as by having actually witnessed the commission of the offense; (3) a confession privately made by the client; and (4) such an "assemblage of probabilities," whether resulting from the weight of the evidence in favor of conviction or otherwise, as to amount to a moral certainty. This classification appears to me to be exhaustive. It is obvious that, in the first case supposed, no question of legal ethics is involved, since a defendant in pleading guilty instantly brings to an end the prosecution against him by his own solemn and deliberate act. It is likewise obvious that, in the second case supposed, the ethical question involved is a very simple one—no man ought to appear in the same proceeding both as a witness and as an advocate, and accordingly a lawyer should refuse professional employment in a cause in which he has such a knowledge of the facts at first hand as might require him to offer himself for examination on the witness stand.

The duty of a lawyer to whom a client has made a private confession of guilt is, under ordinary circumstances, equally simple—he ought to advise his client to plead guilty, and if the client refuses to do so he ought to withdraw from the case. In practice private confessions are much less common than is generally supposed. I can give but two instances from my own experience.

On the first occasion, I was retained by a Negro who had been indicted for larceny. I asked him what his defense was, and he replied that he was guilty, but that he guessed he "had better deny it in court," and that, if he did so, his "word would be as good as hers" (the prosecutrix's). I told him that in my opinion he ought to plead guilty, and after only a very little hesitation he did so with the utmost good humor.

On the second occasion, I was consulted by an intelligent white man who was being prosecuted for conducting a gambling house. He told me that the prosecution against him was a frame-up; he did run a gambling house, but the game was straight and his arrest was the act of players who had lost their money and who had proved to be poor losers. I asked him whether the general public frequented his house and whether he got a rake-off on the game, and he answered both questions in the affirmative. I then said to him that on his own statement it was manifest that he was violating the statute, and that I would not represent him unless he were willing to enter a plea of guilty. He went out of the office without making any special comment on what I had told him. Some weeks afterward it was brought to my attention that he had retained other counsel. Under the circumstances, I felt sufficiently interested in the case to make it my business to find out what happened at the trial. The defendant testified that friends of his sometimes came to his house to play poker and sometimes played for money, but that the public was not admitted; that the game was straight; and that he did not get a rake-off. The verdict of the jury was "not guilty." I do not think for a moment that the reputable and experienced advocate who tried the case for the defense acted improperly. I am satisfied, on the contrary, that the defendant learned some law during the course of his conference with me, and, having duly digested it, amended his story to meet the requirements of an acquittal.

A somewhat novel view, though one not fundamentally inconsistent with what has been said, was expressed by the Earl of Birkenhead, former Lord Chancellor of Great Britain, in an address delivered at a banquet of the American Bar Association, on August 31, 1923. "If," he said, "you take the extremest case of all, the case where it has been put at its strongest against the ethical situation of our profession, the case where a confession has been made by a prisoner to an advocate—I would meet that case without hesitation. It arose once at a critical stage of a great English litigation. I would meet that by saying, 'You are not to be the judge of whether that confession is made under an aberration, under a delusion, in hysteria; you are to put the whole facts of that case as those facts are known to you before the jury and before the judge, and they and not you are to decide as to the facts that have been proved, and as to the reliability of that which has been admitted.' " This amounts to saying to the defendant, "Do not plead guilty, because guilt and innocence are matters of law which you are incompetent to decide. Tell the whole truth in open court, and the judge and jury will draw the proper conclusion." I am disposed to think that I should adopt this procedure in a capital case, because false confessions of guilt, whether induced by mental abnormalities or an unselfish though perhaps misguided wish to shield the real offender, are not particularly uncommon. But in cases of minor importance, where the facts are comparatively simple and there is no reason to suspect hysteria or deliberate deception, it seems to me unnecessarily scrupulous to oppose the defendant's willingness to enter a formal plea of guilty.

The "great English litigation" to which Lord Birkenhead referred was doubtless that resulting from the death of Lord William Russell, an old man, who was found murdered in his bed in May 1840. His valet, Courvoisier, who was a Swiss citizen, was arrested and tried for the murder and was defended by Mr. Charles Philips, an eminent barrister of that day. The defendant denied his guilt, and the evidence against him was purely circumstantial. On the second day of the trial, which lasted three days, Courvoisier was identified in the yard of the prison by Mrs. Charlotte Pioalaine, the wife of a Frenchman who kept a hotel in a neighborhood of doubtful repute. According to her statement Courvoisier had placed in her hands for safe keeping a package which, on being opened, was found to contain silverware marked with the Russell coat of arms. Courvoisier saw her when she was inspecting the prisoners and immediately afterwards demanded an interview with his counsel. In the course of this interview he confessed that he had murdered his master, but insisted nevertheless that Philips should defend him to the uttermost.

What happened thereafter is unfortunately disputed, but I state the facts as Philips contended them to be. In great distress of mind Philips laid the situation before Baron Parke, who was sitting in the case with Chief Justice Tindal but who had taken no active part in the trial, and was advised that under the circumstances he was bound to go on with the case and to advance on his client's behalf every fair argument arising from the evidence. This Philips did. Under the rules of evidence then in force the defendant in a criminal prosecution was not permitted to testify. Accordingly Courvoisier was not called, and could not have been called, as a witness. In a closing speech which Baron Parke afterwards characterized as "perfectly unexceptionable," Philips pointed out the weaknesses and defects in the evidence produced by the Crown and exhorted consideration and pity by the jury for a stranger in a strange land who stood charged with so frightful a crime against one of their own people. The jury rendered a verdict of guilty and Courvoisier was duly executed.

It is apparent that the course which Baron Parke advised Philips to adopt cannot be reconciled with the one which Lord Birkenhead has said he would himself follow in a similar case.

Though the rules of evidence to which Philips was required to conform made it impossible for him to call Courvoisier as a witness, the real issue is one of ethics rather than of law and is not to be obscured by artificial rules. The underlying principle at least is clear enough—*in any case, whether civil or criminal, an advocate may properly do and say on his client's behalf whatever the client might properly do and say on his own behalf if he possessed the requisite legal training and skill.* It follows that a lawyer to whom an accused person has made a private confession of guilt may not permit the accused to testify to what he knows to be untrue. He may not offer evidence in support of an alibi or other affirmative defense which he knows to be untrue. He may not advance any argument (as Philips was charged with doing in the Courvoisier case) the effect of which might be to cast suspicion on an innocent person. So much may be taken for granted.

It has been argued,[1] however, that no legal or moral duty rests on a criminal to confess his guilt, and that in consequence his attorney may without impropriety object to the competency of the court or to the admissibility of evidence and may argue (as Philips admittedly did) that the evidence as a whole is insufficient to prove that the accused is guilty of the offense charged.

The reasoning in support of the premises on which this conclusion is founded may be summarized as follows. A criminal is under no legal duty to confess his crime, because no statutes exist either commanding confession or penalizing a failure to confess. On the other hand the moral duties of a criminal are those of every wrongdoer—to repent and (if possible) to make restitution. If a further duty of confession exists, it must be because the offender believes, or ought to believe, either that his punishment will benefit himself; or that it will deter others from committing like offenses; or, finally,

[1] E.g., by Harrison Hewitt, Esq., in the *Connecticut Bar Journal* for April 1927.

that he is so dangerous a person as to make it necessary that he be imprisoned or executed for the protection of society. The first two of these reasons may be shown to be unsound, and a proper evaluation of the last requires in any given case a detachment of view which a criminal can hardly be expected to possess.

Speculations such as these lead far into the realm of fine-spun casuistry. Let it suffice for present purposes that I cannot accept the general proposition that a criminal is under no moral duty to confess his crime. As it seems to me, the rule must be stated otherwise, though the existence of exceptions must instantly be admitted. If the death penalty were imposed (as it once actually was) for the theft of a loaf of bread, I should not advise a hungry man who had stolen a loaf of bread to plead guilty to an indictment charging him with the theft. If there were a state in the Union (the condition is happily contrary to fact) in which a statute made it a criminal offense for a father to teach the theory of evolution to his child, I should not advise a father who had taught his child what he believed to be true to submit himself to the penalties prescribed by the statute. A discussion of the reasons giving rise to real or apparent exceptions of this sort would involve an inquiry into the source of the sanctity of law—a subject which is touched upon in other chapters of this book and which has no place in the present connection.

Defenders of the conduct of Philips in the Courvoisier case have been accustomed to base their defense upon the extraordinary circumstances of a confession made to an advocate in the actual course of trial and to point out that if Philips had abandoned the case the legal rights of his client would have been seriously compromised. I am not impressed by this argument. Courvoisier had presented himself to Philips as an innocent man. Upon his statement to that effect Philips had advised him to enter a plea of not guilty and had consented to undertake his defense. Having undertaken it, Philips was in duty bound to express to the court and jury his client's contention respecting the matters charged against him. If Courvoisier's version of the facts changed during the course of the trial, he could not complain, as I see it, if his attorney's advice to him underwent a similar change. In my opinion Philips should have withdrawn from the case, unless Courvoisier had been willing either to plead guilty or to authorize Philips to present in some other way to the tribunal trying the case the substance of the statement which he had received from his client in private.

But though one accused of crime persist in a denial of the charge against him both in public and in private, the evidence of his guilt may be little short of overwhelming. Moreover, his statement of what occurred may be inherently improbable, and his reputation, both generally and in connection with the previous commission of offenses like the one concerned, may be equivocal or notorious. These considerations and a hundred others, slighter perhaps but none the less persuasive, may create a settled conviction in the mind of his attorney that the accused is indeed "guilty in manner and form as he stands indicted." Of course a lawyer is not in the position of an innkeeper and a common carrier—that is, bound to render service to whosoever claims it—and he is professionally free to withdraw from such a case. He is likewise professionally free to proceed with it.[2] But is he morally free to do so?

It is, I think, here rather than in the instance of a private confession that the current of public opinion sets "at its strongest against the ethical situation" of the legal profession. A lawyer who continues to defend a client from whose lips he

[2] "It is the right of the lawyer to undertake the defense of a person accused of crime, regardless of his personal opinion as to the guilt of the accused; otherwise innocent persons, victims only of suspicious circumstances, might be denied proper defense."—Canons of Ethics adopted by the American Bar Association.

has received a private confession of guilt is, after all, in most instances only a dishonest lawyer; but a lawyer who urges a defense which he believes to be false may be held, arguably enough, to be at the least a disingenuous man, and his disingenuousness may well appear the more significant and corroding because he is subjected to no sort of professional discipline or censure on account of it. The first judgment condemns only the particular advocate who has been false to his trust, but the second condemns all advocates and calls into question not only trial by jury but every system of administering justice of which advocacy is a part.

Whatever the system may be, the *dramatis personae* of all criminal prosecutions are the same, an accuser and an accused person, and the problems presented are those of determining what actually happened in respect to the matters with which the defendant stands charged and what the consequences to the defendant ought to be. Our ancestors experimented with a number of ways of solving these problems, such as trial by ordeal and by wager of battle, and finally adopted the expedient of submitting disputed matters of fact to the finding of twelve laymen and matters of law to the decision of a single judge. With the merits and defects of the jury system I am not at the moment concerned. Let it suffice, for present purposes, that it represents our method of answering the question, "What happened?" and that this question must be answered somehow whenever a criminal accusation is made on the one hand and denied on the other.

In the conduct of trial by jury, "the advocate," as Dr. Johnson said, "is not to usurp the functions of the judge; the advocate is to make himself the mouthpiece of him who is accused." He is likewise not to usurp the functions of the jury. To suggest that he ought to do so is in effect to propose that the jury system be replaced by some other method of finding facts.

When, therefore, the argument is advanced—as I heard it advanced not long ago by a professor in a theological seminary—that a lawyer ought not to defend a prisoner whom "all the decent people in the community know to be guilty," the criticism really intended is rather of due process of law as at present constituted in the United States than of the conduct of any particular lawyer or even of lawyers in general. Since the defendant in the case giving rise to the discussion had in fact been acquitted, the form of the criticism is perhaps to be attributed to righteous indignation at a real or supposed miscarriage of justice. Certainly the substitution of what "all the decent people in the community know" for the verdict of a jury which has at least listened to evidence and had an opportunity of seeing the parties face to face would seem to amount to a reversal of the classical precedent by appealing from Philip sober to Philip drunk. But in any event it is contrary to a common sense of fairness to try accused persons more than once for the same offense. If we are prepared to abolish trial by jury as the method by which legal guilt or innocence is to be determined, let us amend our laws accordingly. But until we do so, and until we make a law that a man shall be deemed guilty when his defense does not succeed in convincing his own lawyer, an advocate has no more justification for sitting in judgment on his client's cause than the members of a jury have for assuming the roles of partisans, or than a judge has for passing upon the credibility of witnesses.

But the assumption by a lawyer of a judicial attitude is not merely bad as a matter of logic. It is bad in practice as well, because a lawyer's opinion as to guilt or innocence is as fallible as that of anyone else. One of the first criminal cases in which I ever took part was a prosecution in which I was retained by the defendant, who had been indicted for stealing a dog. I asked him what his defense was and he told me that the dog had been given to him by a man whose name he had forgotten. Since the defendant had been in jail awaiting trial for about six weeks and presumably had had ample time to think matters over, this lapse of memory appeared to me exceedingly odd. Moreover, the defense on which he relied is humorously referred to by lawyers as the "mysterious stranger" defense, and there is a tradition that when it is interposed unsuccessfully, as it almost invariably is, the court is accustomed to add a few months to the usual sentence, on the theory that the defendant is not only guilty but gifted with very poor powers of invention besides. In brief, I did not believe a word of what my client told me. Being somewhat influenced by that fact as well as very inexperienced, I tried the case badly. For some reason which I have never been able to understand the defendant was acquitted. Perhaps the jury thought that, under the law, he was entitled to a better lawyer.

About six months afterward an accident put me in possession of the true facts of the case. The story told by my client was, as I had suspected, false, but he was nevertheless entirely innocent. The dog had been stolen by his sister's husband, and the defendant, who was unmarried, had come to the conclusion that with winter coming on it would be better for him to go to jail than to have his sister and her children deprived of the support and comfort to be expected from his erring brother-in-law.

Perhaps it may fairly be asked whether this incident is better suited to "point a moral or adorn a tale," and whether a proper answer would not confine it to the latter purpose. Certainly its hero, though he was innocent of being a thief, was an unabashed perjurer who remains, so far as I know, unrepentant to this very hour. And yet when, as happens from time to time, I see him working at his trade as a stonemason on some building in course of erection and he waves a greeting to me as I pass, I cannot help feeling grateful that the legal conviction of a defendant is not made to depend upon the conscientious conviction of his attorney.

That "the advocate is to make himself the mouthpiece" of his client is a figure of speech which is not entirely accurate. But taking the figure at its strongest we are still a long way from the conclusions of Dr. Paley. According to that authority, a lawyer may assert "his belief in the justice of his client's cause," and, though the assertion be a "falsehood," it is nevertheless "no lie." Any respectable lawyer can preach a simpler and sounder doctrine.[3] It is his duty to present to the court and jury his client's version of the facts, as well as every argument and inference which may fairly be drawn in the latter's favor. It is the duty of the jury to decide the case on the evidence as it comes from the mouths of the witnesses and the law as it comes from the mouth of the trial judge. If, therefore, an advocate makes by way of argument an honest statement of his opinion, he nevertheless acts improperly, since his opinion is either relevant—as it might be on the subject of previous good character—in which event he ought to have been sworn as a witness, or irrelevant, in which event he ought to be silent. If, on the other hand, his statement is dishonestly made, he is in no different position either personally or professionally from any other man who makes dishonest statements.

Perhaps no formal code of ethics can do more than to condemn the expression by an advocate of his personal beliefs about the character and conduct of his client. To stop here is nevertheless to leave something unsaid. Everyone who

[3] "It is improper for a lawyer to assert in argument his personal belief in his client's innocence or in the justice of his cause." Canons of Ethics adopted by the American Bar Association.

has sat for any considerable period of time in a courtroom has listened to the closing speech of at least one lawyer, who, like the player in Hamlet,

> Could force his soul so to his own conceit
> That from her working all his visage wann'd,
> Tears in his eyes, distraction in 's aspect,
> A broken voice, and his whole function suiting
> With forms to his conceit.

Whatever words may be used by such a pleader, it is obvious that he makes a representation as to the state of his emotions which is intended to incline the scales in his client's favor by the weight of his own influence. Jury speeches of this kind are, I believe, both less common and less generally effective than they were a half century ago—a result which is no doubt to be attributed as much to an improved taste as to a regenerated morality. The degree of conscious deception involved differs, of course, in individual cases, and no hard and fast rule can be laid down.

In this and in every like connection there is, however, one proposition from which no escape can be found. There is no room for an esoteric morality in the legal profession or in any other. Sir Edward Coke's classic definition of a burglar is "he that by night breaketh and entereth into a mansion house with intent to commit a felony." Accordingly, one indicted for burglary at common law was entitled to an acquittal upon showing that he broke into a mansion house by day instead of by night, or that he entered with the consent of the owner instead of by breaking, or that he broke into a shop instead of a mansion house, or that his original breaking was without intent to commit a felony.

It is beside the point to say that these are technical defenses. The answer is that they are no more technical than the crime itself, and that crime will always be to a greater or less degree a technical matter. But sin is not a technical matter. The conscience is a more sacred tribunal than any court. A righteous lawyer is first of all a righteous man. What is candid and honorable in private life retains those characteristics before a judge and jury, and no principle of ethics is sound which declares a liar to be a less despicable figure in a courtroom than anywhere else.

V

THE CASE FOR THE JURY

DOUBTLESS the way to administer justice most efficiently would be to abolish trial by jury and put a Solomon in every courtroom; just as the way to govern the world most efficiently would be to abolish democracy and put a Marcus Aurelius in every capital. The supply of supermen is, however, never equal to the demand for them; nor is the supply itself either constant or predictable. Every Solomon is as likely as not to be followed by a Rehoboam, and every Marcus Aurelius by a Commodus. These considerations suggest that in every discussion of the merits of the jury system the question involved is not so much whether trial by jury is good or bad in an absolute sense, as whether something reasonably more promising has been offered to replace it. Among the substitutes which have been suggested are trial by a single judge, by a court consisting of "three or more expert judges," [1] and by a tribunal composed of a judge, a junior member of the bar, and a "substantial business man." [2]

It may be noted in passing that while expertness is a quality which must always be regarded as desirable in judges, the reputation for wisdom enjoyed by the "substantial business man" has been somewhat impaired since the last of these suggestions was made. But indeed the practical answer to all such proposals is that if experience has shown that some juries are stupid, capricious, and corrupt, it has likewise shown that some judges (as well as some lawyers and business men) are stupid, capricious, and corrupt, too. Moreover, in the nature of things, no jury can render more than one bad verdict; whereas a bad judge may, and usually does, remain in authority for life or for a long term of years. A further answer

[1] Gregory Mason in *World's Work*, November 1928.

[2] Russell Duane in *The Forum*, October 1928.

is that some incorruptible judges are nevertheless—as juries never are—arrogant, unduly technical in their decisions, unfeeling and dilatory. No jurists in English history were more justly celebrated for learning than the Chancellors; but it was in the High Court of Chancery—where juries never sat—that men, seeing only ruined and disappointed suitors and undetermined causes, cried out bitterly for law and trial by jury, if what they saw was equity.

But we who are heirs to the political traditions of England and of those English rebels who became the first citizens of the United States, must, unless we reject our heritage, dismiss as inconclusive any argument against the jury system which is based on efficiency alone. We must dismiss any such argument because trial by jury is part and parcel of that sort of democracy which, as nearly all authorities agree, constitutes the special and peculiar contribution of the Anglo-Saxon race to the political wisdom of the world. Its underlying principle is that the sanctity of law arises not from the fiat of any potentate, however benevolent, nor from the vote of any majority, however enlightened, but from the common judgment and consent of the whole body of the people. This principle is reiterated in nearly all our great state papers, and in the practical application of it the jury system plays, and has always played, a vital and important part. In other words, no consideration of trial by jury can be adequate which ignores its political and legislative significance, and seeks to reduce it to the mere method of finding facts which the passion for logic of judges and lawyers has tried to make it.

When I came to the bar there was no class of cases in which juries were so much criticized as in suits for damages arising from industrial accidents. The courts had laid down a variety of rules as to the master's liability in such cases. They had held, of course, that the injured servant or employee could not recover if he had been guilty of contributory negligence. They had likewise held that, under certain circumstances, the servant had "assumed the risks" of his employment, and that even though no act or omission on his part had contributed to his injury he was not entitled to damages if his injury resulted from the negligence of a fellow servant. These determinations constituted what is sometimes called "judge-made law." (I am not using the words in a derogatory sense; here, as always, the important question is: "Is it good law?")

At all events, the juries, if they got a chance to decide the cases at all, invariably found in favor of the plaintiffs, no matter what the evidence was; and it was widely stated that the jury system had broken down in the determination of causes brought by injured employees against their employers, and that some change in the law would have to be made. The latter part of this conclusion, at least, was sound, though belated. The result was that the legislatures of a large majority of the States adopted Workmen's Compensation Laws providing for the care and partial reimbursement of injured employees, irrespective of the nature of the accidents in which they were injured. This is exactly the principle which juries had followed as best they could from the very beginning of the industrial age. Nor are Workmen's Compensation Laws in any objectionable sense class legislation, because they have proved quite as satisfactory to employers as to employees. I doubt, indeed, whether any respectable number of employers can be found who would return to the old system.[3]

A man may, if he pleases, dismiss this entire illustration by saying that it proves merely that juries in a given sort of case consistently violated their oaths for almost a hundred years. In the light of history this seems to me a foolish saying. Or

[3] I am indebted for this excellent illustration to "The Present-Day Jury System: a Defense," an article by Mr. Connor Hall which appeared in the *American Bar Association Journal* for February 1924.

he may say—as I think wisely—that in this particular connection it took our formal legislative machinery almost a hundred years to respond to the popular will, and that the fact that justice was done in the end is to be attributed very largely to the results of trial by jury.

For justice, in the sense in which the law seeks to enforce it and in the sense in which I am using the word, is not something conceived by *a priori* reasoning in the mind of a philosopher. Though it be true, as Spinoza said, that God is beyond our little good and evil, yet it is precisely with this human good and evil that the administration of justice is chiefly concerned. Still less is justice to be defined by the technical rules and refinements of judges and lawyers. Almost numberless legislative enactments—of which one of the earliest is the Statute of 12, Edward I, and one of the latest the Act of Congress of February 26, 1919—declare that in the decision of cases the courts shall not be bound by form or method, but shall give judgment according to the very right of the cause, and bear witness to the passionate insistence with which the men of our race have protested, generation after generation, against inherent professional formalism.

Justice is rather, for every man, the product of the changing definitions of his own race and age. It must assert social and economic convictions as they are, not as they might be. It must hold him who steals my purse to be a criminal, though posterity may perhaps conclude—as I think it will not—that communism is preferable to a system of private property. To speak wisely and well, it must speak humanly and in the present tense. In a word, common justice is the only justice worth having in this world, and the only way to make it better is by the slow process of breeding better men.

I once took part in a public debate on the subject of trial by jury. In the course of it my opponent quoted a saying of Wendell Phillips to the effect that the jury system "worked out a rough, average justice," and added that if each of two litigants had a just claim to $5,000, and a jury were to give $2,000 to one and $8,000 to the other, the kind of justice administered would be both "average" and "rough." No one will dissent from this conclusion; but the language used implies a determination of the very point which is in issue in every lawsuit: What constitutes *a just claim* to recover a judgment for money or some other relief against the defendant?

Suppose that a petty tradesman negligently injures, on successive days and in an identical manner, a millionaire and an unskilled laborer, and that both injured parties bring suits for damages. Shall the millionaire and the laborer be awarded like amounts because they have sustained like injuries? Shall the millionaire receive more than the laborer because his time is of greater value? Shall the laborer receive more than the millionaire because the loss of his time has inflicted upon him a relatively greater hardship? Finally, shall the financial situation of the defendant be considered in determining the several amounts which he must be called upon to pay? These are questions concerning which not all candid and intelligent men will agree, and on which a professional opinion is intrinsically no more representative or persuasive than any other. It is precisely the merit of trial by jury that it brings into our courtrooms, from day to day, the simple though deliberate views of those not technically trained as to what justice really is.

I should feel much less confidence in the results obtained if anything less than a unanimous verdict might be rendered. *The function of a jury is not to vote. Its function is to deliberate*—and thus to come to a general opinion in the way in which Quakers are said to arrive at "the sense of the meeting." In the course of the enforced deliberation which takes place in every jury room it is the well-grounded and conscientious opinion which usually prevails.

Not long ago I listened to the trial of a Negro for the theft of approximately twenty dollars in bills of small denominations. No money had been found on the defendant's person at the time of his arrest. In other respects the evidence against him, though entirely circumstantial, was strong. The verdict of the jury was not guilty. After the verdict had been rendered one of the jurors came to my office on business and in the course of our conversation discussed the case with me. On the first ballot the jurors had stood eleven to one for conviction. The single dissenter was a woman who had been born and brought up south of the Mason and Dixon line. During the discussion occasioned by the failure of the jury to agree on the first ballot she pointed out that although three or four days had elapsed between the commission of the crime and the defendant's arrest, and although the defendant's whereabouts and behavior during this period had been fully accounted for, there was no evidence that he had spent any money or that any money had been seen in his possession. On the basis of these facts she argued that he must be innocent. She assured the other jurors that she knew all about Negroes of the class to which the defendant belonged and that the theory of the case presented by the Commonwealth was psychologically impossible—if the defendant had been guilty he could not have resisted the temptation to spend the money at the first opportunity or at least to show it to his friends. The eleven jurors who had voted to convict were so much impressed by this argument that after a discussion lasting only about half an hour they voted unanimously to bring in a verdict of not guilty.

I have no opinion as to the guilt or innocence of the defendant who was acquitted or as to the validity of the reasoning on which his acquittal was founded, though my informant, a man of much more than ordinary intelligence, was satisfied in both particulars. The point with which I am concerned is that he and his fellows were convinced by an argument which not only had not occurred to any of them in the first place but *which would never have had a hearing if anything less than a unanimous verdict had been permitted.*

Even wilful misbehavior on the part of one or more jurors is not always sufficient to defeat the ends of justice. I have in mind a case which was recently tried in the courts of my own county, in which the evidence against the defendant, a public official, was so overwhelming that no verdict other than that of guilty appeared to be possible. The jury to which the case was submitted twice reported to the court that it had been unable to agree, and on each occasion was simply instructed to resume its deliberations. At the end of almost thirty hours the expected verdict of guilty was rendered. The moment the jury had been discharged it was plain to be seen what had gone on in the jury room—two of the jurors stood apart from their fellows and were visibly shaken men. If, as seems almost certain, they had corruptly held out in the defendant's interest, they had learned at first hand that the weight of righteous conviction is a phrase which amounts to more than a mere figure of speech. I am persuaded that for every case in which the requirement of a unanimous verdict results in a miscarriage of justice, there are a dozen cases in which a small minority of the jury—sometimes even a minority of one—induces the voluntary acceptance by the majority of a sound and sensible conclusion which, except for the requirement, would never have been fairly considered.

I might very well stop here and rest my defense of the jury system upon the propositions that trial by jury is an essential part of Anglo-Saxon democracy; that, in the complicated legislative process which democracy entails, "jury-made law" has on the whole proved more authentic and more truly representative of the popular will than "judge-made law;" and that for practical purposes common justice is preferable to justice of any other sort—even to that which might be held on theoretical grounds to be actually "more just." It is worth mentioning in this connection that the British in Afghanistan and elsewhere in the East have found it necessary to accept the last of these propositions and to enforce judicially merely the custom of the country, rather than to impose on Eastern peoples the alien, though perhaps higher, standards of the West.

Still, the charge is often made that jurors are generally incompetent, by reason of ignorance and prejudice, to decide the cases which are submitted to them; or, as I once heard the charge somewhat naïvely expressed, that the jury system compels the "business magnate" to accept judgment at the hands of "less than his peers." I am aware that statements of this sort cannot be established or refuted by mere assertions or denials, but I cannot leave the subject without recording my own opinion for whatever it may be worth.

"Is it likely," asks Mr. Jerome Frank in his recent book, *Law and the Modern Mind*, "that twelve men, summoned from all sorts of occupations, unaccustomed to the machinery of the law, unacquainted with their own mental workings and not known to one another, can, in the scant time allowed them for deliberation, do as good a job in weighing conflicting testimony as an experienced judge? Can they as well see through the story of the glib liar, or of the unconsciously biased but conscientious witness, or as ably allow for the stage fright which often makes the honest but cautious man speak falteringly on the witness stand?"

The reader will remember that the "three judges" who were presented to him at the beginning of this chapter were described as "expert." Mr. Frank's judge is "experienced" and his jury consists of "twelve men . . . unacquainted with their own mental workings." As a piece of pure dialectics I suppose the answer to Mr. Frank's questions must be that one man assumed to be competent is certain to do a better job in anything from laying bricks to weighing conflicting testimony than twelve men assumed to be incompetent—which is a truism or worse. However, not all judges are either expert or experienced and—since even psychologists are subject to call for jury duty—it can hardly be argued that all jurors are unacquainted with their own mental workings. Incidentally, where abuses in the selection of jurors exist, and corrupt politicians fill the jury wheel with the names of ward-heelers, it is entirely likely that the judges whom these same politicians place upon the bench are no better than they should be.

But my quarrel with Mr. Frank does not end with his experienced judge and his ignorant jurors. These characterizations are indeed not always or necessarily correct, but his reference to the scant time allowed to jurors for deliberation is never correct. The deliberations of a judge result solely from his own sense of humility and responsibility; the cocksure and opinionated judge rarely deliberates. On the other hand—and for reasons already shown—the deliberations of the jury room arise in the very nature of the case and require the evaluation and reconciliation of the conflicting points of view of the twelve jurors concerned.

Subject to the corrections noted, I am now ready to set down my answers to Mr. Frank's questions. In my opinion, twelve jurors usually do a much better job in weighing conflicting testimony than a judge. This is so partly because the jurors are "summoned from all sorts of occupations"—and therefore bring to their task a more diversified experience than is likely to be possessed by a single judge; partly because they are "unaccustomed to the machinery of the law"—and therefore listen to the testimony without technical preconceptions; partly because they are "not known to one another"—and therefore attach no special authority to one another's opinions; and very largely because of the automatic deliberation which trial by jury insures. Such men usually "see through the story of the glib liar or of the unconsciously biased but conscientious witness" much better than a judge, and in particular allow more sympathetically than a judge for the stage fright of the honest but cautious witness, because their own unfamiliarity with the routine of the courtroom subjects them, to some extent at least, to the same sense of embarrassment by which the witness is affected.

Finally, I am not impressed by the argument of the business magnate that the judgment which he receives from the average jury is the judgment of less than his peers. If most litigation turned on the statement and restatement of complicated accounts this argument—at least within some definitions of greater and less—might very well be sound. As a matter of fact, however, the question really at issue in the great majority of cases is not one of mathematics but of human veracity—a question which is at once one of the simplest and one of the most complicated under the sun. In the solution of it—and in the solution of every question involving the fundamentals of life, liberty, and property—I do not believe that the average business or professional man is wiser than the average farmer or carpenter. He is better educated in the formal sense and superficially more polished. He has a somewhat wider knowledge of current events and a more nearly adequate understanding of financial matters. On the other hand he has spent fewer hours alone, and accordingly has thought less for himself and is more easily influenced by stereotypes and catchwords. He is less simple and natural and his prejudices are at least as deeply rooted. These are general observations of the widest sort, and are, of course, without value unless clearly understood to be such. As among themselves, business magnates may, if they please, submit their differences to trial by a single judge or to arbitration by psychologists. I can only say that in a matter of the last moment to myself I had rather submit the issue to an "impartial jury of the vicinage."

VI
THE SANCTITY OF LAW

A GREAT Chief Justice of Massachusetts once said, "Obedience to law is liberty," and intended thereby, as I understand his words, to express the nature of liberty in terms of law. At the present time, much is being spoken and written in the United States about the menace of a growing disrespect for the sanctity of law, and much is likewise being spoken and written about the menace of a growing disrespect for the sanctity of liberty. If, therefore, there is such a connection between liberty and law as to warrant the definition of one in terms of the other, we ought to ask ourselves what this connection is. Or, to put the question less generally, if liberty is indeed obedience to law, we ought to ask ourselves what law is and whence comes that sanctity which it is said to possess.

The concept of law is, I suppose, one of the very oldest in the history of civilization. In every moderately advanced state of society except that of early England the word "law" has had only one significance—namely, a rule prescribed by a superior. A given situation has arisen and people have said, "What was the decree of the chief in cases like this?" or "What is the decree of the chief in this case?" or "Let the tribe vote to decide what shall be done," or "What do the wise men say?" or, what is in practice the same as the last, "What is the will of the god?" Now our Anglo-Saxon ancestors, at least in England, never asked questions or made statements at all like these. Instead they asked a paradoxical question. Whether the paradox implied in the question is true or false or partly true and partly false will appear hereafter. But the question was: "What is the law?" This means that our ancestors regarded the law, not as a rule laid down by anybody to meet the exigencies of a particular case or set of cases, but as an existing thing and a thing which had existed from "time whereof the memory of man runneth not to the contrary." To borrow a theological expression, they habitually thought of law as something begotten, not made.

One of the necessary results of this conception is interest in and regard for ancient customs. If the law is indeed immemorially old, there is no better evidence of what the law is than time-honored practices, and the older a practice is the better evidence it becomes. You remember what Sir Richard, the Norman, says about his Saxon friend in *Puck of Pook's Hill:*

> His Saxons would laugh and jest with Hugh, and Hugh with them, and—this was marvelous to me—if even the meanest of them said that such and such a thing was the Custom of the Manor, then straightway would Hugh and such old men of the Manor as might be near forsake everything else to debate the matter—I have seen them stop the mill with the corn half ground—and if the custom or usage were proven to be as it was said, why, that was the end of it, even though it were flat against Hugh, his wish and command. Wonderful!

So it came about in England that all men knew the exact rights of a widow in her deceased husband's estate and the precise penalty for cutting off a man's hand, not only centuries before there was a written law governing these subjects, but centuries before there was any formal declaration, whether written or oral, that a widow had any rights in her deceased husband's estate, or any formal prohibition against doing hurt to one's neighbor. And in theory, as I have said, a man did one thing and avoided another, not out of deference to custom, but out of deference to law. The law already existed and the custom was evidence of it—that was all.

A second paradox ought to be mentioned. In early English legislation the words "custom" and "liberty" were used almost interchangeably. Thus in chapter 13 of Magna Carta the "*liberties and customs*" of London and other cities and seaports were confirmed, and in chapter 39 of one of the first republications of the Charter it was provided that no freeman should be "disseised of his freehold or his *liberties or his free customs* or be outlawed or exiled or otherwise destroyed but by lawful judgment of his peers, or by the law of the land."

All this is interesting enough as a mere matter of legal history, but the really important questions are how much truth there is in the proposition that the law exists antecedently to any oral or written statement of it and in the seemingly disconnected proposition that, for some purposes at least, a custom is the same thing as a liberty.

In one sense—though a sense which is, I think, both narrow and superficial—the first proposition is certainly not true. I mean that when a new condition arises in the world—as, for instance, by the invention of the aeroplane—it is too much to suppose that there already exists a "rule of the sky," like the time-honored "rule of the road," to meet the precise condition thus created. All that the common law has to say about aeroplanes is that the owner of land owns the air above the land as high as to the sky—a pronouncement which was born in an age when a man could not make use of air to a greater height than he could build, and which consequently will not square with the facts of the present day.

But in a much wider and deeper sense, common law—if I may use that phrase somewhat loosely to refer to that sort of law which is practised before it is promulgated—is one of the most real and practical things under the sun—as real and practical as that common sense of which it is the legislative product—and all the major sanctions of our penal code are founded upon it.

Most people, for example, do not kill their neighbors or burn their neighbors' houses or steal their neighbors' goods, and in consequence we are all agreed that murder, arson, and robbery ought to be punished as crimes. Almost no one disputes these conclusions, least of all the very small percentage of persons who do in fact commit murder or arson or robbery. Even in the midst of the vile sort of sentimentality which sometimes surrounds a sensational murder trial, no special pleader is heard to argue, even by implication, that murderers ought to go unpunished. He only argues that for some reason or other his client is not really to be regarded as a murderer at all. In effect, this argument means that most persons in like situation with the defendant would have done exactly what he did. In the usual case the argument is a bad one because it is not true—most persons in like situation with the defendant would not have done what he did. The technical objection to defenses based upon the so-called "unwritten law" is that it is not written, but in the majority of cases the real objection is that it is not law.

What is even more important than the fact that most people do not commit crimes is the further fact that most people do not wish to commit them. The deepest of all the differences between the average good citizen and the average criminal is not a difference in will-power or self-control, but rather in the line of conduct which each is instinctively moved to follow. Where there is little will to obey there is little obedience among either good citizens or criminals. Anyone doubting this may, I think, profitably ask himself how many laws he has actually been tempted to break and what the result of his temptation was.

Until the present year there was a statute in my own state which forbade the operation of an automobile, under any circumstances, at a rate of speed greater than forty miles per hour. This statute set up a purely *a priori* standard of safety, which was at variance with that determined by current practice and judgment. The consequence was that most owners of automobiles, who had habitually driven at speeds in excess of forty miles per hour and believed that they had done so with entire safety to themselves and others, paid no attention to the statute. On the other hand, the great prohibitions of the penal code are founded upon a consensus of opinion and conduct just short of unanimity. If a man steals my purse he is said to be a robber—that is to say, a criminal. But if he sees no reason why he should not steal it he is said to be a kleptomaniac—that is to say, a madman.

But the effective obligation of customary law is not limited to those subjects on which its terms have been incorporated and expressed in some formal statute or decree. No such statute, for example, enjoins the payment of what are sometimes called "debts of honor"—or, less euphemistically, gambling debts. Indeed, the whole of our legislative and judicial logic is against their collection. If I seek to recover a thousand dollars on a note, the statutes will place at my disposal the courts with their writs and the sheriff with his bailiffs. I can seize and sell my debtor's tangible property and I can attach debts due him by others, including, in some states, his wages and earnings. As a last resort, I can go into the courts of the United States and procure the appointment of a trustee in bankruptcy to take charge of his estate. But if I seek to recover a thousand dollars on a bet the statutes will not help me at all. And yet, year in and year out, the most carefully managed corporation, which investigates and reinvestigates every customer to whom it extends credit, cannot, with all the machinery of the courts within its reach, collect so large a proportion of its debts as any gambler can collect without lifting a finger.

I am not arguing for or against the morality of gambling or of paying gambling debts, any more than I was arguing, a moment ago, as to the wisdom or safety of driving automobiles at any particular speed. I am only concluding the last of three observations of fact, which may be restated as follows. In the first place, when the requirements of a statute are the same as those of common opinion, as in the case of high crimes and misdemeanors, the statute is almost universally obeyed. In the second place, when the requirements of a statute are greater than those of common opinion, as in the case of the operation of automobiles, the statute is disobeyed by nearly all those who are without the will to obey it. In the third place, when the requirements of a statute are less than those of common opinion, as in the case of gambling debts, the latter is, nevertheless, almost universally obeyed, and it would seem —perhaps perversely—a little the more willingly because all the implications of the statute are the other way.

With these observations in mind we may now inquire what significance is to be found in the statement that a custom is a liberty. In pursuing this inquiry, something must be said, if only by way of definition, about the nature of democracy.

The word "democracy" is commonly used to mean, first, a political party—in the United States—as opposed to Republicanism; secondly, a form of government—sometimes called a pure democracy—as opposed to a republic; and, thirdly, a form of state, as opposed to a monarchy or an aristocracy. In what follows I am using the word only in the third sense.

Now democracy in this sense is indeed partly conceptual and approximate—becoming rather than being, evolving rather than evolved. The ideal democracy, like the kingdom of God, does not exist, and perhaps will never exist, on earth; but a faith in democracy presupposes, and the practice of democracy requires, the existence of a popular will which may be determined at least with a working degree of accuracy from day to day. Let me illustrate what I mean by referring to the common experience known as "making up one's mind" —a phrase which, rightly considered, is itself enlightening.

I suppose a man approaches most of the important questions of his life with conflicting preferences. Ambition urges him, let us say, to run for public office. Prudence suggests that in doing so he will be likely to neglect his business. Perhaps what he conceives to be his duty to his family impels him in one direction and what he conceives to be his duty to his state or nation in another. A dozen other considerations pull him this way and that. Some of these considerations may be selfish and some unselfish, or they may be all selfish or all unselfish. At any rate, after a longer or shorter period of indecision, the man is said to "make up his mind," and thereafter the whole man is determined to run for office or not to run, as the case may be. Democracy has staked everything upon the proposition that the mind of a people may be made up in like manner from the discordant inclinations of all the individuals concerned.

I am aware that the proposition just stated has been regarded as fanciful by certain modern writers who contend that democracy means the rule of the majority and nothing more. I do not wonder that these writers have little zeal for democratic institutions. If the United States were governed by a single despot who ordered my execution without trial, I should feel, to put it mildly, exceedingly ill used. But if the United States were governed by an oligarchy of one hundred and this oligarchy ordered my execution without trial, I should feel equally ill used. Finally, if the Constitution of the United States were amended in a perfectly lawful way—as it might be—so as to permit the President to prepare a list of persons to be executed, and the President, in the exercise of the discretion vested in him, selected me as one of his victims, I should not be comforted in the smallest degree by the assurance that a substantial majority of my fellow citizens were in favor of the whole proceeding. If this be democracy, there is indeed only one reason for being a democrat, and that a very selfish one—namely, that, whereas I should have only one chance in a hundred million of being the absolute monarch of the United

States and only one chance in a million of belonging to an oligarchy of a hundred, I have, as between myself and the whole number of voting electors, a little more than one chance in two of being on the winning side at every election. In brief, such a theory leaves the individual citizen, if he happens to be in the minority, as completely forgotten in a democracy as anywhere else.

But democracy, as I see it, is not fundamentally concerned with majorities or minorities at all. What democracy assumes is unanimity—that is to say, a common mind. This assumption is, in practice, never entirely true, and yet, as George Santayana has pointed out in a passage which I shall have occasion to quote at length in discussing the Fourteenth Amendment, we vote only about minor matters. The really significant fact about a presidential election in the United States is not how many voters are Democrats and how many Republicans, but rather that all of the voters presumably regard either a Democratic or a Republican administration as desirable from one point of view and at least tolerable from any other.

> Were this not the case, a decision by vote would be as alien a fatality to any minority as the decree of a foreign tyrant, and at every election the right of rebellion would come into play. . . . To leave a decision to the majority is like leaving it to chance—a fatal procedure unless one is willing to have it either way. . . . It is therefore actually required that juries, whose decisions may really be of moment, should be unanimous; and parliaments and elections are never more satisfactory than when a wave of national feeling runs through them and there is no longer any minority nor any need of voting.

Democracy, says Santayana, in substance, presupposes fundamental unanimity, and in a hearty and sound democracy the office of a representative assembly is only to announce the decision which has already been arrived at. The common law presupposes that laws are first born and afterward declared by judges and legislators. It is clear that these two suppositions are really one and the same; or, to put the matter in another way, that the Anglo-Saxon conception of law is essentially democratic in character.

The story of Robinson Crusoe may be regarded for political purposes as a parable in two parts. The first part is concerned with Crusoe alone upon his island. The poet has made him say that he was monarch of all he surveyed and that his right there was none to dispute; but his monarchy consisted of an uninhabited wilderness, and if there was none to dispute his right there was likewise none to assert it or to whom it might be asserted. Such a right is in effect no right at all.

In the second part of the story, Crusoe and Friday lived together on the island. The coming of Friday converted a solitude into a sovereign State, and Crusoe, like Louis XIV, was the State. Instead of shooting Friday, as he might have done, Crusoe told him that he might keep his life so long as he behaved himself in a specified way. What happened was not the proposal of a contract, but the publication of a constitution. The assent of Friday did not matter in the least. Because Crusoe had a gun, he had absolute power—that is to say, sovereignty—and a constitution is the declaration of a self-limited sovereignty. If Crusoe had afterward revoked the constitution and had shot Friday, the result would have been a sin but not a crime. On the other hand, if Friday had attempted to kill Crusoe, the result would have been treason if he had failed and revolution if he had succeeded. A revolution is either an actual shifting of sovereignty or a practical demonstration that the power theretofore believed to be sovereign is not really so.

Now the situation of Crusoe and Friday is, in miniature, that which has always existed and must always exist in every sovereign State, and it suggests the answer of the political philosopher to the question as to what law is. Law is the voice of sovereignty, and the essence of sovereignty is power. In the field of politics there are no "unalienable rights," because in the last analysis the power which grants a right can necessarily take it away. I do not think for a moment that the framers of the Declaration of Independence meant to assert the contrary. To suppose that they did so is to misread the very words of the declaration which they signed. When men take up arms, protesting that they do so to defend rights with which they have been "endowed by their Creator," they are not talking politics. Such men stand exactly where Friday would have stood if he had attacked Crusoe with a club—exactly where history shows that the framers of the Declaration of Independence actually did stand—that is, on the brink of revolution. Revolutions may be spoken of as political phenomena only in the way in which miracles may be spoken of as natural phenomena. They are outside of politics, just as miracles are outside of nature, and they are to be justified or condemned in the light of history and on moral rather than political grounds.

Nor is the essential quality of sovereignty different in a democracy from what it is in any other form of State. We are accustomed to speak of a system of checks and balances as one of the characteristics of our American form of democracy. The powers of Congress are limited by those of the President, and the powers of both Congress and the President are defined by the Supreme Court. In addition, various rights and immunities are expressly guaranteed, in whole or in part, by the Constitution of the United States. But a system of checks and balances and a bill of rights are no more than effective limitations upon the organs of government. Since the days of the Medes and the Persians, no people has been so foolish as to suppose that there can be, in logic or in fact, a law or a constitution which cannot be amended. If a constitutional provision set up the Supreme Court, a constitutional provision can strike it down; and if Congress is prohibited by the Constitution from making any law respecting an establishment of religion, the authority which declared that prohibition yesterday can revoke it tomorrow. There is somewhere in every sovereign State absolute, unlimited, and illimitable power, and from the decrees of this power the citizen of a democracy, as well as the subject of a monarchy or aristocracy, has, of necessity, no lawful protection and can take no lawful appeal.

And yet there is, as all men are aware, some vital and tremendous difference—reflected and expressed in a sort of fundamental optimism, whether well or ill founded—which distinguishes a democracy from a monarchy or an aristocracy more widely than either of these political forms is to be distinguished from the other. This difference is not to be found in the quality of sovereignty in a democracy, but rather in the source of it. For if, in a monarchy or an aristocracy, one man or a few men have sovereign power and the people are subject to them, in a democracy sovereign and subjects are, by definition, the same. The people are conceived as making those very laws which they are bound to obey.

"The common law," said Mr. Justice Holmes, "is not a brooding omnipresence in the sky but the articulate voice of some sovereign . . . that can be identified." In the act of identification we come face to face with the meaning of the saying that a custom is a liberty. There is no intrinsic sanctity in the decree of a monarch or the vote of a majority. In either case, the law laid down is merely good or bad according to the facts. But a law declaring the usage of a people is a holy law, because it finds its authority and verification in the hearts of those who are called upon to obey it. *When men obey such a law they are free men, because they command themselves.*

VII

THE TWO FOURTEENTH AMENDMENTS

THE Fourteenth Amendment to the Constitution of the United States was proposed by Congress to the legislatures of the several states on June 16, 1866, and was declared ratified by proclamation of the Secretary of State a little more than two years afterwards. The first section—which is the only living part of the amendment and which is sometimes referred to in what follows as if it were the whole—reads as follows:

All persons born or naturalized in the United States, and subject to the jurisdiction thereof, are citizens of the United States and of the State wherein they reside. No State shall make or enforce any law which shall abridge the privileges or immunities of citizens of the United States; nor shall any State deprive any person of life, liberty, or property, without due process of law; nor deny to any person within its jurisdiction the equal protection of the laws.

As a matter of political theory, this language is that of the people of the United States. I propose, in the first place, to attempt to determine its intended meaning by an examination of the principal arguments advanced both for and against the adoption of the amendment in the debates in Congress, in the debates in the legislatures of the several states, and in discussions before the people at large. I call this intended meaning the first Fourteenth Amendment. The text of the Amendment has been many times considered and construed in decisions of the Supreme Court of the United States. I propose, in the second place, to refer to some of these decisions in order to discover the actual meaning of the language used as determined from day to day by our constitutional court of last resort. I call this actual meaning the second Fourteenth Amendment. Finally, I shall attempt to evaluate the political significance of the discrepancies which appear between the Constitution by electoral intention on the one hand and by judicial interpretation on the other.

1

The purpose of the Fourteenth Amendment was plainly remedial. The Civil War had come to an end. Slavery had been abolished by the Thirteenth Amendment. Nevertheless, Negroes remained subject to various disabilities in all the states south of the Mason and Dixon line and in many of those north of it. The Civil Rights Bill, directed by its express terms against discrimination among the inhabitants of any State or Territory on account of race or previous condition of slavery, had been passed over President Johnson's veto, but was generally believed to be unconstitutional. On these accounts the supporters of the Fourteenth Amendment were content in most instances to rest their case on a mere recital of the familiar sequence of the old law, the mischief and the remedy.

On May 8, 1866, Thaddeus Stevens, speaking in the House of Representatives, said:

> The first section [of the amendment] prohibits the States from abridging the privileges and immunities of citizens of the United States, or unlawfully depriving them of life, liberty, or property, or of denying to any person within their jurisdiction the "equal" protection of the laws.
>
> I can hardly believe that any person can be found who will not admit that every one of these provisions is just. They are all asserted, in some form or other, in our DECLARATION or organic law. But the Constitution limits only the action of Congress, and is not a limitation on the States. This amendment supplies that defect, and allows Congress to correct the unjust legislation of the States, so far that the law which operates upon one man shall operate *equally* upon all. Whatever law punishes a white man for a crime shall punish the black man precisely in the same way and to the

same degree. Whatever law protects the white man shall afford "equal" protection to the black man. Whatever means of redress is afforded to one shall be afforded to all. . . . Now different degrees of punishment are inflicted . . . according to the color of the skin. . . . I need not enumerate these partial and oppressive laws. Unless the Constitution should restrain them those States will all, I fear, keep up this discrimination, and crush to death the hated freedmen. Some answer, "Your civil rights bill secures the same things." That is partly true, but a law is repealable by a majority. And I need hardly say that the first time that the South with their copperhead allies obtain the command of Congress it will be repealed. . . .

Fifteen days later Senator Jacob M. Howard of Michigan presented to the Senate the joint resolution proposing the adoption of the amendment. Senator Howard had served as a member of the Reconstruction Committee by which the text of the amendment had been drafted, and therefore spoke with at least apparent authority. In the course of his remarks he pointed out that the citizens of each of the states had long enjoyed "a mass of privileges, immunities, and rights, some of them secured by the second section of the fourth article of the Constitution . . . some by the first eight amendments of the Constitution"; but that these privileges, immunities, and rights were protected only from legislation by Congress and not from legislation by the several states. The Senator continued:

The great object of the first section of this amendment is, therefore, to restrain the power of the States and compel them at all times to respect these great fundamental guarantees. . . . The last two clauses of the first section . . . disable a State from depriving not merely a citizen of the United States, but any person, whoever they may be, of life, liberty, or property without due process of law, or from denying to him the equal protection of the laws of the State. This abolishes all class legislation in the States and does away with the injustice of subjecting one caste of persons to a code not applicable to another. It prohibits the hanging of a black man for a crime for which the white man is not to be hanged. It protects the black man in his fundamental rights as a citizen with the same shield which it throws over the white man. . . . If adopted [the amendment will] . . . forever disable [the States] from passing laws trenching upon those fundamental rights and privileges which pertain to citizens of the United States, and to all persons who may happen to be within their jurisdiction. It establishes equality before the law, and it gives to the humblest, the poorest, and most despised of the race the same rights and the same protection before the law as it gives to the most powerful, the most wealthy, or the most haughty. . . .

The statements of Mr. Stevens and Senator Howard unquestionably represented the official attitude of the Republican majority in Congress, and were substantially repeated by other Republicans in the debates on the amendment which took place in the House and Senate. They were likewise substantially repeated in addresses to other deliberative bodies and in discussions directed to the general public.

Governor Andrew G. Curtin of Pennsylvania, in his message to the State Legislature which afterwards ratified the amendment, said:

I present, for your consideration, the amendments to the Constitution of the United States, proposed . . . by . . . Congress. . . . The amendments are so moderate and reasonable in their character, that it would [be] astonishing, if the people [should fail] to approve them. That every person, born in the United States, and free, whether by birth or manumission, is a citizen of the United States, and that no State has a right to abridge the privileges of citizens of the United States—these are principles which were never seriously doubted anywhere, until after the insane crusade in favor of slavery had been for some time in progress. What is called the decision of the Supreme Court of the United States, in the Dred Scott case, has made it expedient and proper to re-assert these vital principles in an authoritative manner, and this is done in the first clause of the proposed amendments. . . .

At that time Pennsylvania was the only state which reported in full the debates in its legislature. Senator Connell, speaking in favor of the amendment, quoted the law of Mississippi for the year 1865 making it a crime, punishable by a fine of not less than fifty dollars nor more than five hundred dollars, for the employee of any railroad to allow any freedman, Negro, or mulatto, except nurses with their mistresses, to ride in first-class passenger cars set apart for and used by white persons. After citing this statute, Mr. Connell declared that the adoption of the amendment was a political necessity on account of the state of things in the South. He added: "Not much Shakespeare about that. That section [of the statute quoted] gives one a glimpse of the poetry, refinement and humanity of Mississippi life."

Similar arguments—which perhaps appear to have been more temperately worded only because they were incompletely reported—were presented to the legislatures of Ohio, Illinois, Missouri, Indiana, Minnesota, Massachusetts, and various other states.

The issue raised by the proposal of the amendment was, of course, widely discussed in the press.

Carl Schurz, writing in the *Atlantic Monthly* for March 1867, declared that the first section was "intended to engraft the main provisions of the Civil Rights Act upon the Constitution," and thus formed "a necessary complement of the abolition of slavery." To the same effect were editorial comments in the *New York Times*, *Harper's Weekly*, and other newspapers and periodicals. The *Times* particularly commended Senator Howard's opening statement in the Senate as "frank and satisfactory," and his exposition of the conditions leading up to the proposal of the amendment as "clear and cogent."

For present purposes, the grounds on which the amendment was opposed are of less importance than those on which it was supported. It is worth mentioning, however, that its opponents generally accepted without question the definition of the issue propounded by their adversaries. Samuel J. Randall, a Democrat from Pennsylvania, replying in the House to the arguments of Mr. Stevens and his followers, declared that the first section proposed to make an equality in every respect between the white and black races, notwithstanding the policy of discrimination which had theretofore been exclusively exercised by the states. In the opinion of this speaker there was "no occasion whatever for the Federal power to be exercised between the two races at variance with the wishes of the people of the States." In the same debate, Andrew J. Rogers, of New Jersey, a Democratic member of the House, called attention to the fact that the first section was admittedly neither "more or less than an attempt to embody in the Constitution . . . [the] outrageous and miserable civil rights bill," and asserted that since a Negro who was refused the right to be a juror would be deprived of his privileges and immunities as a citizen of the United States, the result of the amendment would be a revolution worse than the one through which the country had passed. Mr. Wallace, an opponent of the amendment in the legislature of Pennsylvania, said that the first and fifth sections taken together declared who were citizens and conferred upon Congress power to protect that citizenship. He defined privilege as "everything that . . . is desirable," and immunity as "a privileged freedom from anything painful," and contended that under the power conferred upon Congress by the second clause of section one, "the dearest rights" could be bestowed upon Negroes. The *Memphis Avalanche* said that the amendment had been the "war cry of the partisan leaders in the late struggle on the hustings and at the ballot-box," and that it meant to the Northern people Negro equality, social and political, not, however, applicable to themselves. The *Montgomery Mail* said that the chief objection to the amendment was the first section, which prohibited a state "from depriving [a Negro] of any rights or privileges which a white man [might] possess." The *New Orleans Picayune* characterized the first section as an incorporation into the Constitution of the Civil Rights Bill. Another opponent of the amendment asserted that it secured for the Negro the right to vote, to sit on juries, to enter hotels, lecture rooms, and so forth. A press correspondent, seemingly a Republican, said that the Democrats of Kentucky feared that Congress would be empowered by the amendment to confer the suffrage on Negroes; that it admitted Negroes to the witness stand, the jury box, street cars, good seats in public conveyances, good accommodations at hotels, the public schools, and all other civil rights which white people enjoyed; and that if it went this far, the Democrats reasoned that it might go farther.

In the nature of the case the foregoing summary is by no means exhaustive. *It is, however, sufficiently exhaustive to justify the statements that the purpose of the framers of the Fourteenth Amendment was to complete the work of emancipation by writing into the Constitution the provisions of the Civil Rights Bill, and that a large majority of its supporters and opponents believed that its principal, if not its only, effect would be to confer additional rights and immunities on members of the Negro race.*

At least one (and presumably a majority) of the members of the Supreme Court were originally of the same opinion. The amendment was first considered by the Court in the *Slaughter House Cases* decided in 1873. Mr. Justice Miller, who delivered the opinion of the Court, said:

> The institution of African slavery, as it existed in about half of the States of the Union, and the contests pervading the public mind for many years, between those who desired its curtailment and ultimate extinction and those who desired additional safeguards for its security and perpetuation, culminated in the effort, on the part of most of the States in which slavery existed, to separate from the

Federal Government, and to resist its authority. This constituted the war of the rebellion, and whatever auxiliary causes may have contributed to bring about this war, undoubtedly the overshadowing and efficient cause was African slavery.

The learned Justice then reviewed at some length the events leading up to the adoption of the Thirteenth, Fourteenth, and Fifteenth Amendments, and proceeded as follows:

> We repeat, then, in the light of this recapitulation of events, almost too recent to be called history, but which are familiar to us all; and on the most casual examination of the language of these amendments, no one can fail to be impressed with the one pervading purpose found in them all, lying at the foundation of each, and without which none of them would have been even suggested; we mean freedom of the slave race, the security and firm establishment of that freedom, and the protection of the newly made freeman and citizen from the oppressions of those who had formerly exercised unlimited dominion over him. It is true that only the fifteenth amendment, in terms, mentions the Negro by speaking of his color and his slavery. But it is just as true that each of the other articles was addressed to the grievances of that race, and designed to remedy them as the fifteenth.
>
> We do not say that no one else but the Negro can share in this protection. Both the language and spirit of these articles are to have their fair and just weight in any question of construction. . . . But what we do say; and what we wish to be understood is, that in any fair and just construction of any section or phrase of these amendments, it is necessary to look to the purpose which we have said was the pervading spirit of them all, the evil which they were designed to remedy, and the process of continued addition to the Constitution, until that purpose was supposed to be accomplished, as far as constitutional law can accomplish it.

These remarks were followed by a discussion of the several clauses composing the first section of the amendment. As to the concluding clause—"nor shall any State . . . deny to any person within its jurisdiction the equal protection of the laws"—the learned Justice observed:

> The existence of laws in the States where the newly emancipated Negroes resided, which discriminated with gross injustice and hardship against them as a class, was the evil to be remedied by this clause, and by it such laws are forbidden.
>
> . . . *We doubt very much whether any action of a State not directed by way of discrimination against the Negroes as a class, or on account of their race, will ever be held to come within the purview of this provision. It is so clearly a provision for that race and that emergency, that a strong case would be necessary for its application to any other.* (Italics added.)

In the entire field of judicial dicta it would be hard to find a prophecy which has been more completely discredited by the event.

2

Since the determination of the *Slaughter House Cases* the amendment has been interpreted by the Supreme Court in more than a thousand decisions. Many of these decisions have been concerned with the inevitable work of definition.

Thus a child born in the United States of Chinese parents becomes a citizen of the United States at the moment of his birth by virtue of the first clause of the amendment; but an unemancipated Indian, though born in the United States, is not subject to the jurisdiction thereof, and on this account is not a citizen within the meaning of the clause in question. A corporation is not a citizen and consequently does not enjoy those privileges and immunities which are secured to citizens against legislation by the states, but is a person and as such is protected against deprivation of property without due process of law and against a denial of the equal protection of the laws.

The prohibitions of the amendment are directed exclusively against action by the states and not against the misconduct of individuals. Since, however, a state can act in no other way than by its legislative, executive, or judicial agencies, the amendment is directed against the power of a state by whatever organ it may act, and applies not only to a state constitution or statute, but also to municipal ordinances or regulations adopted by state authority, and to wrongful action by a state court or by the officers of a state in administering a valid statute, though not to the unauthorized (and therefore merely advisory) instructions of a state officer such as a superintendent of weights and measures.

Contrary to the "great object" of the amendment as understood by Senator Howard, the privileges and immunities which are thereby protected are not the "great fundamental guarantees" enumerated in the Bill of Rights, but only those that belong to citizens of the United States as distinguished from citizens of the states, or those that arise from the Constitution and laws of the United States as contrasted with those that spring from other sources. It follows that while a state may not abridge the right of a citizen of the United States to pass from one state to another, or to protection on the high seas and in foreign countries, it may, if it sees fit, abridge his right to trial by jury in a state court.

Trial by jury is not only not a privilege of national citizenship, but is not a requisite of due process of law. Deprivation of due process, though not defined in the Constitution, may result from the taking of the property of a railroad company for private use under the asserted authority of a state board of transportation, from the attempted imposition on a utility company of confiscatory rates, and from the attempt by a state to subject to taxation property and rights not subject to its jurisdiction. A litigant has been denied due process of law where his case has been decided by a state supreme court in such a way that he has not had a proper opportunity to present his evidence, but not where a state court has erroneously admitted evidence or entered an erroneous decree after a full hearing. Freedom of contract and freedom of speech and of the press, though not included in the privileges and immunities of citizens of the United States, are nevertheless—the first under earlier and the second under later decisions—among the liberties protected by the due process clause.

All these liberties are, however, subject to regulation by the police power of the states. A state statute which restricts freedom of contract by fixing maximum hours of labor for both men and women constitutes a valid exercise of the police power, but until quite recently a similar statute fixing minimum wages for women exceeded the limits of that power and was unconstitutional and void. The same power justifies an act forbidding the advocating or teaching of the doctrine of resorting to violence as a means of changing industrial and political conditions, but not an act denouncing the display of a red flag as a sign, symbol, or emblem of opposition to organized government.

The equality guaranteed by the final clause of the first section is legal equality, not social equality. In consequence, equality is not denied by state statutes requiring separate railway carriages for the white and colored races or prohibiting the teaching of white and Negro pupils in the same corporate educational institution. Neither is it denied by a statute prohibiting adultery and providing a heavier penalty when the crime is committed by persons of different races than when both guilty parties belong to the same race, nor by the refusal of the managers of a primary (as distinguished from a general) election to permit Negroes to vote therein. On the other hand, an anti-trust statute, imposing fines for unlawful combinations of capital or skill but containing a proviso exempting agricultural products or livestock while in the hands of the producer, is unconstitutional by reason of the inequality resulting from the exemption contained in the proviso; and a municipal ordinance which vests in supervisors the right to grant or withhold their assent to the use of wooden buildings as laundries is likewise unconstitutional as applied to one who has complied with every requisite precaution both for the protection of neighboring property from fire and against injury to the public health.

In each of the cases in which the amendment has been construed, its application to particular states of fact has been declared or denied by the Court, and the rights and obligations of individual litigants have been finally determined. If all these determinations were stated, the result might well be described as the amendment in fact, as distinguished from either intention or theory.

If such an attempt were made we should make an end of speaking about rights and liberties and begin to speak about men and things. We should have to record that the amendment protected Wong Kim Ark, the American-born son of Chinese subjects, when he was refused permission to land at San Francisco on returning to this country from a visit to China, but not John Elk, an American Indian, when he was denied the right to register as a voter in the Fifth Ward of Omaha; the Indianapolis Water Company against the water rates fixed by the Public Service Commission of Indiana, but not the Knoxville Water Company against the water rates fixed by the City of Knoxville; August Bartels against the penalties imposed upon him by an Iowa statute for teaching German to children in a parochial school, but not Albert W. Hamilton against a regulation of the University of California requiring him to take a course in military science and tactics; Yick Wo, a subject of the Emperor of China, when he was imprisoned in San Francisco for engaging in the laundry business in a frame building, but not Soon Hing, also a Chinese subject, when he was imprisoned in the same city for engaging in the laundry business between the hours of ten P.M. and six A.M.; L. A. Nixon, a Negro, when he was prohibited by a

Texas statute from voting in a primary election in that state, but not R. R. Grovey, also a Negro, when he was prohibited by the resolution of a party convention from voting in a similar election in the same state; Joseph Tipaldo when he was indicted for failing to comply with the provisions of the New York Minimum Wage Act, but not West Coast Hotel Company when it was sued by Elsie Parrish, a chambermaid in its employ, for the difference between the wages which she had actually received and the amount to which she was entitled under the provisions of the Washington Minimum Wage Act; and Yetta Stromberg when she directed the children in a summer camp in a ritual which consisted of raising a red flag and pledging allegiance to the cause for which the flag stood, but not Benjamin Gitlow when he arranged for the publication of a manifesto advocating the forcible overthrow of the established political system of the United States.

These illustrations are not given to call attention to any real or supposed conflict in the decisions of the court, but only to emphasize two conclusions which are in any event too plain to be controverted: (1) *In a number of respects the amendment does not mean what its proponents intended.* (2) *In an even greater number of respects it does mean what its proponents never intended. In short, both by way of exclusion and by way of inclusion, the second Fourteenth Amendment is radically different from the first.* The political significance of this antithesis remains to be considered.

3

Hardly anyone any longer denies that judges make law, at least within some definitions of that regrettably elastic word. From what has been said it is clear that they make not only law of the ordinary sort, but also constitutional provisions. The extent of their contribution to a particular article or section depends on the generality of the language of the text, and on the variety and nature of the questions presented for determination in actual litigation. Where the language used is clear and specific, as in the case of the attempt to establish national prohibition by the Eighteenth Amendment, the judicial contribution is comparatively small. On the other hand, where the language of the text is as vague and general as that of the due process clause, the contribution of the judge may well prove even more important than that of the legislative draftsman. It is a gross understatement to say that the representatives who voted for the Fourteenth Amendment did not intend all the consequences which have resulted from its adoption. The simple truth is that most of these consequences were neither considered nor foreseen by anyone, whether representative or elector, at any time during the period in which the adoption of the amendment was discussed. The question before us is how we are to characterize that part of the amendment which has been written by the Supreme Court. The question comes to this: Admitting that judges, though ostensibly only interpreters, make law and make constitutional provisions, what is a "good" law or a "good" constitutional provision, and what is a "bad" one?

There is a school of thought which seeks to make social utility the test of legislative and judicial excellence. If this test is a correct one, we must describe as "good" every interpretation of the amendment, not plainly unreasonable, which was adopted by the Court against an alternative less likely to promote the general welfare; and we must describe as "bad" every interpretation adopted against an alternative not plainly unreasonable and more likely to promote the general welfare. In short, since the Court acts in a sense involuntarily and answers only the questions propounded by particular litigants, "good" and "bad" must sometimes be understood to mean "better" and "worse"; but the standard by which better and worse are to be distinguished is the social advantage or detriment which seems likely to result from the decision announced.

I agree that the field of judicial legislation is limited in the nature of the case by the not unreasonable alternatives between which the Court must choose.[1] I do not agree, however, that these alternatives are to be evaluated on the basis of their social utility. Within the limits stated, the test of lawmaking by courts is no different from that of lawmaking by any other of the instrumentalities by which, in a democracy, the popular will is expressed and enforced. Our theory of government presupposes a representative endowed with common sense—not a mere mouthpiece for the electors who supported him—and a judge learned in the law—neither a creature of the executive on the one hand nor an irresponsible eclectic on the other. The representative is to enact statutes and constitutions, and the judge is to give a reasonable construction to the statutes and constitutions so enacted. Both representative and judge must do honest work in their respective fields if the democratic process is to function properly. In the long run, however, their work must stand or fall not on the ground of social benefit or detriment, but on the accuracy with which it conforms to the dominant forces of usage and opinion. Where no such conformity exists, either the representative or the judge has failed. The elaborate mechanism of democracy has broken down at one point or the other, and has belied the sovereign power which it was called into being to express. "The people," said John Marshall in *Cohens* v. *Virginia*, "made the constitution, and the people can

[1] "I recognize without hesitation that judges do and must legislate, but they can do so only interstitially; they are confined from molar to molecular motions. A common-law judge could not say, 'I think the doctrine of consideration a bit of historical nonsense and shall not enforce it in my court.'" Mr. Justice Holmes in *Southern Pacific Company* v. *Jensen*. In other words, the refusal of the judge to enforce the doctrine would amount to the adoption of an unreasonable alternative.

unmake it. It is the creature of their will, and lives only by their will. But this supreme and irresistible power to make or unmake, resides only in the whole body of the people; not in any subdivision of them."

It must be admitted that the conception of law made by "the whole body of the people" tends to become metaphysical, indeed almost mystical, if carried to its logical limits. According to some of its expositors, the only duty of both representative and judge is to declare the law as it already exists in the mind of the people. Such a theory ignores some of the realities of the legislative process. It would be absurd to argue, for instance, that the recent and useful "lame duck" amendment may be justified only if it was proposed and adopted in response to a popular demand; or that the twenty-six judges who considered in *Di Santo* v. *Pennsylvania* [2] the right of the legislature of Pennsylvania to require the licensing of persons engaged in the sale of steamship tickets might have been guided in their deliberations by a proper responsiveness to the general will on the particular point in controversy. To admit so much is not, however, to say that there is no general will about efficiency in government or about the right of a state to the exercise of the police power.

As was aptly observed by Mr. Justice Holmes, "no one denies that there is a difference between night and day," and

[2] In this extraordinarily close case the Court of Quarter Sessions of Dauphin County, Pennsylvania, which consisted of three members, held that the statute was constitutional. The Superior Court of Pennsylvania held that the statute was unconstitutional and reversed the judgment of the lower court. Two of the seven judges of the Superior Court dissented. The Supreme Court of Pennsylvania, consisting of seven members, held that the statute was constitutional and reversed the judgment of the Superior Court. The Supreme Court of the United States held that the statute was unconstitutional and reversed the judgment of the Supreme Court of Pennsylvania. Three justices dissented. Assuming that the three judges of the Court of Quarter Sessions of Dauphin County, Pennsylvania, were unanimous, a point on which I am without information, fifteen of the twenty-six judges thought that the statute was constitutional and eleven thought that it was unconstitutional. The case was not decided under the Fourteenth Amendment but under the Commerce Clause.

"the fixing of a point when day ends is made inevitable by the admission of that difference." When only one manufacturer out of a hundred has installed in his factory a given safety device, the device in question is certainly not in customary use. When ninety-nine of the same manufacturers have successively adopted the device, it certainly is in customary use. The admission of this difference makes it necessary to assert that the act of a single manufacturer converted an unusual practice into a usual one. To say that the effective act was that of the fifty-first manufacturer is only to apply a rule of thumb to the solution of a doubtful point. Both law and politics are beset with difficulties of this sort. For present purposes it is sufficient that there are statutes and decisions which represent the popular will, and other statutes and decisions which misrepresent it. The validity of the distinction remains unaffected by the fact that there is a twilight zone in which the attempt to apply it requires determinations which are necessarily arbitrary and sometimes even unreal.

The premises of democracy have been stated by no one more clearly than by George Santayana. He says:

> The practice of English liberty presupposes two things; that all concerned are fundamentally unanimous, and that each has a plastic nature, which he is willing to modify. If fundamental unanimity is lacking and all are not making in the same general direction, there can be no honest coöperation, no satisfying compromise. Every concession, under such circumstances, would be a temporary one, to be retracted at the first favorable moment; it would amount to a mutilation of one's essential nature, a partial surrender of life, liberty, and happiness, tolerable for a time, perhaps, as the lesser of two evils, but involving a perpetual sullen opposition and hatred. To put things to a vote, and to accept unreservedly the decision of the majority, are points essential to the English system; but they would be absurd if fundamental agreement were not presupposed. Every decision that the majority could conceivably arrive at must leave it

still possible for the minority to live and prosper, even if not exactly in the way they wished. Were this not the case, a decision by vote would be as alien a fatality to any minority as the decree of a foreign tyrant, and at every election the right of rebellion would come into play. In a hearty and sound democracy all questions at issue must be minor matters; fundamentals must have been silently agreed upon and taken for granted when the democracy arose. To leave a decision to the majority is like leaving it to chance—a fatal procedure unless one is willing to have it either way. You must be able to risk losing the toss; and if you do you will acquiesce all the more readily in the result, because unless the winners cheated at the game, they had no more influence on it than yourself—namely none, or very little. You acquiesce in democracy on the same conditions and for the same reasons, and perhaps a little more cheerfully, because there is an infinitesimally better chance of winning on the average; but even then the enormity of the risk involved would be intolerable if anything of vital importance was at stake.

It is easy to set down some of the fundamental unanimities upon which our American polity depends. We are all agreed, for example, that government is better than anarchy and that a democracy is a better form of government than either a monarchy or an aristocracy; that a system of private property is to be preferred to communism; that church and state should be completely separated; that accused persons should be tried in accordance with the traditions of English liberty; that monogamy is the best form of the marriage relation; and that freedom of speech and of the press is one of the essential rights of citizenship. All of these convictions are expressed in the laws of every state of the Union. Most of them are also expressed, in whole or in part, in the Constitution of the United States. Yet all of them have been rejected in one country or another during the course of recorded history, and some of them are rejected today in countries as highly civilized as our own.

To take a single illustration out of many available, the framers of our Constitution wrote into it a provision that no religious test should ever be required as a qualification to any office or public trust under the United States. The article in question is declaratory of a customary point of view by which the religious opinions of public officials are not regarded as matters of vital political importance. If Alfred E. Smith had been elected President, a large body of citizens would doubtless have been displeased, but I do not suppose that any experienced observer believes that a rebellion would have occurred. In Ireland, however, where the memory of old wrongs makes it as intolerable for Catholics to be governed by Protestants as for Protestants to be governed by Catholics, a decision by vote becomes, as Santayana says, "an alien fatality" by which it is known in advance that the minority will refuse to be bound. The difference has nothing to do with relative degrees of civilization or national enlightenment. It results rather from the almost universal acceptance in the United States of an attitude toward religious issues which is not accepted in Ireland. This attitude is the cause rather than the effect of our constitutional provision. The fundamental agreement which democracy presupposes must exist in fact before popular lawmaking becomes a working possibility.

If the people set up constitutional provisions, they also strike them down. When the great Chief Justice spoke of the supreme and irresistible power by which constitutions are unmade, he might well have cited *Chisholm* v. *Georgia* in illustration of his statement. In that case the Court over which he was afterwards called to preside had decided that the judicial power of the United States extended to a suit brought against a state by a citizen of another state. The decision—which would perhaps attract little attention today—proved to be at variance with the spirit of the age in which it was rendered.

In less than five years the supreme and irresistible power had declared by the adoption of the Eleventh Amendment that the Constitution should not be construed in the way in which the Court had construed it. In a somewhat similar way the decision in *Pollock* v. *Farmers Loan and Trust Company*, which denied to Congress the power to impose an income tax, was set aside by the adoption of the Sixteenth Amendment. The Fifteenth Amendment has been virtually nullified in the only part of the country in which its provisions were of any moment. The Eighteenth Amendment, which in my opinion never represented customary morality, was repealed by the Twenty-first Amendment. The Dred Scott decision was overthrown on the battlefields of the Civil War. Mr. Benét has stated one of the plainest facts in our constitutional history, in language which oddly echoes that of John Marshall:

> Sometimes an image that has stood so long
> It seems implanted as the polar star
> Is moved against by an unfathomed force
> That suddenly will not have it any more.
> Call it the mores, call it God or Fate,
> Call it Mansoul or economic law,
> That force exists and moves.

I have suggested the canons of criticism by which I think the decisions under the Fourteenth Amendment ought to be evaluated. The preamble of the Constitution is in the first person plural. The theory behind the grammar seems to me on the whole to correspond to a political reality. On the affirmative side, the mores tend to write our fundamental unanimities into the law of the land. On the negative side, legislation, whether formal or judicial, which proves offensive to the mores, is set aside after one fashion or another—by amendment or repeal, by judicial interpretation or reinterpretation, by nullification or by force—and ceases to be the law of the land. Both sorts of legislation partake, though in varying degrees, of the interstitial character to which Mr. Justice Holmes has referred.[3] The molecular motions of the judge are confined within the intervals of the text which he is called upon to expound. The molar motions of the legislator are likewise confined, though within the larger and vaguer intervals of the usage and opinion which he is chosen to render articulate.

It has been shown that the interpretation of the Fourteenth Amendment has defeated many of the purposes which its proponents intended, and has accomplished other purposes which nobody intended. Neither of these statements necessarily amounts to an indictment of the Court.

On the first point it should be remembered that the amendment was proposed before the passions arising from the Civil War had had time to cool, and that it was adopted at the instance of a "subdivision" of the people, to make use of Marshall's word, against the bitter opposition of a defeated but unreconciled minority. Unlike most articles of the Constitution, its prohibitions were not directed against action by the National Government but against action by the states. These prohibitions might have been so construed as to destroy the essential characteristics of our dual form of government and to impose social equality between the white and black races on the white inhabitants of the South. Without attempting to justify all the decisions of the Court, I venture the opinion that the judges who refused to construe the amend-

[3] The saying that a common-law judge could not refuse to enforce the doctrine of consideration because he happened to regard it as a piece of historical nonsense is the statement of a standard of judicial self-restraint. If the judge did refuse to enforce the doctrine, he would be a bad judge and his view of the law would not ultimately prevail. Within much wider limits, the products of formal legislation are subjected to the same sort of practical revision. That this revision actually takes place is a commonplace of politics. The so-called legal realism which can find law only in the latest decision of the latest controversy seems to me a truism from one point of view and grossly unrealistic from any other.

ment in this way more truly expressed the considered judgment of "the whole body of the people" than did Thaddeus Stevens and the so-called radical Republicans.

The unintended consequences of the amendment have resulted in part from the very nature of a constitution. Herbert Spencer defined life as "the continuous adjustment of internal relations to external relations." When the adjustment ceases to exist, the man is dead. When a constitution can no longer be adjusted to meet the needs of a changing world, the constitution is dead.

> I speak first of the Constitution [says Mr. Justice Cardozo] and in particular of the great immunities with which it surrounds the individual. No one shall be deprived of liberty without due process of law. Here is a concept of the greatest generality. Yet it is put before the courts *en bloc*. Liberty is not defined. Its limits are not mapped and charted. How shall they be known? Does liberty mean the same thing for successive generations? May restraints that were arbitrary yesterday be useful and rational and therefore lawful today? May restraints that are arbitrary today become useful and rational and therefore lawful tomorrow? I have no doubt that the answer to these questions must be yes. . . . The content of constitutional immunities is not constant, but varies from age to age. "The needs of successive generations may make restrictions imperative today, which were vain and capricious to the vision of times past." "We must never forget," in Marshall's mighty phrase, "that it is a *constitution* we are expounding." Statutes are designed to meet the fugitive exigencies of the hour. Amendment is easy as the exigencies change. In such cases, the meaning, once construed, tends legitimately to stereotype itself in the form first cast. A constitution states or ought to state not rules for the passing hour, but principles for an expanding future. In so far as it deviates from that standard and descends into details and particulars, it loses its flexibility, the scope of interpretation contracts, the meaning hardens. While it is true to its function, it maintains its power of adaptation, its suppleness, its play.

We are not to conclude, therefore, that the extension of the Fourteenth Amendment to subjects not considered in the generation in which it was adopted amounts, in itself, to an abuse of the judicial function. I will give two illustrations from decisions which have been widely discussed. Since I regard one of them as good and the other as bad, and since the effect of both was to limit the power of the states, it is apparent that if I approach the questions adjudicated in a spirit of prejudice, the prejudice is not concerned with the subject of states' rights.

I think *Adkins* v. *Children's Hospital*, which denied to the states the power to pass minimum wage laws, was a bad decision and that it was properly overruled in *West Coast Hotel Co.* v. *Parrish*. Both decisions were approved by only a bare majority of the Court, and we may accordingly assume that neither of the alternatives presented was legally unreasonable. I do not characterize the Adkins decision as bad because the subject of minimum wage laws was not considered by the framers of the due process clause, or because I personally regard such laws as desirable, or even because I think most Americans regard them as desirable. I characterize the decision as bad because I think most Americans believe that the states should not be hampered in making experiments intended to promote public health and social security.

I think *Stromberg* v. *California*, by which freedom of speech and of the press was definitely placed beside freedom of contract among the liberties protected by the due process clause, was a good decision. I might easily be brought to share the doubts more than once expressed by Mr. Justice Brandeis about the correctness of the earlier decisions which extended the language of the clause beyond procedural matters. The extension has been made, however, and has met with universal acquiescence, if not with universal approval. Here again I am not concerned with the intention of the framers or with the meaning which they attached to the word "liberty." I characterize the Stromberg decision as good because I think most Americans believe that freedom of speech and of the press is as much a liberty as freedom of contract.

In stating these conclusions I am attempting to determine the will of the sovereign power which made the Constitution yesterday and can unmake it tomorrow, whose effects have been identified in the moving forces of usage and opinion and which has been variously referred to as the mores and the spirit of the times. Mr. Justice Cardozo has noted regretfully that "in every court there are likely to be as many estimates of the *Zeitgeist* as there are judges on its bench." I understand this saying to mean no more than that it is hard to be a good judge. I may be mistaken about what the will of the sovereign is. But if I am also mistaken about the source of sovereignty, I am persuaded that there is no meaning in democracy.

VIII

TWO SINS AGAINST TOLERANCE

In a catechism which I used to study there was a classification of sins on the basis of virtues in the somewhat discouraging ratio of two to one. The path of godliness, it appeared, was beset with temptations on either side. One could have too much or too little of the quality of every virtue, but whether one sinned by way of excess or by way of deficiency one was equally far from being in a state of grace. Thus it was said that the sins against Hope were Presumption on the one hand and Despair on the other.

I hold no brief either for or against such a method of classification as a piece of abstract casuistry, but I am interested in its present application to the theory and practice of Tolerance, which is the newest and therefore the least generally understood of the cardinal virtues. Moreover, at the risk o seeming unduly dogmatic, I am willing to assert that the sins against Tolerance are Skepticism and Bigotry, and that, paradoxical as it may seem, we Americans are simultaneously in danger of becoming skeptics as a matter of philosophy and bigots as a matter of fact.

1

The roots of skepticism lie in the very general modern acceptance of what I have come to regard as one of the most pernicious heresies under the sun—the doctrine, namely, that truth and error are subjective matters which rest on nothing more enduring than personal opinion and which have no relation to objective reality. I am not attacking the teachings of any formal school of philosophy. I am only trying to express the attitude of most of the people who think of themselves and speak of themselves as liberals. Go into any church which calls itself liberal or advanced, and you will be told in substance that it is not necessary to be right but only to think that you are right.

This is not only a very soft doctrine, but it is softer than the facts. Upon the very fabric of life is stamped the stern command that you must be right at your peril. Not for nothing was it written that it must needs be that offenses come, but woe to that man by whom the offense cometh. To say that polygamy is a meritorious practice for Mormons because they honestly believe in it is to say that the world was flat before Columbus proved that it was round. To say that Democrats and Republicans are equally patriotic is to state a perfectly evident fact, but to say that their political opinions are equally sound is to state an absurdity. Moreover, it is an absurdity which no one is so foolish as to commit in practical affairs. No one for a moment supposes that a clear conscience will heat a cold room or turn a bad meal into a good one. We live our lives subject to rigorous physical laws, and when we violate them we take the consequences. What we are to eat and how we are to live are questions which we are bound to answer at our own risk. If we fail to answer them correctly, mere goodness of intention will not help us a whit.

Much good work has been done in recent years in the field of prison reform, but some of it has been marred by a failure to remember that a prisoner is, after all, a man who has committed a crime. It is utterly beside the point to answer that if we knew all we should forgive all. There is respectable authority for the proposition that it is our duty to forgive all whether we know all or not. God alone can measure the length and breadth of human sin in the light of his infinite mercy. But neither our knowledge nor our forgiveness is any reason, so far as I can see, for supposing that a murderer is any the less a murderer because he has added unwritten amendments to the text of the Ten Commandments. It is precisely the case of the man who is out of step with the regiment. As a piece of pure logic, it is possible (though unlikely) that the man and the regiment are both out of step with the music. But it is unthinkable that they are both in step with it, and at the same time out of step with each other.

Nor do I think that any more can be said on behalf of this particular kind of liberalism if we pass altogether outside the field of individual ethics. It is generally conceded, for instance, that the Civil War was the most tremendous domestic crisis through which America has passed up to the present time. Every mind indignantly rejects the idea that sin can in any wise be imputed to the men who faced each other on the battlefields of that war. We are humbly conscious rather that their conduct was equally above all praise. And yet it is a mockery, which they would be the first to resent, to suggest that the cause which prevailed was neither better nor worse than the one which was defeated.

Another national crisis is upon us today. As I write these words, a battle is being waged, behind the rights and wrongs of puzzling specific instances, between those who are seeking to fulfill and those others, whether fascist or communist, who are seeking to destroy, the social and political hopes and aspirations to which the American Commonwealth was dedicated. In the issue thus joined it is altogether likely that each side honestly believes in the justice and wisdom of its cause. It is certain, however, that one side or the other is mistaken, and neither idealism, however unselfish, nor loyalty, however devoted, can abate the awful consequences of that certainty. Let our citizens look to it—the welfare of their children will depend on the course which they adopt and not on the purity of the motives which may lead to its adoption.

It must be admitted, of course, that truth is one thing and our idea of it another; but this is only the tacit admission behind every human affirmation. If we never spoke except upon certain knowledge, we should always be silent. "A decent respect to the opinions of mankind" bids us beware of a wayward cocksureness; but pure skepticism implies an indecent disrespect to our own opinions, which is one of the clearest of the stigmata of decadence. It was the disciples of Pyrrho and not of Socrates who doubted whether they doubted. Our forefathers professed "a decent respect to the opinions of mankind," but they nevertheless had no scruples about pitching several thousand pounds of tea into Boston harbor. They also hanged witches at Salem, and did many other fierce and wrong acts; but they never committed the sin of Pontius Pilate, whose name has been detestable for two thousand years, because, at a stupendous crisis, he could do no better than to ask, "What is truth?"

I have a friend, a lawyer, who has frequently had occasion to examine two medical experts as witnesses on his side of various important cases. The physicians in question are in all respects equally distinguished practitioners, but my friend considers one of them a much safer witness than the other. He bases this belief on the answer which each is accustomed to make to a usual question in the course of cross-examination. This question is whether the witness may not be mistaken in his opinion. The first physician always says, "Certainly," without more. The second replies, "I may be mistaken, *but I think not*"; and my friend is satisfied that the emphasis on the added words carries great weight with juries.

Logically, the second answer is a piece of tautology, because in stating any opinion one necessarily expresses a belief in its correctness; but the tautology springs from unfairness inherent in the question itself. An admission of possible error is the unspoken preface of every speech. Fallibility is the inertia against which a man moves when he undertakes to speak at all. How positively he may be justified in speaking depends upon "an assemblage of probabilities" of which he must be the judge. This "assemblage of probabilities" may be so strong as to amount to a moral certainty, or so weak as to make the adherence to a judgment based upon it mere stubbornness. In either case tolerance certainly demands nothing so absurd as a concession that one opinion is as good as another because both may be wrong.

Now tolerance is a by-product of democracy, professing the the same doctrine and subject to the same limitations. The essence of democracy is not equality, but equality before the law. The essence of tolerance is not doubt, but charity and a sense of fair play. The vice of the bigot and the despot is not certitude, but a refusal to hear both sides of the case. Freedom of thought no more implies an approval of heresy than freedom of action implies an approval of crime. Everyone has a right to a hearing, just as everyone has a right to a chance in the world; but truth and worth are, none the less, solemn and detached realities which nothing can controvert.

All this is, in a sense, a protest against a modern point of view. In another sense it is a personal profession of faith. The objective distinction between good and evil, and our fitness to make that distinction, seem to me first principles which increase in importance with our own perplexities. If the world is indeed a wilderness, it is both untrue and foolish to keep repeating that all paths lead straight to the broad highway; and it is equally foolish to follow only half-heartedly what seems to us the best path, for the reason that our neighbor may possibly have hit upon a better one. There is no way out of the labyrinth except to find the clue. Nothing will discharge our obligation to find it except performance. On such a theory, life is a perilous quest which may end in achievement. On any other, it is a meaningless nightmare without an end in view. It was Shakespeare who wrote, "for there is nothing either good or bad but thinking makes it so."

But it is worth remembering that he put these words in the mouth of Hamlet, who was either a madman or a sane man successfully feigning madness, as the critics may prefer.

2

But if the sin of skepticism lies in a perversion of liberal thinking, the menace of bigotry is chiefly to be found in an equally dangerous perversion of conservative conduct and leadership.

The American people are just now confronted with the wave of social and political unrest which has been sweeping over the world since the end of the World War. It is, I suppose, impossible to approach the questions which are now before us for consideration without some mental predisposition one way or the other. In approaching them I am aware that my own predisposition, both innately and as a matter of training, must be described as conservative, unless the meaning of that word has lost all relation to its etymology. I really believe, for instance, that a democracy is a more desirable form of state than either a monarchy or an aristocracy, and I desire to preserve what seem to me the essentials of the particular form of democracy which our forefathers established. I am as far as possible from being a fascist, a communist, or an anarchist. I believe in an economic system founded on private property and in an industrial system supported by private capital and conducted by private initiative. I am opposed to any change in the established distribution of powers among the executive, the legislative, and the judicial branches of our government.

These are simply my own conclusions, which may be quite incorrect as a matter of fact, though, like my friend's witness, *I think not.* But, so far as my fellow citizens are concerned, my conclusions are, in a certain sense at least, entirely irrelevant.

They are part of a composite judgment, nothing more, and they are entitled to only so much weight as their own intrinsic worth, backed by the weight of my personal authority, be that much or little, is able to win for them. "All power," says the Constitution of my own state, in words which fairly express the political philosophy underlying the Constitution of the United States as well, "is inherent in the people and all free governments are founded on their authority and instituted for their peace, safety and happiness. For the advancement of these ends they have at all times an inalienable and indefeasible right to alter, reform or abolish their government in such manner as they may think proper."

But the right thus stated is, in the United States, happily more than the abstract product of any paper constitution. It is a perfectly practical fact, and every American knows it. Whenever a substantial majority of our fellow citizens, having soberly considered both sides of the case, desires to adopt the social and political theories of Stalin or Hitler, it not only has a theoretical right so to do, but it has, by means of constitutional amendments, the actual power to accomplish such a result. Precisely because this is the case, the right of free speech, even as its warmest advocates have defined it, affords no protection to the agitator whose words create a clear and present danger of an attempt to overthrow by force our present form of government. The crime for which such an agitator may be indicted is of statutory origin, but logically it is treason —not treason against the United States in the technical sense, but treason against the basic principle of democracy, which is that the will of the whole people (provisionally determined from day to day by the instrumentality of the ballot) is paramount to the will of any part of the people.

Now, if it be true that the people have a right "to alter, reform or abolish" their government at will—and we Americans should be the last to dispute it—and, further, if it be true that it is here and now treason against democracy and tolerance for a minority, either radical or reactionary, to attempt the forcible overthrow of a political order with which they happen to disagree, it is equally—and for the same reasons—treason against democracy and tolerance for a conservative majority forcibly to prevent a full and free discussion of the views of political thinkers with whom they happen to disagree. Indeed, one proposition necessarily depends on the other. Revolution by force is a crime only when revolution by argument and persuasion is an ever present possibility. Free speech is not merely one of the results of democracy; it is likewise one of the continuing causes of democracy. When free speech ceases, public opinion ceases; and when the rule of public opinion ceases, despotism begins. The American tradition affirms that the forcible overthrow of despotism is not base but noble.

Not long ago a well-known clergyman and educator delivered a public lecture in the city in which I live. In the course of his remarks he said that if he were President of the United States he would order the arrest of every communist in the country, would have them taken to New York harbor, and thence "on a ship of stone with sails of lead" would "start them straight for the closest port of Hell." The speaker was an educated native-born citizen and was speaking in a small and thoroughly American inland city, but one seldom hears more seditious language on the lips of an illiterate immigrant haranguing foreigners in the heart of one of our great centers of population. In principle such an utterance is quite as bad as that for which the so-called criminal anarchist may be sent (as I think rightly) to jail. In practice it is a great deal more sinister and alarming. The number of radical agitators in the United States is said to be about twenty thousand. The number of influential conservatives is many times as great.

It is, therefore, chiefly upon the temperance and fortitude of conservative leadership that the safety of America depends.

I have said that I have faith in our political institutions. I have faith in our people as well. "It is not uninteresting to the world," said Thomas Jefferson, "that an experiment should be fairly and fully made whether freedom of discussion, unaided by power, is not sufficient for the propagation and protection of truth." We find ourselves in the midst of this experiment, and I for one am willing to engage in debate with the apostles of the totalitarian state, not only because tolerance entitles both sides to a hearing, but because I believe I have a better case than they have and because I have confidence in the court and jury.

The Constitution of the United States can claim for itself none of the sacred character which the Hebrews attributed to the laws of Moses. It was devised by wise and patriotic men after a score of compromises. It was adopted after the most unrestricted consideration in the forum of public opinion. It stands vindicated in the record of a century and a half of progress and development without a parallel in the history of civilization. If, then, the form of government which the Constitution set up cannot now win for itself vindication as a working success from the same tribunal which approved it as a mere experiment, the obvious conclusion would seem to be that our government is not really so good as I think it is—in other words, that my own conclusion on this point is quite wrong. In that case we ought by all means to avail ourselves of the first opportunity to replace our present political structure by a better one.

There is only one other possible point of view, and that is that the people are incompetent to select their own form of government. If that is true, democracy has failed; and if democracy has failed, America has failed. Personally

I have no fear on this point, but even if I had, being an American and remembering the aspirations, the self-denial, the blood and tears, the anguish and longing that have gone into the making of America—it seems to me that I would at least give democracy the benefit of the doubt and continue, albeit with a waning faith, along the old paths, even as Peter, though he denied his Lord, nevertheless "followed afar off . . . to see the end."

IX

AN OPEN LETTER TO THE CONSERVATIVE MAJORITY

A CONSERVATIVE is one who seeks to preserve the existing order; a progressive, one who seeks to improve it; a reactionary, one who seeks to destroy it in order to restore an earlier order; and a radical, one who seeks to destroy it in order to make a new beginning. If any reader is disposed to quarrel with these definitions, let him accept them tentatively and for present purposes only. Assuming this done, it immediately becomes necessary to make two preliminary observations.

In the first place, it must be apparent that the points of view which I have denominated conservative, progressive, reactionary, and radical are in themselves quite without ethical significance. By their fruits they are to be known and iudged. Abraham Lincoln and Nicholas II were both conservatives; if the world will long remember the President and will forget the Czar, the reason lies, at least in part, in the judgment of history that the American Union was better worth saving than Holy Russia. The despotism of Louis XIV was as progressive a development of the power of the French kings as was the glorious Revolution of that of the English Parliament; if we prefer the latter to the former, we do so because we are accustomed to set more store by the rights of man than by efficiency in government. Joan of Arc, the peasant girl who freed France, and Napoleon III, the Emperor who enslaved her, were equally reactionary. The logic of events made the signing of the Declaration of Independence as radical an act as the storming of the Bastile; but the American Revolution was followed by the Constitutional Convention of 1787, and the French Revolution was followed by the Reign of Terror and the despotism of the First Empire. It is, after all, the quality of the things which men seek to preserve, to develop, to restore, or to build anew that justifies or condemns their conduct.

In the second place, it must be apparent that of the four attitudes under consideration the conservative and the progressive have at least this in common, that they depend on a faith in the continuity of human history and experience; and the reactionary and the radical have at least this in common, that they spring from a complete dissatisfaction with things as they are. Of course a man may be simultaneously a conservative or a progressive in one connection and a reactionary or a radical in another, but it is still true that in any given connection the difference between a conservative and a progressive is simply a matter of emphasis, and the difference between a reactionary and a radical is simply a matter of opinion as to what ought to be done after the status quo has been destroyed.

As everyone knows, both reaction and radicalism are abroad in the world at the present time. How much of either actually exists in the United States is perhaps a debatable point, but at any rate there is, here as elsewhere, a great hue and cry about them. In its extreme form this agitation is expressed in statements to the effect that in the long run America is certain to become either fascist or communist, and that the only issue for our citizens to decide is which of the two alternatives to adopt. Most Americans find one horn of the dilemma as piercing as the other. The consequence is that the preservation of our form of government seems to them for the time being even more important than its improvement. It is to the conservative majority thus constituted that the following communication is addressed.

1

At the outset I ought to say that I write as one of you. The ancient Greeks were better philosophers than we Americans are and, man for man, were better men. The Romans were better law-givers. The Hebrews were more religious. The Germans are certainly more painstaking and possibly more profound. But we belong—at least by virtue of our political traditions—to the Anglo-Saxon race, and the Anglo-Saxon race has made a unique contribution to the accumulated wisdom of the world, viz., the development of a special sort of democracy which is exemplified in the system of government which our fathers set up in the United States. We agree in believing that this system of government is, all in all, eminently worth preserving.

But in politics, as in war, it is a great deal easier to attack than to defend. Some of us have forgotten exactly what it is in our institutions that we have reason to be grateful for, just as children sometimes forget what they are crying about, though keeping none the less a sense of having been wronged. And so our replies to the attacks of both reactionaries and radicals have often been confused and stupid. Among other things, we have sometimes answered the charge that our government was all wrong in such a way as to suggest that we believe it to be all right. We are likely to fare badly in any argument joined on such an issue, because of course it is not all right, and as soon as we attempt to prove that it is we are bound to get into all sorts of difficulties. In point of fact it is full of defects and inequalities, but our reply to our adversaries ought to be simply that it is better, both in theory and in practice, than any substitute they have to offer, and that it can be made better still. That is part of our task today; in a plainer sense it will be the task of our children tomorrow. We know, however, that they cannot build that City of God of which the fathers dreamed unless we transmit to them uninjured the foundation upon which its superstructure is to stand.

But it is not only in debate that we have been forgetful and stupid. Let me illustrate what I mean by referring to events with which most of us are entirely familiar. Not long after the end of the World War the Assembly of the State of New York refused on two occasions to seat duly elected representatives of the Socialist Party, solely because they were Socialists. Much more recently, in 1935, the Congress of the United States adopted virtually without debate or dissent the so-called "Red rider," under the official construction of which no teacher in the public schools of the District of Columbia might discuss, even in his own home, the theory or practice of Communism without forfeiting his salary as a teacher. More recently still Earl Browder was arrested and prevented from speaking in Terre Haute while campaigning for the Presidency of the United States on the Communist ticket. These things were done in the name of Americanism—that is, in our name as conservatives—and by agencies of our government itself, so that it seemed as if they were the fruits of the very system which we are seeking to preserve. I say "seemed," because in the narrow sense in which I am now using the word our government changes from year to year, almost from day to day, and these particular acts were committed by groups of men who had been placed in power directly or indirectly by us and could have been removed by us as soon as their terms of office expired. But to unthinking persons such a distinction was by no means obvious.

Now in this state of affairs it is perfectly clear, for several reasons, that the cause of the radicals was not really menaced at all. In the first place, all history bears witness to the truth of what was wittily observed by Mr. Justice Holmes in declining during the Prohibition era an invitation to discuss the subject, "Freedom of Speech," that "with effervescing opinions, as with the not yet forgotten champagnes, the quickest way to let them get flat is to let them be exposed to the air." The Czars of Russia deported all the radicals they could lay their hands on for five hundred years. It might seem in consequence that at the end of that period there would have been no radicals left in Russia. But the facts show that there were, unhappily, almost no conservatives left in Russia.

Furthermore, the position of the radicals was strengthened rather than weakened by repression, because the very fact of repression gave color to their repeated and continued assertion that the existence of a free popular government in the United States is more apparent than real. When a man says that his government is not free, and is immediately persecuted—or seems to be persecuted—for saying so, it looks very much on the face of things as if he were right in his contention.

Finally, the success of the radicals was not jeopardized by any of the acts of which we are speaking, because these acts, though done in our name, were thoroughly reactionary in character. The things which were jeopardized by them were representative government in the first instance cited, and civil liberty in the second and third. Now representative government and civil liberty are inextricably bound up with the political ideals and traditions of the United States. Our ancestors have cherished them on two continents and for almost a thousand years. If they were to be struck out of the framework of our government, there would be an end of that government as we now know it. In brief, there would be an end of the existing political order. But the radicals had nothing to fear on that account, because the destruction of the existing order is, as we have seen, the one aim which is held by reactionaries and radicals alike.

In view of all these considerations, it would have been very good tactics on our part—to say nothing of anything else—to go to the defense of the radicals with all the strength we had. If we had done so, we could have stopped the forces of reaction almost at the outset, and our cause would have gained the immense credit of defeating a menace quite as revolutionary as that of communism. It is gratifying to remember that some of our leaders and representatives did speak out, and speak out plainly. But too many of us were guilty of the incredible folly of sitting idly by, while a radical minority, many of whom were not native-born Americans and some of whom were not Americans at all, fought the battle of Americanism for us. In so far as they won it, we may rejoice with all our hearts at the result, but it is impossible not to feel that our own authority has been tremendously discredited. Moreover, the nature of the case makes complete reparation impossible. The "Red rider" has been repealed, but as Mr. Grenville Clark has forcibly pointed out,[1] no act of legislation or decree of court can compensate Mr. Browder for the loss of his right to speak on the particular day on which his right was denied.

2

I have said that the justification of our point of view in present-day politics is to be found in the fact that the institutions of the United States exemplify a special and unique sort of democracy, and further that representative government and civil liberty are inextricably bound up with these institutions. Such a statement falls short of the whole truth of the matter. Representative government and civil liberty are more than necessary incidentals of that form of democracy which exists in the United States. They are in themselves the very essentials of its significance and uniqueness. In them is summed up the whole of our contribution to what the world has learned about the science of politics. The Greeks knew something about the despotism of majorities, if that be democracy, and the Germans know something about obedience to law, if that be liberty. But neither the Greeks nor the Germans nor any other people have understood representative

[1] "Constitutional Rights," Pamphlet Series, No. 6, The American Academy of Political and Social Science, Philadelphia, 1938.

government and civil liberty as we have understood them. Without them experience teaches that no democracy can succeed. Our fathers had faith to believe that with them our own could not fail. We conservatives have professed, at least with our lips, the faith of our fathers.

But if representative government and civil liberty are the objects of our peculiar care, they have no place in the programs of our adversaries. "Fascism," says Mussolini, "combats the whole complex system of democratic ideology, and repudiates it, whether in its theoretical premises or in its practical application. . . . We solemnly bury that lie—democratic universal suffrage. We do not care a damn for this public opinion." "The working class," says Trotsky, "cannot guarantee the democratic character of its dictatorship without transgressing the limits of its democratic program." "The syndicalist," says Mr. A. D. Lewis in *Syndicalism and the General Strike*, "has a contempt for the vulgar idea of democracy; the vast unconscious mass is not to be taken into account when the minority wishes to act so as to benefit it."

Language such as this, which at least has the merits of clearness and candor, leaves nothing at issue between the fascist and the communist except the method of determining the things which are likely to prove beneficial to the "vast unconscious mass"—in any case the views of the mass are not to be considered at all. On the other hand, democracy cannot survive except for the existence of a public opinion which is enlightened as well as governing. It is the office of civil liberty to create such a public opinion, and that of representative government to express it. If we accepted the premises of Mr. Browder, there could be no logical objection to our putting him and all of his followers in jail. Doubtless it is what they would do to us if the destinies of the American people were in their hands and circumstances made such a course seem expedient. But the destinies of the American people are in our hands. Just here we come, definitely and finally, to the parting of the ways.

For it is manifest that an obligation rests upon us which depends on considerations much deeper than expediency and more compelling than an abstract sense of fair play—an obligation, moreover, by which we alone are bound and which differs in kind from any assumed by our opponents. We must protect free institutions at the peril of everything else, because free institutions are the fundamentals of our own case in chief. Without them our cause cannot prosper or even endure. To compass or permit their abridgment in the the name of saving democracy is suicidal, because it cuts away the foundation on which democracy stands. It is, politically speaking, the sin against the Holy Ghost—democracy denying itself. A fascist and a communist ought to be liberals perhaps, but a democrat must be one.

When, therefore, those who would persuade us to change our form of government have been silenced without due process of law, they have suffered nothing but the personal inconvenience of imprisonment or discrimination. But we have suffered the moral consequences of apostasy. Due process of law is our phrase and not theirs. It is we who have hitherto asserted the principles which make for free speech and a free press, and they who have denied them. When the Socialists walked out of the New York Assembly, they had lost nothing but their seats. But we had lost, in that particular connection, a part of our birthright. It is we and not they who have quoted with pride the saying that taxation without representation is tyranny. If Mr. Browder can persuade a majority of our fellow citizens to adopt the tenets of communism, no man knows, indeed, what the result will be. But we have one abiding comfort—whatever it is, it will not be communism according to his definition and it will be democracy according to ours.

All this is neither visionary nor unduly optimistic. It is not visionary because it is only a restatement of the axioms which underlie every noteworthy political achievement of the Anglo-Saxon race from Magna Carta to the Constitution of the United States. And it is no more optimistic than democracy itself. If the success of our government depends on the ability of the people to govern themselves, it is surely a very simple thing to say that we, who have risked everything on that supposition, ought reasonably to act as if we had faith in it. For faith, as has been finely said, "is, on the practical side, just the resolution to stand or fall by the noblest hypothesis," and without faith no hypothesis, even though it be true in fact, is worth anything in practical affairs. The human body is really lighter than water, but that fact will not help a man who is out of his depth and insists on trying to walk—he must act as if he believed in the laws of physics before the laws of physics will help him. In like manner, if we wish to justify democracy, it is of first importance that we give democracy a chance to justify itself.

But is our hypothesis true in fact? I have assumed its truth from the outset, because I have been writing as a conservative to conservatives, and such an assumption is, after all, our only reason for being what we are. And yet the question is an important one, though the issue is not in our keeping. As surely as no act of the swimmer could change the inevitable result if the laws of gravity were against him instead of being in his favor, so surely the deluge impends if the premises of democracy are ill founded.

Our fathers have proved some of them to be true. And how about those which remain to be proved by us and by our children? Well, they still constitute, as it seems to me, the noblest hypothesis. For democracy implies more than the fitness of the people to govern themselves. It presupposes a world in which truth, if let alone, will in the end prevail over error, and righteousness be vindicated. Some of you will remember the words of Gamaliel. He was speaking of men who taught what seemed to be so revolutionary a doctrine that certain of their countrymen took counsel to slay them. "Take heed to yourselves," he said, "what ye intend to do as touching these men. For before these days rose up Theudas, boasting himself to be somebody; to whom a number of men, about four hundred, joined themselves; who was slain; and all, as many as obeyed him, were scattered, and brought to naught. After this man rose up Judas of Galilee in the days of the taxing, and drew away many people after him; he also perished; and all, even as many as obeyed him, were dispersed. And now I say unto you, Refrain from these men and let them alone; for if this counsel or this work be of men, it will come to naught; but if it be of God, ye cannot overthrow it; lest haply ye be found to fight even against God." The men to whom he referred were progressives rather than radicals, because they spoke in the name of One who said that He came not to destroy but to fulfil. In the fullness of time it was their cause before which "the prejudices of the Synagogue, and the doubts of the Academy, and the pride of the portico, and the fasces of the Lictor and the swords of thirty legions were humbled in the dust." Gamaliel was a conservative. The fact that he was a conservative at that particular time and place shows that he lacked vision. But he was a good democrat for all that, and his doctrine is our doctrine.

X

A BRIEF ON THE PLAY SCENE

THE recent trilogy of Professor J. Dover Wilson [1] has served to direct attention anew to the subject of *Hamlet* and particularly to the play scene, which Professor Wilson correctly regards as "the climax and crisis of the whole drama." In the course of his elaborate reconstruction of this scene he comes face to face with the problem of the identification of the "speech of some dozen or sixteen lines" which Hamlet undertook to "set down and insert" in *The Murder of Gonzago*, a play already in the repertory of the strolling players. As every reader of Shakespeare will remember, the avowed objects of Hamlet in having the play produced were to test the honesty of the Ghost, and, if that were established, to "catch the conscience of the King." In explaining his plan to Horatio immediately before the performance began he said that one scene came "near the circumstance" of his father's death as narrated by the Ghost, and added that if the King's "occulted guilt" did not "itself unkennel in *one speech*" he was prepared to regard the Ghost as an impostor from Hell instead of the spirit of his father. When the play was presented the King rose in terror when Lucianus, the Player-Murderer, poured the mock poison in the Player-King's ears. Thereupon, on the order of Polonius, the play was abandoned in the middle of a scene and with Lucianus still on the stage.

Professor Wilson concedes that the identification of Hamlet's lines presents a vexed question "over which much paper and ink have been expended." An examination of the notes in the Furness Variorum edition of *Hamlet* abundantly justifies this statement. According to one opinion, the lines are contained in the long and moralizing speech of the Player-King which immediately follows the gratuitous promise of his con-

[1] *Hamlet*, *The Manuscript of Shakespeare's Hamlet*, and *What Happens in Hamlet.*

sort not to remarry in the event of his death. On the other hand, much support may be found for the conclusion adopted by Professor Wilson that the inserted speech is the one spoken by Lucianus at the moment when the play murder is committed. The purposes of this paper are to show that both conclusions are mistaken; to advance as the true explanation that the performance of the play was interrupted before Hamlet's speech had been delivered; and, finally, to suggest what the subject of the missing speech was.

The lines of Lucianus selected by Professor Wilson are as follows:

> Thoughts black, hands apt, drugs fit, and time agreeing,
> Confederate season, else no creature seeing,
> Thou mixture rank, of midnight weeds collected,
> With Hecate's ban thrice blasted, thrice infected,
> Thy natural magic and dire property
> On wholesome life usurps immediately.

I pass over the fact that if this is Hamlet's speech his intended dozen or sixteen lines were reduced to six in the course of composition. There are "grounds more relative than this" on which to rest the statement that the lines cannot be his. The moment we assume, as Professor Wilson agrees that we must, the structural coincidence involved in the existence of a play presenting the exact means by which Hamlet's father was murdered, it is manifest that so far as the portrayal of the murder is concerned the important thing is not what the Player-Murderer says but what he does. The murderer has made his entrance, however, and *must say something*. Having this in mind, I cannot imagine more ineffective lines than those which are placed in his mouth. Not only is the poetry of the poorest—as generally throughout what we are permitted to see of the Gonzago-play—but the language used is as vague and general as possible. It is precisely the sort of bombast which we should expect to find in an old play of the sort which

Shakespeare had in mind and at which he took the opportunity to poke a little fun.

Professor Wilson argues that the lines of Lucianus are "but a condensation of the description of the poisoning in the Ghost's speech" and that the words "mixture rank of midnight weeds collected" bring back to the vision of Claudius "in dreadful detail that scene four months before when he too was bending over a sleeping king, about to poison him with 'cursed hebona in a vial.' " Such an argument surely verges on the absurd. When Claudius saw a reproduction of the very method (certainly not a usual one in any age) by which he had poisoned his predecessor, it is not easy to suppose that the ranting lines of the Player-Murderer were required to bring back to his vision the details of the scene enacted four months before. Indeed, since the information received by Hamlet from the Ghost was concerned (with an exception of the first importance to be noticed later) with what had been done rather than with what had been said at the time the murder was committed, any attempt to enlarge or rewrite the speech assigned to Lucianus would necessarily have involved the risk of emphasizing differences rather than likenesses and thus of diminishing the effect of the scene on Claudius. If, however, Hamlet had arrived at an opposite opinion and had decided to rewrite the speech, can there be any doubt that he would have been as concrete as possible? Can there be any doubt, for instance, that instead of referring vaguely to "midnight weeds" (I suppose there are several varieties of midnight weeds from which poisons may be compounded) he would have been careful to mention hebona, which was the poison actually administered? No! No! Even if Hamlet had been so foolish as to think that the impression of the play murder on Claudius would be enhanced by a speech, he could not have been guilty of the malevolent platitudes which fall from the lips of Lucianus.

An equally strong case may be made out against the passage in which the Player-King prophesies to the Player-Queen that she will break her promise not to contract a second marriage after his death. Now we are nowhere told that Gertrude had made any such promise to King Hamlet. If she had, her breach of it must be reckoned as the least of her misdeeds. She had (as Professor Wilson thinks and as I think) committed adultery with Claudius. In marrying her deceased husband's brother she had also committed what Shakespeare's audience clearly understood to be incest. Even in the hysterical violence of the closet scene Hamlet, though he talks about marriage vows, says nothing about the making of a promise to his father not to remarry.

But what is much more important, if the lines under consideration were composed by Hamlet, they must be understood as an attempt to catch the conscience of Gertrude rather than that of Claudius. We know, however, from Hamlet's own words in the "rogue and peasant slave" soliloquy that his intention was otherwise. Like Gertrude, the King was guilty of adultery and incest. In addition he had murdered his brother and his sovereign and had usurped the throne. In the light of this record it can hardly be supposed that Hamlet expected his guilt to unkennel itself merely because he was reminded, however forcibly, that the Queen, in addition to her other misdemeanors, had violated a promise about remarrying which she had made to her first husband.

What, then, are we to conclude: that Shakespeare forgot about Hamlet's inserted speech or did not trouble himself to write it because he was sure that the audience would not notice its omission?—that Hamlet abandoned his plan and did not set down the lines which he had in mind?—that the speech is to be found in some passage in the Gonzago-play other than those to which reference has been made?—or that, for some reason, the speech which Hamlet prepared was never delivered? I am content to rest my case against the first of these alternatives on the statement of Professor Wilson (though his opinion is expressed in a connection slightly different from the present one) that Shakespeare was not "a bungler, a slipshod dramatist, who [left] loose ends and banal obscurities thickly scattered over the central scene of his most famous drama." A conclusive answer to the second alternative is that the dialogue between Hamlet and Horatio shows that the inserted speech had actually been prepared and was ready for delivery a few moments before the performance of the Gonzago-play began. As to the third alternative, it is enough to say that three centuries of criticism have failed to identify Hamlet's speech with any passage in the text other than those which have already been discussed.[2] Before disposing of the final alternative it becomes necessary to say a few words about the posture in which Hamlet stood toward the other persons in the drama and about the practical difficulties with which he was confronted.

Dr. A. C. Bradley, who seems to me the soundest of all Shakespearean critics, has discussed at some length what may be described as the "external theory" of the cause of Hamlet's delay. As Dr. Bradley summarizes the arguments by which this theory is supported, it may be asked what Hamlet was to do "when the Ghost had left him with its commission of vengeance. The King was surrounded not merely by courtiers but by a Swiss body-guard; how was Hamlet to get at him? Was he then to accuse him publicly of the murder? If he did, what would happen? How would he prove the charge? All that he had to offer in proof was—a ghost-story! . . . Obviously, then, even if the court had been

[2] An exception must be noted in the person of Professor J. Q. Adams, who appears to think that Hamlet wrote the entire scene which was presented before the King. I cannot resist the comment that if this be so he certainly talked much better than he wrote.

honest, instead of subservient and corrupt, it would have voted Hamlet mad, or worse, and would have shut him up out of harm's way." While Dr. Bradley regards considerations such as these as insufficient explanations of Hamlet's behavior, and therefore concludes that the external theory will not hold water, he admits that it is "quite probable that, when Hamlet was 'thinking too precisely on the event,' he was considering, among other things, the question how he could avenge his father without sacrificing his own life or freedom," and that "assuredly, also, he was anxious that his act of vengeance should not be misconstrued, and would never have been content to leave a 'wounded name' behind him."

I fully agree that Hamlet's delay was not caused "merely, or mainly, or even to any considerable extent" by external difficulties, but it seems to me that the points admitted by Dr. Bradley are to some extent understated. It was surely not "thinking too precisely on the event" for Hamlet to realize that in order to justify the blow by which Claudius was to be struck down it was essential to denounce him before the whole court. Only three persons—Claudius, Hamlet, and Horatio, to whom Hamlet had recounted the tale unfolded by the Ghost—knew the method by which the late King had been murdered, or knew indeed that he had been murdered at all. If, therefore, the behavior of Claudius were such as to satisfy both Hamlet and Horatio of his guilt, it was certain that the inference of guilt would be drawn by nobody else. The plot of the Gonzago-play made it a perfect instrument to serve notice on the King that Hamlet had discovered his guilt, but as an instrument of public accusation it was entirely worthless. In order to make it serve the latter purpose something had to be added, not for the benefit of the King but for the benefit of the court. Until this something was added, until the King was openly accused of murder, Hamlet could strike only at the peril of his own life and reputation. If we are to take him at his own words, he did not set his life "at a pin's fee," but he valued his reputation so highly that he charged Horatio with his dying breath to "report [his] cause aright to the unsatisfied."

Professor Wilson has not overlooked the force of at least a part of what has just been said. In his opinion it may be taken for granted that "if the interlude proved the Ghost honest Hamlet intended to finish his uncle off immediately afterwards," but he nevertheless pauses to inquire what reason Hamlet was to give the world for the assassination. He calls attention in a footnote to the suggestion of a friendly critic that the suspicions of the courtiers would be aroused by the fact that the scene of the play murder is laid in a garden and that Hamlet's father was known to have died in a garden, but dismisses the suggestion with the apt remark that to accept it "is surely to find Scotland Yard at Elsinore." His own solution of the difficulty is that by a sudden afterthought Hamlet intended the Gonzago-play to have two meanings. To the guilty Claudius the Player-King was of course to represent the murdered King Hamlet, and Lucianus, the Player-Murderer, was to represent himself. On the other hand to the court the Player-King was to represent Claudius and Lucianus was to represent Hamlet. In this way, says Professor Wilson, Hamlet "uses the play to threaten his uncle" and to "prepare the court for the execution to follow."

I am bound to say that this theory seems to me a very strange one. No support whatever is to be found for it in the text. Professor Wilson makes much of the fact that upon the entrance of Lucianus Hamlet describes him as "nephew to the king," and argues that the purpose of Hamlet's remark was to identify himself with Lucianus in the minds of the audience. But what reason is there to doubt that in the original Gonzago-play Lucianus was actually nephew to the King? The plot of Shakespeare's drama had already required him to present to his audience the extraordinary coincidence of an existing play in which a sleeping king was murdered by poison administered through the ears and in which the murderer got the love of the King's wife. Nothing was to be gained and something was to be lost by insisting on the further coincidence involved in making the murderer brother to the King. Doubtless it was on this account that Shakespeare caused Hamlet to tell us in his soliloquy that the players were to present "something like" the murder of his father, and in his conversation with Horatio to say that one scene in the play came "near the circumstance" of his father's death. If Lucianus had been brother to the King in the Gonzago-play, the circumstance of the death of King Hamlet would have been exactly reproduced and the improbability of the entire situation would have been needlessly emphasized.

But a much graver objection to Professor Wilson's theory becomes apparent when we inquire what possible motive Hamlet could have had in seeking to be associated in the minds of the courtiers with the villain of the Gonzago-play. "The Ghost's commands," says Professor Wilson, "the salvation of Gertrude, the family honor of the House of Denmark, forbade any disclosure of the truth. The real meaning of the Gonzago story, the King's meaning, could not be revealed, because the Queen herself was involved. Hamlet was, therefore, obliged to furnish the court with some theory which would explain the Gonzago-play, account for the open discomfiture of his uncle which he hoped it would effect, and justify (*or at any rate make explicable*) the assassination that was to come after. His own rights (i.e., his rights to the throne as his father's son and heir) gave him everything he required."

The weakness of this argument is implicit in the words in parentheses which I have placed in italics. Hamlet could not hope to justify (and surely did not wish to make explicable) an attack on the person of the King by presenting himself to the court in the guise of a cowardly and treacherous assassin about to poison his lawful sovereign. To do so would have been deliberately to misreport his cause to the unsatisfied. Moreover, in charging Claudius with murder Hamlet was not required to involve the Queen in any way. There was no necessity for revealing her adultery, and apart from adultery her only fault had been her "o'er hasty" and incestuous second marriage. As Hamlet's comments on the dialogue between the Player-King and Player-Queen show clearly enough, he had no scruples about calling attention to this fault in public.

It follows from what has been said that while I agree with Professor Wilson that if Hamlet struck the King down, he was under the necessity of giving the world a reason for his act, I find myself strongly in disagreement with the view that the reason which he intended to give was other than the true one—namely, that the King was the murderer of his father. I believe, in short, that in the Gonzago-play the Player-King was to be identified for all purposes with King Hamlet and Lucianus with Claudius, and that at least one of the difficulties with which Hamlet was confronted was to make these identifications as clear to the courtiers as they were likely to be to his uncle.

With the foregoing considerations in mind, we may now proceed to an examination of the last of the alternatives propounded—namely, that the inserted speech was never delivered. So far as I know, only three critics have discussed this possibility. Dr. Furnivall, as quoted in Dr. Furness's note, holds "very strongly that Lucianus's speech is not the [inserted] speech, and that, in fact, the speech is not in the printed play. Either the King's conscience was more quickly stung than Hamlet anticipated, and so the written speech was never needed; or . . . Shakespeare contented himself with showing us . . . that Hamlet altered the play and put his 'dozen or sixteen lines' into action instead of words." Mr. Malleson, also quoted by Dr. Furness, says that if the King had not blenched, "we should have had probably the rest of the dozen lines, which might have contained a hint of the Poisoner's next aim, the seduction to a second marriage of the seeming-virtuous Queen." Dr. Bradley, evidently sharing Mr. Malleson's view that the lines of Lucianus constituted only the first half of the inserted speech, feels that "Hamlet's device proves a triumph far more complete than he had dared to expect. He had thought the King might 'blench,' but he does much more. When only six of the 'dozen or sixteen lines' have been spoken he starts to his feet and rushes from the hall, followed by the whole dismayed Court." I cannot bring myself to believe that Hamlet was the author of any of the wretched lines delivered by Lucianus. Nevertheless, the comments of Mr. Malleson and Dr. Bradley do justice to one of the realities of the situation. When the play was interrupted Lucianus was in the center of the stage. If no interruption had occurred he would (at the least) have had to make his exit, and, as in the case of his entrance, *he would have had to say something*. It is certain, therefore, that his speech was not at an end when the King rose.

It will be observed that only Mr. Malleson has ventured to conjecture what the unspoken lines would probably have contained. In his opinion they "might have contained a hint of the Poisoner's next aim, the seduction to a second marriage of the seeming-virtuous Queen." The suggestion is an acute one, which, in my view of the matter, just misses the mark. The dumb show had already made it clear that the Poisoner was to get the love of his victim's wife and the dialogue between the Player-King and Player-Queen had been full of references to second marriages. In view of the situation existing in Elsinore, these references must have seemed to the courtiers in exceedingly bad taste. They could not, however, standing alone, have been understood as an accusation of murder directed against Claudius.

I am persuaded that the key to the solution of the entire problem is contained in the observation already made that, *with a single exception*, the tale unfolded by the Ghost had been concerned with things done rather than with things said at the time of King Hamlet's death. The exception is to be found in these lines of the Ghost:

> 'Tis *given out*, that sleeping in my orchard,
> *A serpent stung me*, so the whole ear of Denmark
> Is by a forgèd process of my death
> Rankly abused.

Now I think I need not labor an argument in order to show that the Queen was not guilty of complicity in her husband's death. She stands acquitted by the almost unanimous voice of competent criticism. There is not a word in the text to imply, however remotely, that Claudius acted with any other accomplice. It follows that the cause of death must have been "given out" by Claudius. Under circumstances which we can only conjecture he must have said to the Queen, or said to someone, that *King Hamlet had died from the sting of a serpent. The courtiers knew, of course, the cause of death which had been given out; what they did not know was that the process of the death was forged.*

Let us return now to the Gonzago-play and to the necessity for converting it from a secret into an open denunciation of Claudius. My conclusion is that when Claudius rose he prevented the delivery of Hamlet's inserted lines, which were to be spoken by Lucianus either in a soliloquy or in a scene with the Player-Queen. In the former case the lines would have disclosed the intention of the murderer to ascribe the death of his victim to the sting of a serpent. In the latter case the forged process of the death would have been presented directly to the Player-Queen. In either case the effect on the court would have been positively electrifying. The murder of a

King in a garden had been depicted. There had been unseemly talk about second marriages. The extraordinary behavior of Hamlet must have impressed the courtiers that something important was about to take place. The moment Lucianus referred to the sting of a serpent the purport of the Gonzago-play would have been as clear as crystal to everyone in the room. Moreover, the impact of the scene on Claudius would have been doubled. He would have known at once that no attempt to control himself and to brazen matters out could save him. Hamlet not only knew of his guilt but was about to denounce him publicly.

It will no doubt be said that there is no basis in the text for the theory which has just been expounded. I do not agree with any such statement. The last line of Hamlet before the interruption of the play is an attempt to direct the attention of both Claudius and the court to what is about to happen: "You shall see anon how the murderer gets the love of Gonzago's wife." But Claudius has already seen and heard enough and rises in confusion. Hamlet immediately says, "What! frighted with false fire?" There is not a single note on this line in the Furness Variorum edition of *Hamlet.* To me its import is exceedingly plain—*Claudius had been frighted with false fire because the real fire was about to come.*

One other possible objection ought to be noticed. How, it may be argued, if the purposes of Hamlet in the play scene partially miscarried, do we find him in almost hysterical high spirits when conversing with Horatio immediately after the play had been interrupted? I can do no more than to state my answer to this objection. The first purpose of the Gonzago-play had been brilliantly accomplished. The guilt of the King was apparent to both Hamlet and Horatio, and any possibility of doubting the Ghost's word was at an end. I agree with Dr. Bradley that Hamlet's doubt on this point had never been a "genuine doubt" but was rather "an unconscious fiction, an excuse for his delay—and for its continuance." The second purpose of the Gonzago-play—the public accusation of the King—had failed, not because of any weakness on Hamlet's part but because the King had been frighted by false fire. Because it failed—because the King had rushed from the room—Hamlet had been reprieved from the necessity of acting. The high spirits which possessed him in the scene with Horatio were equally compounded of triumph at the discomfiture of the King and relief that he had not been compelled to strike. But I am aware that this argument can only be suggested. To make it good would require an analysis of the character of Hamlet. The subject is a large one, and perhaps too much about it has been written already.

XI
DIVERSITIES OF GIFTS

Now there are diversities of gifts, but the same Spirit
I CORINTHIANS 12.4

1

MORE than a century ago an Irish priest was appointed rector of St. Mary's Church, which stood then, as it stands today, at the corner of Prince and Vine streets, one square to the south of King Street. St. James Episcopal Church is situated at the corner of Duke and Orange streets, an equal distance to the north of King Street. When the appointment of the priest of St. Mary's was only four years old, the vestry of St. James called to its pulpit a young man who had begun as a lawyer a career which he was destined to end as a bishop. At almost the same time a new minister came to Trinity Lutheran Church, whose lofty spire has overlooked King Street from the south since the concluding decades of the eighteenth century.

They became fast friends. The priest was an ardent Democrat. The Lutheran minister was a Whig. The Episcopal rector regarded parties—"faction," as George Washington would have expressed it—as the besetting sin of Church and State. In spite of these political differences all three were elected to the school board. When President Zachary Taylor died in office, the board met in the Court House in order to pass resolutions of respect. At the close of the meeting the three friends walked, arm in arm, to Trinity Church in order to take part in a religious service in memory of the dead President. The picture which they presented was never forgotten by those who saw it, and has become for us on King Street a symbol of not the least part of the contribution which America has made to the wisdom and charity of the world.

But indeed the precedents which make for tolerance among us run back much further than a century. A decade before the last of the witches was hanged in Salem, the "Great Law" of William Penn had provided that no person who acknowledged one Almighty God to be the creator and ruler of the world, and who professed himself obliged in conscience to live peaceably and justly under the civil government, should in any wise be molested or prejudiced by reason of his conscientious persuasion or practice. Relying on this assurance, several families from the Palatinate, descendants of the distressed Swiss Mennonites, settled on the Pequea Creek, whereupon Penn sent to the Conestoga Indians a present—consisting, somewhat inappropriately, of powder and shot—and a message requiring their friendship to "the Palatines, settled near Pequae." The Indians made a conciliatory reply, and in the course of a few years the Mennonites were followed by coreligionists of Penn himself; by Amish, called in early days Beardy Men and Hooker Mennonites—the latter because of the hooks and eyes which they still use on their clothes instead of buttons; by Dunkers or Tunkers, with beards as long as those of the Amish, but without the distinguishing hooks and eyes; by Moravians, who founded a congregation of which Count Zinzendorf is reckoned as the first pastor; and by one Conrad Beissel, who lived first as a hermit on the banks of the Cocalico and afterwards founded a monastic society whose members attained such excellence in music as to be publicly rewarded by the King of England, and such skill in printing as to be chosen printers of money for the Continental Congress.

If to these little-known sectarians, referred to locally by the collective designation of "plain people," there be added representatives of the usual Protestant denominations and the Catholics who laid the foundations of St. Mary's—the women mixing the mortar while the men gathered the stones from the adjoining farms—it is not hard to credit the statement of an authority on the subject that a pedestrian on King Street may meet representatives of as many as thirty sects during the course of a walk on that thoroughfare.

2

He who would see the plain people of the present generation can make no better beginning than by following King Street to our market house on any market day. The land on which we are standing was set apart in 1730 "for the erection of a market within the town" and has ever since served its appointed purpose, the stalls in the market house being rented annually by the city to the highest bidders at a public auction.

Here is a placid Mennonite housewife who, with the help of her little daughter, is selling vegetables raised on her husband's farm, and in addition a variety of products of her own handiwork—yellow noodles for "schmaltzing" (baking with bread crumbs) or making soup, pickled pigs' feet called "souse," dried apples or "schnitz," "schmierkaes," and thick sugar cookies which are known as "pepper nuts." If the time of the year were near Shrove Tuesday, her wares would also include "fasnachts"—raised doughnuts without holes—which are eaten on that feast day.

Being indoors now, she has removed the black bonnet, shaped like a short pokebonnet, in which she came to market, and in so doing has uncovered a small white cap resembling a miniature sunbonnet, the strings of which are tied under her chin. She wears a black garb (it might also be gray or, indeed, any quiet print) consisting of a waist buttoned close to the neck, but without a collar, and a long full skirt. A cape made of the same material as the dress completes as plain a costume as may well be imagined. It is curious, nevertheless, to observe the universality of the experience that the effort to avoid distinction in dress inevitably defeats its purpose. In a somewhat similar connection the Quakers, in attempting to abolish ritual, have unwittingly created an exceedingly effective ritual out of silence.

The little girl does not wear a garb. She has not yet renounced the world and joined the church—has not "come out" and "given herself up," as the Mennonites themselves express it. She will make her own decision on that point when she has arrived at years of discretion. Perhaps she will never give herself up, and unless she does so she will continue to dress as her own taste and that of her mother determine. If, in due time, she concludes to take the momentous step, she will appear some morning attired like her mother, and from that day forward the vanity of personal adornment will be a thing of the past.

If her father had come to market it might be possible to tell whether the family belongs to the Old Mennonites, who are the more numerous and the less rigid, or to the New Mennonites, who claim to have returned to an earlier and more excellent standard. Among the former, the wearing of beards is optional; among the latter, beards are considered productive of both pride and envy, and are consequently forbidden. A Mennonite with a beard is, therefore, certainly an Old Mennonite, but one without a beard may belong to either of the two branches of the church. Old Mennonites vote at elections and are allowed to hold such public offices as school director and road supervisor, but not to be members of the legislature. Their ministers are expected not to vote. New Mennonites do not vote at all. If one of them becomes a backslider in the eyes of the church, the other members of his own family are not allowed to eat at the same table with him, and his wife withdraws from him.

Old Mennonite ministers are chosen in the following manner. When a vacancy occurs and a new appointment is required, several men go into a small room and receive privately oral nominations to fill the vacancy. After this has been done, an opportunity is given to any nominee to excuse himself from the service. Those who are not excused, if, for instance, six in number, are brought before six Bibles, in one of which a lot has been placed. Each candidate takes up a book, and the one within whose book the lot is found is the chosen minister.

3

Across the aisle of the market a portly Amishman, his hollow-chested wife, and their little son are engaged in selling poultry and potatoes. The rule among the Amish requires that the men shave their upper lips and allow their beards to grow, whence, as already stated, they were formerly known as Beardy Men—a name which went out of use when the wearing of beards became generally fashionable during the period of the Civil War. Our Amishman has kept the rule to the letter, and his beard, which is reddish brown in color, is a full and noble one. Except for the necessary absence of a beard, the little boy is a perfect manikin. His hair, like that of his father, has been cut straight over the forehead and hangs almost to his shoulders, and he wears the characteristic Amish garb consisting of a dark coat and waistcoat fastened with hooks and eyes, long trousers (which are worn without suspenders), and a round-crowned black felt hat with an extremely wide brim. Though he may not know it, the hooks and eyes on his clothing are symbols of an inherited pacifism and express the abhorrence which his ancestors felt for the brass buttons which have always played such conspicuous parts in adorning the uniform of a soldier.

The Amish mother, though she too wears a garb, is much less restricted in her choice of colors than her Mennonite neighbor. Her bonnet—which has a long visor hiding her face and a "curtain" reaching to her shoulders—and the folded shawl or handkerchief meeting demurely over her breast are black, but her closely fitting dress is a dull magenta and the apron which she wears over it is royal blue. She has selected these colors, not because she mistakenly believes them to be inconspicuous, but because she regards them as "unworldly"—that is, not in general use. Certain shades of green and purple, as well as magenta and royal blue, appear to have been definitely approved by her coreligionists as unworldly colors. The implications of this approval are not altogether unnoticed by the world itself. A merchant on King Street once told me of a customer of his who hesitated about buying a piece of cloth which was otherwise acceptable to her on the ground that the color "looked Amish." He hastened to assure her that she was mistaken, and she completed the purchase.

The Amish love of color is not limited in its expression to the dress of the women. Houses and barns are sometimes gayly painted. A blue gate is said, though perhaps incorrectly, to be a sign that a marriageable daughter is to be found within. Before the days of automobiles every Amish family possessed a wagon covered with yellow oilcloth. These wagons were built without dashboards and usually without whip sockets—the latter being regarded, except among one faction of the Amish, as symbolical of compulsion or force. Some members of the church now drive automobiles, but this practice is strongly disapproved by others.

One becomes a member of the Mennonite Church by conversion, but one is born into the Amish communion. There are less than twenty family names in the entire fellowship, and I have never heard of an Amish convert. On the other hand, instances of voluntary withdrawal from the church are exceedingly rare. The small number of surnames sometimes creates difficulties. A public-school teacher with whom I was acquainted was elected to teach at an ungraded country school having thirty-four pupils, all but two of whom were named Stoltzfus. In order to avoid confusion it became necessary to invoke medieval precedents, and to speak of "Hickory John" and "Black Isaac." A client of mine prefixed the word "Spring" to his given name because of a large spring which was located on his farm, and invariably signed his name in its revised form to checks and legal documents.

Though in nearly all connections the Amish have been content to accept the views and continue the practices which have been handed down to them, it by no means follows that they are lacking in natural spirit and gayety. Indeed, their young men sometimes display a wildness of behavior which seems altogether out of keeping with the soberness of their appearance. Time out of mind they have had a passionate interest in fast and spirited horses. In spite of a traditional adherence to the Republican Party, which originally resulted from their opinions on the subject of slavery, they voted the Democratic ticket in the presidential election of 1932 because of their deep-seated hostility to national prohibition. At wedding parties, called "infares," the revelry frequently continues all night. On these occasions both young and old join in a game not unlike "Hunt the Slipper," which is played with what is known as a "bloom-sock"—a handkerchief or towel, twisted and doubled, with the ends tied in a knot. In the course of the game the bloom-sock is passed secretly from hand to hand in order to confuse that one of the players whose obligation it is to find it. As opportunity offers, the other players hit him with the bloom-sock. If he is able to seize it, his obligation is discharged and another takes his place.

4

You may well suppose at first glance that the man in charge of the next market stall is also an Amishman. A second glance, however, will serve to correct your mistake. His shaven upper lip and full beard are suggestive of the Amish practice, but his gray coat of clerical cut is both lighter in color and finer in material than that of any Amishman. Most of all, the large buttons with which his coat is fastened show conclusively that he belongs to some other denomination. As a matter of fact, both beard and garb result from his own choice and are not rendered obligatory by the discipline of his church. He is one of the Dunkers, or, as they prefer to be called, the Brethren. As the commonly accepted name indicates, he believes in "dipping"—that is, in baptism by immersion.

The members of the various "plain" denominations do not greatly differ from one another in theological beliefs. All of them have retained the ordinances of baptism, whether by pouring or immersion, and of the Lord's Supper. Some of them also practise feet-washing.

An eyewitness of a generation ago [1] has described a feet-washing and love feast among the Dunkers. The ceremony was held in the evening and in church, the seats of which were so constructed that by turning down the backs of some of them tables could be formed. At the appointed time the presiding bishop rose in his place and read the account of the feet-washing contained in the Gospel according to Saint John. In front of him stood four men, who, at the words "laid aside his garments," took off their coats, and, at the words "took a towel and girded himself," put on long white aprons tied around the waist. Two of these men washed feet and two wiped, and, having thus ministered, were ministered to by four others who took their places, and who were in turn replaced until all had taken part. The women, who occupied a separate side of the church, performed the same ordinance for themselves in a similar manner. At its conclusion all present

[1] Mrs. Phebe Earle Gibbons, whose essay, "Pennsylvania Dutch," appeared in the *Atlantic Monthly* for October 1869. I have made use of her observations in a number of other places throughout this paper.

partook of a love feast consisting of soup, bread, butter, and meat, without salt or other condiment. When all had eaten, a young bishop rose at the center of the main table, shook hands with the sister on his left, and kissed the brother on his right. From brother to brother and from sister to sister the kiss went around the congregation until the last sister, who had no one to kiss, went forward and kissed the first one with whom the bishop had shaken hands, thus completing the chain of unity. This ceremony was followed by communion, which was administered with bread or cakes, unleavened and sweetened, and home-made wine.

But if theological differences among the plain sectarians are slight and unimportant, there are many differences in customs and practices which rest indirectly on theological grounds, and of which the lawyer who maintains an office on King Street is bound to take notice. All of the plain denominations forbid their members to institute legal proceedings under any circumstances whatever, though both Dunkers and Mennonites are permitted, in extremity and by way of last resort, to defend themselves against unjustified suits and to appeal to the police for protection.

The latter permission, which is not accorded to the Amish, is founded upon a passage in the Acts of the Apostles in which it is narrated that forty Jews entered into a conspiracy to kill Paul. But Paul sent his nephew to the chief captain to inform him of the conspiracy, and the latter put Paul under the charge of soldiers to be brought safe to Felix, the governor. For some reason, however, a Dunker may defend himself in court or ask for protection *only once*. If the verdict goes against him he may not appeal, and if his request for help is unanswered he may not renew it but must take the consequences.

The idea of nonresistance is not entirely confined to human relationships. Among the striking peculiarities of a branch of the Dunker fellowship is a strong opposition to the use of lightning rods. "If," said one of their preachers, "God wishes to preserve the building, he can preserve it without the lightning rod. If he does not wish to preserve it, I am willing to submit to the result."

5

Only a few persons may now be found who claim membership in the monastic society founded by Conrad Beissel. The brothers and sisters wore a habit similar to that of the Capuchins or White Friars and lived in separate houses, sleeping on benches with blocks of wood for pillows and eating with wooden forks from plates made of thin octagonal pieces of poplar board. Even the flagons, goblets, and trays used in the communion service were made of wood. The celibate brothers and sisters met only in religious exercises and at love feasts. Celibacy was recommended, though not enjoined, and no vows with reference to it were taken. The strictest simplicity was practised by all.

On one occasion a brother who had taken the name Onesimus, and who, though designated as prior, was subordinate to Beissel, ordered a bell from Europe without the knowledge of the society and caused to be placed on it a Latin inscription in which his name was included. When the bell arrived it was duly paid for, but a council was held in order to determine what to do with it. The first decision was to break the bell and bury the pieces in the earth. The next morning, however, Beissel appeared before the council and said he had reflected that, as the brothers were poor, the bell should be pardoned. This was accordingly done and the bell was sold. For many years the pardoned bell, still bearing the name of the innovating prior who had caused it to be cast, was used to summon worshipers to Trinity Lutheran Church. Afterwards it passed into the hands of one of the fire companies on King Street.

DIVERSITIES OF GIFTS

Though Beissel was surpassed both in education and in native powers of mind by a number of his monastic associates, he was a first-rate musician and composer. He developed an unusual style of singing, founded on the music of nature as found in the tones of the Aeolian harp. The music was set in four, six, and eight parts. All the parts save the bass were led and sung exclusively by women, the men being confined to the bass, which was set in two parts, the high and the low bass. The former, in combination with one of the female parts, is said to have been an excellent imitation of the concert horn, and the latter to have resembled the deep tones of the organ. An early visitor to the monastery reported that the singers scarcely opened their mouths or moved their lips, and added that the effect was to throw the voices up to the ceiling of the chapel, which was not high, so that the tones seemed to be entering from above with almost superhuman softness and devotion.

The commissioners who were sent by the English Government to visit the society after the French and Indian War were so charmed by what they heard that they requested that a copy of the music be sent to the royal family in England. This request was cheerfully complied with. About a year afterwards a box was received, three or four feet long and two or two and a half feet wide, containing a present in return. What the present was is not certainly known—none having seen it but Beissel and one Jaebez, who was then prior and into whose care the box had been consigned. On this occasion Beissel had no afterthoughts. He caused the box and its contents to be buried secretly. From a hint dropped by Jaebez it is supposed that the contents consisted of images of the King and Queen in full costume. Perhaps something may be said in justification of the feeling that it is harder to pardon an image than a bell.

6

The history of religious differences would appear to show that it is harder to pardon a heretic than either an image or a bell. If so, the views of some of Beissel's coreligionists must be regarded as exceptional. "We deny eternal punishment," said one of them. "Those souls who become sensible of God's great goodness and clemency, and acknowledge his lawful authority . . . and that Christ is the only true Son of God, are received into happiness; but those who continue obstinate are kept in darkness until the Great Day, when light will make all happy."

But a belief in universal regeneration has played no appreciable part in the spirit of tolerance which, from those early and vivid days

> When reds and blues were indeed red and blue,

has always manifested itself on King Street. For tolerance, as I have tried to show elsewhere, is a by-product of democracy, and though rooted in the greatest of the divine virtues, must be reckoned as a civil virtue rather than as an ecclesiastical one. It does not result from theological views about human regeneration. Still less does it depend upon the acceptance of that curious modern point of view which regards a judicial attitude as one by which judgment is withheld rather than given. Its practice is summed up for us on King Street in the memory of a priest and two ministers who thought themselves the better citizens and not the worse churchmen because they were willing to attend a religious ceremony in a Protestant church in order to do honor to the memory of a President of the United States.

XII
A LETTER TO MY FATHER

Dear Father:

I am not sure whether or not you ever read Kipling's *Jungle Book*. If you did so it must have been long ago, when the *Jungle Book* was first published and was read aloud to me as a very small boy, a little at a time, just before we were called to supper on winter evenings. In that case I think you will remember how Tabaqui, the jackal, came for no good purpose to the cave of Father and Mother Wolf and, having made a meal on some bones which they had thrown aside, embarrassed them by telling them how beautiful their children were. As Kipling points out, they were quite properly embarrassed, because there is nothing so unlucky as to compliment children to their faces.

Perhaps it is also unlucky to compliment the old to their faces, but if there is such a precept I do not think that it applies to the dead. I may, therefore, write words now without embarrassment to either of us, which I never spoke, and indeed would not have wished to speak, in times past. If it seems strange to you that in the course of what follows I refer to you chiefly in the past tense, you must set it down to the literary affectation by which we are accustomed to speak and write of the dead in that way.

By a necessity even more compelling—a necessity which, in the very nature of the case, enters into every human relationship—I can think of you only in the form in which I knew you. You were over forty years of age when you were married, and though you lived to see me grow from childhood to be as old as you were on your wedding day, I saw you—at first through the mistaken eyes of childhood, but at last in very truth—always as an old man. So it comes about that in the picture of you that I like best only your eyes are young. You wear a sedate overcoat, hanging loosely from a buttoned top button, and a sedate felt hat. Your beard is not the full and splendid one which you first grew in the year of the Centennial—when, having cut yourself in shaving, you came to the quiet resolution that it would be a long time before you shaved again—but is close-clipped and gray. You stand so straight as to seem to lean backward a little, but your step has lost the spring which made you delight, in your youth, in hunting and fishing for trout, and with which in the days of my own boyhood you set the pace of our Sunday walks together.

"Where shall we walk today?" I would say on each succeeding Sunday, being, like Caesar's Gauls, desirous of new things. "Do you see that barn out there?" you would invariably reply, and we would make the accustomed circuit that took us by the barn, talking on many subjects, but chiefly of the ancient history which I was studying at school and of that other history which you had seen with your eyes in the making.

It would be easy to enumerate here the great events to which you were a witness—how you saw three of the five great wars in which our country has been engaged, the first telegraph, the first telephone, the first (and perhaps almost the last) trolley car, the first aeroplane, the first radio, the discovery of the North and South Poles, and a thousand other events of like moment and significance. But the truth is that you were in general very little influenced by objective events. Indeed, apart from purely personal happenings I can think of only two occurrences in the course of your whole life by which you were greatly affected—the Civil War, and the publication of the works of Emerson.

The Civil War irrevocably fixed your politics. You were born and brought up along the Susquehanna River in the exciting days of the underground railroad. You have told me how a boyhood playmate of yours was charged on a certain day to stay away from the haymow. Boylike, he went there at the first opportunity, and on poking about at random with a fork was startled by a cry of terror from a "black man" —the phrase which you always used—who was hidden under the hay. Doubtless little boys were impressed by such experiences and came to more or less unconscious conclusions about them. You have told me, too, that your father was a Whig who could not quite bring himself to vote for Frémont, and that, four years later, after watching a torchlight parade of some followers of Douglas, you burst into the room where he was sitting, demanding passionately, "Who are we for?" "We are for Lincoln," your father answered slowly, and you went away satisfied. Two years later you read about the fight between the *Monitor* and the *Merrimac* in Hampton Roads, and made a boy's model of the *Monitor* which stands beside me as I write. Later still you watched Lee's cavalry riding down the west bank of the river before the battle opened at Gettysburg, while the smoke from the burning bridge at Columbia darkened the sky.

From such experiences as these came your whole-hearted devotion and loyalty to the Republican Party, which are somehow summed up for me as from a bygone age in the "Battle Hymn of the Republic" and which, though a Republican, I do not share, and a sort of mystical faith in political equality—"the right," as you used to say, "of bad or ignorant men to express their badness or ignorance at the polls"— which I also do not share, but which was doubtless the best element in what seems to me to have been the generally bad business of reconstruction. Perhaps I fail to do full justice to this latter feeling. If so the reason is that I never fully understood it. You were sometimes inclined to leave gaps in your expression of abstract ideas.

There was nothing abstract about your love of Emerson. You planned in your youth to go on a walking trip to Concord in order to see him, but for some reason which I do not know the plan came to nothing, and as a result you never saw him in the flesh. But you read and pondered every word of his prose and verse, and you reread the essays every year of your life with what seemed a growing sense of their majesty and power. A month or two before you died you asked me to have rebound the two volumes that you cherished most (Emerson's *Prose Works*, James R. Osgood and Company, Boston, 1876), saying that you wanted me to have them as my inheritance from you. They stand on my bookshelves now. I do not count them the richest part of my inheritance, but I want you to know that I do not undervalue them.

I shall never forget a night, ten or a dozen years ago, when Professor Bliss Perry, speaking under the auspices of the chapter of the Phi Beta Kappa Society at the college in the city in which we lived, chose Emerson as the subject of his address. The speaker told of Emerson's early life and mentioned the death of his first wife and of his two brilliant brothers. "But," said Professor Perry, speaking after a little pause with a sort of ringing suavity of utterance, "he had pulled himself together, being of the old unbeatable Puritan stuff; he had married again, had bought a house, had published a little book, had backed himself to win against his generation—against the world." I remember nothing else about that address, except that the speaker succeeded in expressing a part of your own love and admiration for your hero. When it was over, your face was quite pink and radiant behind your beard, and your rather small brown eyes were bright with unwonted excitement. I asked you whether you wanted to join those of the audience who were going forward to shake hands with Professor Perry, but you shook your head. You were never a ready speaker and you knew that it would have been useless to try to put into words the delight which the evening had given you. If Professor Perry ever sees these words, he will know that for at least one auditor he made a perfect speech that night.

My own feeling about Emerson has always been that there was in him a sort of superficial optimism which arose from ignoring or denying some of the obvious facts of life. Then I think about you—how you lived and how you died—and I am not so sure.

But all that I have written is beside the point of what I really meant to tell you. You are going to be remembered here on earth for a very much longer time than you would have thought possible, if, indeed, you had thought about that subject at all. I shall tell you why. There is a feeling abroad about you which has been growing in the years which have passed since your death. I have seen it in the face of Herman, the gravedigger—who, in the intervals between the demands of his calling, was accustomed to help you in the garden and in making your grape wine—and in the faces of neighbors and tradespeople who knew and spoke with you during your later years. I have heard of it from the lips of the men who worked for you in the prime of your life on the Elizabeth Farms where I was born. I have heard of it, too, from the lips of those men's sons, who never knew you and who will perhaps speak of it to their sons in after days. This feeling is that you were a very wise man. I think it is true. I write deliberately—I think you were the wisest man I ever knew.

There are many kinds of wisdom. There is the broken but triumphant wisdom of the twice-born, about which you knew nothing whatever. There is the sudden and bewitched wisdom of insight, which belongs to poets and Celts and about which you—who, to use Santayana's wistful phrase, were "almost a poet"—knew something. But there is another sort of wisdom, which was the greater part of yours, founded on patience and simplicity and on watching

> the certain things,
> Swine, and slow moons like silver rings,
> And the ripening of the plums.

It was an unconscious wisdom on your part. I remember asking you once—half shyly, because I was almost sure in advance what your answer would be—whether you thought you had learned anything in the course of your lifetime about the mystery of life. You answered, as I had expected, that you had learned nothing at all. And yet, though you were unaware of the fact itself, it is easy enough to set down some of the sources of your wisdom and some of the things in which it consisted.

I have said that it was founded on simplicity and on the things of earth. You were brought up as a nurseryman, and you spent the happiest years of your life as the manager of more than a thousand acres of farm land. Though you came afterward to live in the city, the house which you chose on King Street was at the city's very edge. You lived there for a generation without taking more than a casual interest in civic affairs and without playing any active part in them. You were somewhat skeptical about what most Americans regard as progress. You were never a leader. Confident and successful men respected you and went their ways. I am not sure you were sorry to see them go. You were not readily impressed by the reputation of success.

At heart you were always a farmer. I do not remember having ever heard you use the word "nature," and it may well be that you would have sympathized with Meredith's caustic reference to "birds and beasts and herbs which ninnies call nature in books." But your interest in individual birds and beasts and herbs was unfailing. I do not think that you could have brought yourself to live anywhere without a garden in which to renew your youth by budding and grafting trees, to grow, among other vegetables, the tomatoes of which you were so proud, and to set up some of the red-and-green wren houses which you made not only for yourself but for half the children of the neighborhood. To the end of your life you found comfort in sitting alone for long hours out of doors. Stevenson has called attention somewhere to the characteristic simplicity of old soldiers and old priests. The comment is acutely made, but it seems to me that he should have added old farmers to his enumeration. The reason for all these simplicities is the same—lifelong adherence to a code which, whatever theories may be, actually works in practice. We are all withdrawals from the earth and in the end she never disappoints us.

No one knew you well who had not heard you speak at one time or another of your way of life on the Elizabeth Farms—of your mare, Nellie, on whose back you rode over the red fields and along the little streams that flow between the hills, and of how, pausing sometimes in the hush of early spring, great thoughts would come to you which you could never quite put into words; of Peter and Annie, the middle-aged couple who kept house for you; of the annual adventures of sowing and reaping; and of the sick animals to whom, for want of a veterinary, you ministered at need. Your successes in this latter connection seemed to give you greater pleasure than any others which came to you. You would tell, in a vein of ingenuous boasting which was otherwise quite foreign to you, how you studied the few medical works which were available in order to interpret the symptoms from which a given patient was suffering, and how, after due deliberation, you decided to prescribe such and such a medication. Then would come a narration of how the medicine was administered, and finally a celebration of the results accomplished. "Jolly!" you would say proudly. "When I went to the stable in the morning anyone could see that that mule was going to get well."

Less often you spoke of the people of that entire countryside —descendants, most of them, of Hessian prisoners of the Revolutionary War—who came to consult you in all the vicissitudes of their lives. I do not say that it is so, but if you were inclined to overestimate your skill and address with animals, you greatly underestimated your influence on the men and women who, in a not very different fashion, were committed to your care. It so happens that I have met few of those people face to face. One of them, who was a child when she knew you, said recently to someone, who repeated the saying to me, that when she felt like punishing her children she always stopped and asked herself what you would think about it. Another of them, who is now an old man, came to see me a month or two ago, bringing with him a letter which you had written him when you were over eighty years of age. He had seen you only once or twice in more than forty years. He thought that I should like to see what you had written and perhaps should like to copy it. The letter itself he would not let me keep. He said he wanted to give it to his son.

The last time you visited Elizabeth in the flesh was even later than the date on which that letter was written. There was to be a reunion of some of the old residents of the neighborhood and you had been asked to make a little speech. We arrived early at the church in which the ceremonies were to be held, and you and I walked alone as far as the bridge over the stream that flows midway between the church and the mansion house. You stood on the bridge, very frail and gray, but erect and unbroken, thinking perhaps on that June afternoon, as Malory thought on a day in May so many years ago, of "old gentleness and old service, and many kind deeds that were forgotten by negligence," and of such other matters to which, it may be conjectured, the thoughts of the very old turn. You called my attention to a fence along one of the fields, which needed to be repaired. "If I were manager of these farms now," you said, "I would say to Peter and John, 'Drop what you are doing for a little while, and let us fix that piece of fence down by the bridge.' " Then you were silent for a long time, evaluating the greater paradox and the less. At last you smiled and said, speaking slowly as your wont was, "In order to do that, all I should have to do would be to get Peter and John out of their graves, and if I were young again I think I could do that."

Though you lacked both the means and the inclination to travel, had never made the four hours' journey by rail which would have taken you to New York, and, indeed, had been only once or twice outside the limits of your own state, you were without exception the least parochially minded man I have ever known, and the one least influenced by classifications and catchwords. You instinctively disbelieved in the existence of

> The Anthropophagi, and men whose heads
> Do grow beneath their shoulders.

If, by some miracle of time and space, you had been set down in the court of the Great Khan, you would not have entertained for a moment that deep-seated human delusion of which even the gifted Greeks were not wholly free, that those who speak an unknown tongue are necessarily barbarians. You would not have reminded yourself that you were a Nordic and that the Khan was of a different race. Setting aside the matter of your personal shyness, of which you had not a little, you would have had no sense of essential superiority or inferiority. You would have met the Khan with perfect simplicity and dignity, and because he was a man you would have known the nature of his hopes and fears and the subjects of his deepest interests.

You used on occasions a ceremonious and stately sort of courtesy which would doubtless have pleased the Khan as much as it sometimes pleased others. A friend of mine has told me of having had a conversation with you on the street, at the conclusion of which he asked you to come to see him and his wife. You answered, "I am an old man and I go out very seldom in the evening, but when I sit at home I think of many delightful things." "Exactly," as my friend said to me, "as if your father sat at home in the evening thinking how delightful it would be to call on Carol and me."

You once sought—I suspect somewhat whimsically—to justify your slowness of speech by saying that you tried never to advance an argument without restating to yourself the truth which you meant to express, as it might be restated from the point of view of your adversary. The whimsicality lay in the fact, which you knew very well, that your slowness of speech was not confined to argumentative matters; but the rule which you laid down is, for all that, the rule of a true liberal. You were a liberal in everything—in your predispositions toward social and economic questions; in your religious views, which, apart from the doctrine of nonresistance in which you did not believe, were strongly similar to those held by the Quakers; in your attitude toward science and scientific research. I remember the interest which you took in the implications of the new physics, and the comment which you made on a book which contained an explanation of the Einstein theory. You read the book twice, and when you had finished it for the second time you said to me, "I did not understand all of this book, but I did understand some of it. I have known all my life that there is only one thing in the world, and the scientists working in their own way are on the track of finding it out." The idea which you expressed is of course as old as Democritus and some of those other Greek philosophers who were half poets, instead of being half scientists, as are the philosophers of today; but I agree with you that in scientific matters the signs of the times are good. If the scientists can keep their verities within five thousand years of the guesses of the poets, they have every reason to be proud.

I have written this much, and yet I have not written what wisdom is or what a man must do or refrain from doing in order to become wise. No man, it seems, may transmit to his son the wisdom that is his. The secret of its attainment is hidden even from himself, and is not to be purchased with money or expected as the certain reward of age and experience or won by taking anxious thought. If it were otherwise, we should all come at last to the full stature of wisdom, and, having done so, we should put away those foolish things whereby we are troubled and made afraid.

"Raphael paints wisdom," said your master Emerson, "Handel sings it, Phidias carves it, Shakespeare writes it, Wren builds it, Columbus sails it. . . ." You, who painted no pictures and carved no statues, whose songs were without notes and whose poems were without words, who built houses only for birds and who never sailed adventuring on any of the Seven Seas, came also to wisdom by a road of your own finding. It was not the road of the gifted and the great of this world. I am mindful, nevertheless, of the saying of the apostle that the foolishness of God is wiser than men.

Perhaps a knowledge of this truth is the greatest of all the blessings which have come to me as

Your Son

www.ingramcontent.com/pod-product-compliance
Lightning Source LLC
LaVergne TN
LVHW011817200926
848484LV00005B/1228
9781512808827

THE LEGAL EFFECTS OF RECOGNITION IN INTERNATIONAL LAW

Published on a fund

established by

William Guggenheim

of the Class of 1889

University of Pennsylvania

The
Legal Effects of Recognition in International Law

as

Interpreted by the Courts of the United States

By

JOHN G. HERVEY, LL.B., Ph.D.

Instructor in Political Science, Wharton School of Finance and Commerce, University of Pennsylvania

PHILADELPHIA
UNIVERSITY OF PENNSYLVANIA PRESS

London
Humphrey Milford: Oxford University Press

1928

PRINTED IN THE UNITED STATES OF AMERICA

LANCASTER PRESS, INCORPORATED
LANCASTER, PENNSYLVANIA

PREFACE

Few phases of International Law have received less study at the hands of international lawyers and research scholars than the effects of recognition upon the determination of individual rights and obligations. Nevertheless, these effects have been of the utmost importance in the courts, and with the continued non-recognition of Soviet Russia by the United States they promise to be of increasing importance. This study is presented in the hope that it will clarify the problems and stimulate further study and research in this field.

Little effort has been made in the course of this study to distinguish between the recognition of a state of insurgency, belligerency and independence. It appears from the cases that these differences have exerted little influence in the courts. However, it should be pointed out that the study is concerned primarily with the recognition of new states and new governments within old states. These have received the major attention of the courts.

The author wishes to acknowledge with pleasure his indebtedness to Hon. Roland S. Morris, at whose suggestion the study was undertaken. His encouragement and help during the preparation of the manuscript have proved invaluable. The writer is deeply indebted to Roland R. Foulke, Esq., whose pertinent criticisms have steered the writer from numerous errors. Special thanks are due Prof. Edwin D. Dickinson of the Law School of the University of Michigan and Osmond K. Fraenkel, Esq., of the New York Bar, and all others whose case notes and comments have appeared in the numerous legal publications.

JOHN G. HERVEY

PHILADELPHIA

TABLE OF CONTENTS

LIST OF CASES

CHAPTER I

Introduction

In recent years the legal aspects of recognition have assumed unprecedented importance. This is especially true as regards the United States and England. New states and new governments within old states have emerged to compel a reconsideration of recognition policies by the Foreign Offices. Likewise new situations before the courts have made it necessary for them to re-examine and restate the fundamental principles which control in recognition cases.

In 1913 Huerta, Madero, and Carranza began to stage a political *corrida de toros* in which at least one participant, Madero, expired, while the Family of Nations stood aghast. The United States was not only a curious spectator, but her Chief Executive protested that "such pretended governments" would not be "countenanced or dealt with." [1]

Carranza emerged as the political chieftain. The United States and eight of the Latin American republics recognized him as the head of the *de facto* government on October 19, 1915.[2] Carranza, in turn, waved a *constitucional capa* before foreign nations through his proposed agrarian reforms, nationalization of subsoil rights, and limitations as to the lands which foreigners may own in Mexico.[3] These anti-foreign constitutional reforms caused strained relations between the United States and Mexico from 1917 to 1920. They stood back of the refusal to recognize the Obregon government and the diplomatic deadlock which lasted from 1921 to 1923.

---

[1] President Wilson, "Annual Message to Congress," *New York Times*, December 3, 1913.

[2] *Oetjen vs. Central Leather Company*, 246 U. S., 1918, 297. In this case the court reviews the events in Mexico during this period.

[3] *New York Times, Current History Magazine*, September, 1927, p. 846.

These difficulties were adjusted at the Niagara Falls Conference in 1923. Thereupon the United States accorded full recognition. But our State Department protested vigorously in the fall of 1925 when the Mexican Congress attempted to put the constitutional provisions into operation.

Soviet Russia has become a thorn in the side of the foreign offices of all the larger states.[4] Some of the powers have granted recognition only to have its withdrawal forced upon them by the non-observance of her solemn undertakings. Other governments have accorded recognition and later have found that the Russian diplomatic representatives were *persona non grata,* while some states have consistently refused recognition only to have their policies crucified upon a lurid cross of economic imperialism.

New states emerged from former empires as a result of the blast from Mars of a decade ago. Czechoslovakia, Jugo-Slavia and Poland suddenly found their ambitions for statehood realized. They constituted new international personalities. They had to be dealt with. They could not be disregarded by the old states. This was early realized by the United States, for in the course of his message to Congress on the Essential Terms of Peace in Europe,[5] President Wilson acknowledged the existence of these problems and their implications. Practical exigencies, political considerations and his belief in the right of self-determination were fused in his recognition policy toward the new states.

This study is not concerned with the wisdom of his or any other policy. It is only incidentally concerned with the recognition policy of any country. It does not purport to be a study of American policy or policies. Admirable studies covering these points have been made.[6] It is not concerned

[4] At this point the words "government," "power," and "state" are used interchangeably.

[5] January 22, 1917.

[6] Julius Goebel, Jr., *Recognition Policy of the United States,* 1915; N. D. Houghton, *De Facto Governments,* 1927; Taylor Cole, *Recognition Policy of the United States Since 1901,* 1928.

with the meaning of recognition, nor with the importance of recognition, except insofar as individual rights before the courts have been involved. A concise study of these points is presented in the succeeding chapter for purposes of clarity.

It is a study of the legal effects of recognition as interpreted and applied by the municipal courts of the United States and England. It deals with cases and controversies before courts of law and equity. The awards of arbitration commissions and mixed claims commissions are outside the scope of this treatise, and for that reason no attention is given to such awards.

A foreign government establishes a credit in the United States and that government is subsequently overturned; a foreign state aids and abets an American corporation in securing a monopoly in that country, and later its acts are called into question in the courts of the United States in a suit involving prosecution for violation of the anti-trust laws; or a foreign public vessel anchors in an American harbor, whereupon the representatives of an insurrectory faction in that country secure an attachment upon the vessel and demand that the courts adjudge that it is the lawful government and entitled to the vessel in question. The adjudication of these and similar cases is illustrative of the complex legal problems which have centered around recognition. The English and the American courts have found from their examinations that certain legal results flow. Under the theory of *stare decisis* these legal results are important.

From an examination of the cases certain postulates stand out. In the first place the courts are unanimously agreed that recognition by the political departments of the government is binding upon the courts. They cannot enter into an independent examination in order to determine for themselves which is the lawfully instituted government in a designated territory: with what results, especially as regards Soviet

Russia, we shall see when we come to examine this point later.

In the second place the courts of the *recognizant* state [7] cannot sit in judgment on the acts of the recognized government. This is subject to certain limitations which will be considered at a later point. However, from the rule that the courts of the recognizant states will not sit in judgment on the acts of the recognized governments the courts have derived a second rule. They regard the effects of recognition as retroactive. It validates everything which has been done by the recognized government from the time of its inception in so far as the courts of the recognizant government are concerned.

Furthermore recognition is necessary to give a state or government a status before the courts of recognizant states. They cannot be parties plaintiff unless they are recognized: they are not entitled to immunity from suit in the absence of recognition. These questions have led the courts into uneasy fields. Finally the protection of property has evoked much consideration and the cases dealing therewith are not uniform.

In most of the recent recognition cases the courts have been gradually feeling their way. They have had few studies to guide them. The rules which were enunciated in the early cases have been blended into the new cases and followed on the principle of *stare decisis* rather than for rational reasons. Recently, in an important English case,[8] the court followed a precedent established by two American cases and the judges pointed out that these American cases laid down the rule with little or no reasoning. However, an examination of these cases shows that the courts reasoned by implication rather than directly.[9]

---

[7] Hereafter the writer will use this term to denote the state or government according recognition.

[8] *Luther vs. Sagor*, 1921, L.R. 1 K.B. 460; on appeal, 1921, L.R. 3 K.B. 532.

[9] The cases referred to were *Williams vs. Bruffy*, 96 U. S., 1877, 176, and *Oetjen vs. Central Leather Company*, 246 U. S., 1918, 297.

The object of the present work is to study the effects of recognition as revealed by the decisions of the courts, and to determine critically the correctness or incorrectness of the positions assumed by the courts with a view toward furnishing a guide for future use in the determination of such cases and controversies.

CHAPTER II

Preliminary Considerations

With the emergence of the "states system" from the Treaty of Westphalia in 1648, the basis of society shifted from a single state to a collectivity of states. The original community, composed only of the Christian states of Europe, gradually expanded and came to include Turkey, Russia, the United States and the Spanish Americas. More recently Japan and China entered, together with the post-war countries of Europe, so that at the present time the "community of states" embraces all the discovered portions of the globe. It is no longer a Christian European system. It is universal in its geographical extent as well as in its religious and cultural embrace.[1]

Incident to the emergence of the "states system" came the so-called fundamental rights of existence, independence, equality, intercourse, respect, and jurisdiction, around which International Law has developed.[2] To call them fundamental, or to call them rights in the Austinian sense, is perhaps misleading. They are fundamental only in the sense that they constitute the basic, underlying assumptions upon which states act in their intercourse with one another. They are assumptions or postulates of action in the international community, rather than interests, in the exercise of which the protection of a superior power can be invoked. This is true because in inter-state life there is no common superior to which resort can be had.[3]

---

[1] Oppenheim, *International Law,* v. I, pp. 31–34.

[2] See 10 *A. J.*, p. 125, for statement issued by the American Institute of International Law. Contra, Sterling Edmunds, *Lawless Law of Nations,* pp. 100–114.

[3] Address of Elihu Root, April 24, 1908, reported in 2 *A. J.*, pp. 451–457. Such sanctions as exist are, "appeal to public opinion, publication of cor-

Nevertheless, they underlie the international structure. States rely upon them for the enforcement of their rights and obligations. Before a state, or a government, may exercise, or claim the right to exercise, these so-called fundamental rights, it must be accorded recognition individually by each of the members which constitute the International Family. An adoption into the family must take place.

In this respect recognition is important because it confers upon a state, or a government, the legal right to exist. Prior to recognition it can claim the right to exist only so far as its subjects are concerned. Subsequent to recognition it not only can claim, but can demand, the right to exist as a member of the Family of Nations. From the moment of recognition a state is entitled to all the rights of an international personality.[4]

A discussion of the legal effects of recognition necessarily must be predicated upon a knowledge of certain elementary considerations. These include the nature of recognition, the kinds of recognition, the methods followed in according recognition, and the arm of the government charged with the exercise of the function. These stand back of any consid-

respondence, censure by parliamentary vote, demand for arbitration with the odium attendant on a refusal to arbitrate, rupture of relations, reprisals, etc.," award of the Hague Tribunal, North Atlantic Fisheries case, *Hague Court Reports, Carnegie Endowment Edition,* p. 167.

[4] On the meaning of recognition see: Philip Marshall Brown, *International Society,* 1923, ch. 4; ibid., *International Realities,* ch. 3; Pitt Corbett, *Leading Cases on International Law,* 1922, pp. 47–50, 68–70, 83–85; G. B. Davis, *Elements of International Law,* 1908, 3d Ed., 34, 42; Sterling Edmunds, *Lawless Law of Nations,* 1925, pp. 115–132; Julius Goebel, Jr., *Recognition Policy of the United States,* 1915; R. R. Foulke, *Treatise on International Law,* v. I, pp. 112–118; W. E. Hall, *International Law,* 1909, 6th Ed., pp. 82–92; H. W. Halleck, *International Law,* 1908, 4th Ed., v. I, pp. 70, 71, 83–92; A. S. Hershey, *Essentials of International Public Law and Organization,* pp. 199–215; C. C. Hyde, *International Law,* v. I, pp. 55–82 and notes; T. J. Lawrence, *Principles of International Law,* 1910, 4th Ed., pp. 83–92; Kent's *Commentary on International Law,* 1866, pp. 95–106; J. B. Moore, *Digest of International Law,* 1906, v. I, pp. 72–163, 206–241; Oppenheim, *International Law,* 1920, 3d Ed., v. I, pp. 134–139; Wharton, *Digest of International Law of the United States,* 1886, v. I, pp. 509–553; Wilson and Tucker, *International Law,* 1922, 8th Ed., pp. 47–55; Q. D. Woolsey, *Introduction to the Study of International Law,* 1899, 6th Ed., pp. 40–43; 33 *Corpus Juris,* pp. 393–395; 15 *Ruling Case Law,* pp. 106–108.

eration given to the question by the courts. For this reason it is necessary that we give brief consideration to each of them.[5]

Turning to the nature of the recognition function, we find that it " is an outward and visible manifestation of the mental comprehension of an existing fact or state of affairs. . . . As used in International Law, the term ' recognition ' is confined to those facts which are material in international life." [6] The facts in international life of which cognizance must be taken include the existence of a state of war, membership of a body politic in the Community of States, or internal changes in state life, such as a turnover in government within the state.[7]

The majority of writers regard the above conception of recognition as too broad.[8] Oppenheim uses the term to connote the process by which non-original members have been initiated into the Family of Nations. He says that for every state, that is not already but wants to be a member, recognition is necessary.[9]

Oppenheim acknowledges that many writers do not agree with him. Hall, Revier and others contend that state existence is a fact to be determined by the state itself. When self-satisfied of such existence it enters of its own right into international life.[10] Nevertheless, these writers acknowledge that recognition is necessary before a new state can demand intercourse with other states. Seemingly they arrive at the same conclusions as Oppenheim. The necessity for the reception of new members arises from facts, i.e. the ex-

---

[5] These are aspects of recognition to which treatment has been given by the courts in dealing with the question.

[6] R. R. Foulke, *International Law,* v. I, p. 112.

[7] *Ibid.,* pp. 112–113.

[8] An excellent collection of the opinions of various writers has been made by Foulke, *op. cit.,* notes pp. 112–113.

[9] Oppenheim, *International Law,* v. I, p. 134. "Those states which are members (of the Family of Nations) are either original members because the Law of Nations grew up gradually between them through custom and treaties, or they are members which have been recognized by the body of members already in existence when they were born."

[10] Hall, *op. cit.,* secs. 2 and 26.

istence of international life and the demand for inter-state intercourse.

However, the controversy over the nature of the recognition function has not involved the courts. They regard a state or government as a self-created entity.[11] It exists without recognition.[12] Recognition is the acknowledgment of an existing fact: it does not create the fact, say the courts.[13]

In *Wulfsohn et al. vs. The Russian Republic,* 1923, in adjudicating the confiscation of certain furs owned by the plaintiff in Russia, for which recovery was asked, Mr. Justice Andrews of the New York courts took this view of the recognition function. He felt that recognition did not create the state, although it might be desirable.[14] The recognition by other states or governments is merely concrete evidence or testimony of friendly relations. It does not create the state or government, said the court, although necessary for certain purposes.

The same opinion was expressed on appeal.[15] A new government springing into existence does not require the recognition of other governments to confirm its international personality. So long as it confines its action to its own citizens, and to the limits of its own territory, it may dispense with such recognition. But if it desires to enter into the society of na-

[11] In *Harcourt vs. Gaillard,* 12 Wheaton, 1827, 523 at 527, the court said: "It has never been admitted by the United States that they acquired anything by way of cession from Great Britain by the Treaty of Peace, 1783. It has been viewed only as a recognition of pre-existing rights. . . . The treaty . . . amounts to a simple recognition of the independence . . . of the United States. . . ." See also *McIlvaine vs. Coxe's Lessee,* 4 Cranch, 1808, 209 at 212.

[12] Obviously in some cases states have been created by treaty, such as some of the post-war European states which received their birthright from the Versailles Conference.

[13] Editorial comment, *Saint Louis Law Review,* 1917, v. 2, p. 37.

[14] "Whether or not a government exists, clothed with the power to enforce its authority within its own territory, obeyed by the people over whom it rules, capable of performing the duties and fulfilling the obligations of an independent power, able to enforce its claims by military force, is a fact, not a theory. For its recognition does not create the state, although it may be desirable. So only are diplomatic relations permitted. Treaties made with the government which it succeeds may again come into effect." 234 N. Y. 372, 138 N. E. 24 at 25.

[15] 195 N. Y. Supp. 472; 202 App. Div. 421.

tions, all the members of which recognize rights to which they are mutually entitled and duties which they may be called upon reciprocally to fulfill, "such recognition becomes essentially necessary to the complete participation of the new state in all the advantages of this society." [16]

This view was taken in 1923 by Mr. Chief Justice Taft as sole arbitrator in the controversy between Great Britain and Costa Rica. Great Britain had refused to recognize the Tinoco regime. Mr. Chief Justice Taft, in the course of his award, held that by such refusal Great Britain was not estopped to urge the claims of British subjects, where the claims were dependent upon acts and contracts of the Tinoco government. The Tinoco government had been recognized by practically all of the Latin America republics and by some of the European powers, although unrecognized by the United States and Great Britain. The regime was shown by the evidence to be a *de facto* government,[17] and Mr. Chief Justice Taft gave judgment against Costa Rica.

This point was raised in the courts of the United States about 1815 in a number of cases involving the activities of the Buenos Ayres government.[18] In the course of one of the cases [19] it was argued that the existence of the United States as an independent power began in 1776 and not with the Treaty of Peace in 1783. It was contended by analogy that the independence of Buenos Ayres began with its declaration of independence, and that since this independence was a matter of notoriety throughout the entire world, our courts were bound to treat it as an independent nation. Mr. Chief Justice Marshall was of the opinion that a nation be-

---

[16] *Wulfsohn vs. Russian Republic,* 195 N. Y. Supp. 472, 202 App. Div. 421 at 422.

[17] 18 *A. J.* 147 at 155. The text of the award is reproduced in full.

[18] *Consul of Spain vs. The Conception,* 1819, Fed. Case No. 3, 137, 2 Wheeler Cr. Cas. 597, Brunner Col. Cas. 497; *The Maria Josepha,* 1819, Fed. Case No. 9,078, Brunner, Col. Case 500, 2 Wheeler Cr. Case 600; *U. S. vs. Hutchings,* 1817, Fed. Case No. 15, 429, 2 Wheeler Cr. Case 453.

[19] *United States vs. Hutchings,* 1817, Fed. Cas. No. 15, 429, 2 Wheeler Cr. C. 543.

comes independent from its declaration of independence only as respects its own government. Before it can be considered independent by the judiciary of foreign nations, it is necessary that "its existence should be recognized by the executive authority of those nations." In the absence of executive recognition of the Buenos Ayres government the court refused to acknowledge its national seal or the validity of documents and instruments bearing the purported seal.

Recognition is not compulsory. It is voluntary or optional.[20] Each state judges for itself whether a new state or a new government within an old state merits recognition. This formed the basis of Mr. John Bassett Moore's observation that "recognition is the assurance given to a new state that it will be permitted to hold its place and rank, in the character of an independent political organism, in the Family of Nations. The rights and attributes of sovereignty belong to it independently of all recognition, but it is only after it has been recognized that it is assured of exercising them. Regular political relations exist only between states that reciprocally recognize them. Recognition is therefore useful, even necessary, to the new state."[21]

The first expression on the point by American courts is found in *Rose vs. Himely*.[22] This case arose after St. Domingo had broken off relations with France but prior to its recognition by the United States. Certain acts of confiscation were at issue. In his opinion Mr. Chief Justice Marshall observed that "it is for governments to decide whether they will consider St. Domingo as an independent nation, and until such decision shall be made, or France shall relinquish her claim, courts of justice must consider the ancient state of

---

[20] Except in consequence of particular conventions, no state is obliged to accord it. "But the refusal may give rise to measures of retorsion. When, after the formation of the Kingdom of Italy, certain German states persisted in refusing to recognize it, Count Cavour withdrew the *exequaturs* of their consuls. Recognition was then accorded." Moore, *Digest*, v. I, p. 72.

[21] Moore, *Digest*, v. I, p. 72.

[22] 4 Cranch, 1808, 241.

things as remaining unaltered, and the sovereign power of France over that colony as still subsisting." This doctrine was quoted with approval in *Clark vs. United States,*[23] and by implication in *The Hornet.*[24]

It has received its latest affirmation in *Wulfsohn et al. vs. Russian Republic.*[25] Justice Rich in delivering the opinion of the court in that case said: " Every other State is at liberty to grant or refuse recognition, and until such recognition becomes universal on the part of other States, the new State becomes entitled to the exercise of its external sovereignty as to those of the States only by whom that sovereignty has been recognized." [26]

A distinction is made by most writers between the recognition of a state and the recognition of a change of government within an old state. Little reference to the distinction is made in the judicial opinions dealing with recognition. Yet several of the cases can best be interpreted with this distinction in mind. This is especially applicable to those cases pending in the courts of the recognizant state at the time of the overthrow of the recognized government.[27]

In the case of a new government within an old state, this does not mean that other states cannot take cognizance of such new government without formal recognition. Indeed, they may. But such cognizance does not necessarily admit the legality of the recognized government.[28] Recognition of a new government may be either as the *de jure* or the *de facto* government. A " *de jure* government in International Law means 'one which, in the opinion of the person using the phrase, ought to possess the powers of sovereignty though

---

[23] 5 Federal Cases (No. 2,838), p. 932; on appeal, 8 Peters, 1834, 436.

[24] 12 Federal Cases (No. 6,705), 1870, p. 529, 2 Abb. U. S. 35, 11 Int. Rev. Rec. 6.

[25] 202 App. Div. 421, 195 N. Y. Supp. 472.

[26] *Wulfsohn vs. Russian Republic, op. cit.* at 422.

[27] *The Sapphire,* 11 Wallace, 1871, 164; *U. S. vs. Trumbull,* 48 Federal, 1891, 94; *Russian Gov. vs. Lehigh Valley Railway Co.,* 293 Fed., 1919, 133.

[28] Hershey, *International Public Law and Organization,* Rev. Ed., p. 210.

at the time it may be deprived of them,' while a *de facto* government is one which is ' really in possession of them, although the possession may be wrongful or precarious.' "[29]

In *Thorington vs. Smith*,[30] which involved the juristic status of the Southern Confederacy, Mr. Chief Justice Chase made the interesting observation that " there are several degrees of what is called *de facto* government."

A *de facto* government " in its highest degree, assumes a character very closely resembling that of a lawful government.[31] This is when the usurping government expels the regular authorities from their customary seats and functions," and establishes itself in their place, and becomes the actual government of a country. The distinguishing characteristic of such a government is, " that adherents to it in war against the government *de jure* do not incur the penalties of treason; and under certain limitations, obligations assumed by it in behalf of the country, or otherwise, will, in general, be respected by the government *de jure* when restored. . . . "[32]

The Commonwealth of England under Cromwell as Protector constituted a *de facto* government. But the Southern Confederacy was not a *de facto* government in the same sense. " No treaty was made by it with any civilized State," as in the case of England. " No obligations of a national character were created by it, binding after its dissolution, on the States which it represented, or on the National Government." [33] This does not mean that the Southern Confederacy was not a government *de facto*. It was, but it was of another type.

In the cases dealing with *de facto* governments, the courts recognize a distinction which depends upon the extent of the

---

[29] Lord Justice Warrington, *Luther vs. Sagor,* 1921, L. R. 3 K. B. 532 at 551; Wheaton, *International Law,* 5th English Edition (1916), p. 36.

[30] 8 Wallace, 1869, 1.

[31] The Chief Justice used the term " lawful " in the sense of a *de jure* government. Such is the implication gathered from a reading of the decision.

[32] *Thorington vs. Smith,* 8 Wallace, 1869, 1 at 8.

[33] *Ibid.*

territorial operation of the *de facto* government in question. "One of them is such as exists after it has expelled the regularly constituted authorities from the seats of power and public offices and established its own functionaires in their places, so as to represent in fact the sovereignty of the nation. Such was the government of England under the Commonwealth established upon the execution of the King and the overthrow of the loyalists. . . . The other kind of *de facto* governments . . . is such as exists where a portion of the inhabitants of a country have separated themselves from the parent state and established an independent government." [34]

This distinction is of practical importance. If the temporary government is in control of only a part of the territory occupied by its predecessor, as was the case of the Southern Confederacy, recognition of such *de facto* government may constitute an affront to the state which has not relinquished authority over the territory in quesion. But a different situation is faced where the temporary government occupies the entire territory. Recognition of such a government does not and by nature cannot constitute an offense against the preceding government when the latter is restored to power. Also, the restored government, as against the recognizing government, is not in general entitled to question the validity of the acts of the temporary government.[35]

The distinction between recognition of a government as a *de jure* and a *de facto* government appears to be unimportant as a matter of municipal law in the courts of the recognizant state. Either form of recognition is binding upon its courts. This exact issue was before the English courts in the *Republic of Peru vs. Peruvian Guano Company*.[36] In that case

---

[34] *Williams vs. Bruffy*, 96 U. S., 1817, 176.

[35] See the award of the Permanent Court of Arbitration at the Hague, Oct. 11, 1921, in the case of the *French Claims Against Peru*, 16 *A. J.* 16, pp. 480–484; Hyde, v. 1, pp. 59–63, on the time of according recognition to a new state produced by revolution.

[36] 1887, L. R. 36 Ch. Div. 489.

one of the principal grounds relied on by the plaintiff was that the agreement had been made on behalf of the *de facto* government of the Republic of Peru which was not the *de jure* government. Justice Chitty, in the course of his opinion, held that the court was bound to take cognizance of the recognition of a *de facto* government by the government of his country as soon as it had been shown that a *de facto* government of a foreign state had been recognized by the government of the country; no further inquiry was permitted in the courts of the recognizant state.

The English court declined to investigate, and indeed had not the proper means for investigating, the title of the actual Government of Peru, or any other foreign state which had been thus recognized by the English government. The court held that the attempted distinction between the *de facto* and the *de jure* government which ran through the statement of claim was untenable.[37] The court felt that the action of the *de jure* government of Peru in declaring void the acts of its *de facto* predecessor was not binding upon a foreign state, England in this case, which had recognized the temporary *de facto* government.

In like manner the courts of the United States have uniformly held that they cannot examine the acts of recognized *de facto* governments. In numerous instances their acts have been before the American courts. For most purposes they have treated their acts as valid, and have refused to sit in judgment on them.[38]

The legal effects of the acts of recognized *de jure vs. de facto* governments were considered by the United States Supreme Court in 1869. In considering the acts of a *de facto* government of the second type, the court said that such government might perhaps be more aptly denominated a

---

[37] *Republic of Peru vs. Peruvian Guano Co.*, 1887, L. R. 36 Ch. Div. 489 at 497.

[38] *United States vs. Rice*, 4 Wheaton, 1819, 246; *Keene vs. McDonough*, 8 Peters, 1834, 308; *Thorington vs. Smith*, 8 Wallace, 1869, 1.

government of paramount force. "Its distinguishing characteristics are that its existence is maintained by active military power . . . against the rightful authority of an established and lawful government; and, that while it exists, it must necessarily be obeyed in civil matters by private citizens who, by acts of obedience, rendered in submission to such force, do not become responsible, as wrong doers, for those acts, though not warranted by the laws of the rightful government." Actual governments of this sort "are usually administered directly by military authority, but they may be administered also by civil authority, supported more or less directly by military force."[39]

In case the recognizant state has expressly refused to accord recognition to such a *de facto* government, or a government of paramount force, it appears from the cases that the courts are free to treat the acts of such *de facto* governments, or states, as voidable, if not void.[40] The status of the acts of a *de facto* government, with which relations have been severed, does not appear from an examination of the cases.[41]

Internationally, the distinction between a government *de jure* or *de facto* is material. The recognizant state may, by *de facto recognition,* enter into relations with the recognized state without affirming the legality of the recognized government. This recognition "by no means implies the recognition of such head as the legitimate head of that state."[42] *De facto recognition* is not an acknowledgment of legal equality. It is rather a formal acceptance and acknowledgment of the existence of certain facts, of which, in its external relations, the recognizant state must be aware.[43]

---

[39] *Thorington vs. Smith,* 8 Wallace, 1869, 1 at 9.

[40] *Sokoloff vs. National City Bank,* 239 N. Y., 1924, 158; *Banque Internationale vs. Goukassow,* 1923, L. R. 2 K. B. 680; *Cia. Minera Ygnacio Rodriguez Ramos, S. A. vs. Bartlesville Zinc Co.,* 275 S. W., 1925, 388.

[41] It does not appear that any cases involving such a point have come before either the English or the American courts. It is conceivable that the point might be raised in the English courts since the severance by England of relations with the Soviet Republic.

[42] Oppenheim, *International Law,* v. I, sec. 342, p. 528.

[43] *Ibid.*

The majority of states have come into existence by severing relations with a mother state. Recognition of the child state is not incompatible with recognition of the mother state. Lawrence points out that such recognition of the new state is considered " a normal act, quite compatible with the maintenance of peaceful intercourse with the mother country." [44] Obviously such would not be true if the new state had not actually severed relations with the mother state and maintained a separate existence. Such action is necessary in order that the new state establish itself as a fact to be dealt with in international life.

Should a proposed state attempt to establish a separate existence, and prior to the consummation of such independence third states should accord it complete recognition, such recognition would be considered as an affront to the parent state. It might be regarded as an act of intervention and could be resented with force by the parent state.[45] This renders it necessary to inquire as to which arm of the government is charged with the power of recognition, and to know exactly how the power may be exercised.

Is the power vested in the central government alone, or is it divided? May it, under appropriate circumstances, be exercised by the local or provincial governments? Is there any prescribed form which must be followed? What are the methods by which recognition is accorded? To what department of the government does the function belong? Can there be such a thing as recognition by the judicial department? Is recognition necessarily executive in nature? These points will be touched upon in the sections which follow. The chief consideration will be given to the United States.

In the United States the control of foreign affairs is vested in the national government, and not in the several states.

---

[44] *Principles of International Law,* p. 88.

[45] Hall, *International Law,* 83; Moore, *Digest,* v. I, 73.

"The United States is a national government, and the only government in this country that has the character of nationality."[46] National matters are entrusted to the government of the Union. "For local interests the several States of the Union exist, but for national purposes, embracing our relations with foreign nations, we are but one people, one nation, one power."

Such an arrangement is not universal, although some publicists argue that it is. But their argument is not in accord with the facts. The German States, prior to 1914, possessed the rights of legation, and under certain circumstances exercised treaty-making powers. They have lost these under the new constitution of 1919.[47]

Judged by the practice of the United States recognition may take place in several ways. In the first place, recognition may be accorded by entering into a treaty for the express purpose. It may be granted by the insertion of such a stipulation in a treaty negotiated for other purposes. If circumstances do not compel the negotiation of a convention, it may be implied from the despatch of diplomatic agents: re-

---

[46] Mr. Justice Bradley, in *Knox vs. Lee, Parker vs. Davis,* more commonly referred to as the *Legal Tender Cases,* 12 Wallace, 1870, 457 at 555. The doctrine so long contended for, that the Federal Union is a mere compact of Sovereign States, "should be regarded as definitely and forever overthrown." A similar view had been expressed by Mr. Chief Justice Marshall fifty years earlier in *Cohens vs. Virginia,* 6 Wheaton, 1821, 264. The noted Chief Justice said: "In war, we are one people. In making peace we are one people. In our commercial regulations, we are one and the same people. In many other respects, the American people are one; and the government which is alone capable of controlling and managing their interests in all these respects, is the government of the Union. It is their government, and in that character they have no other," p. 413. He referred to the states as "constituent parts of one great empire." Mr. Justice Bradley stated that the national government "is invested with power over all the foreign relations of the country, war, peace, and negotiations and intercourse with other nations; all of which are forbidden to the state governments." Later in his opinion he said that "the judiciary has jurisdiction to decide controversies between the states . . . and the government is clothed with power . . . to protect each of them against invasion and domestic violence," op. cit., 555. See also Mr. Justice Field's exhaustive opinion in *Chae Chan Ping vs. United States,* 130 U. S., 1889, 581.

[47] Brunet, *New German Constitution,* 1922, pp. 307–315. Also articles 45 and 78 of the German Constitution, reproduced in McBain and Rogers, *New Governments of Europe,* pp. 185 and 191.

lations which are considered to exist only between independent states.

It is a moot question whether the mere appointment of consuls implies recognition. The authorities are not agreed.[48] Moore has examined the practice in this regard,[49] and it appears from his examination that disagreement turns upon the issuance of the *exequatur*. The issuance of an *exequatur* implies recognition, whereas the mere appointment of consuls does not.[50] Moore, in his *Digest*, points out that the United States recognized several of the Latin American republics by this method. In summary, it may be said that any act which shows a disposition or intent on the part of the recognizant state to treat a new state or government as an International Person may be considered as an act of recognition.

A far more mooted question than the method of recognition, is that of the exercise of the function.[51] To what department of the National Government does the function belong? The constitution of the United States is silent on the point. It does not, by express terms, confer the power upon any one branch of the government.

However, the power vests by implication with the executive branch. The constitution [52] provides that the " executive power shall be vested in a President of the United States." The powers of the President, not being enumerated, are considered to be such powers as naturally inhere in the chief executive of a state. This includes the power of recognition. It is true that certain powers are enumerated,

---

[48] Oppenheim, *International Law*, v. I, p. 596, is firmly convinced that such appointment implies recognition, while Hall, *International* Law, p. 109, is equally certain that such an act does not accord recognition.

[49] *Digest*, v. I, pp. 79, 90, 206.

[50] In 1832, the United States afforded recognition to Belgium through the issuance of *exequaturs*. Similarly, we recognized Venezuela, Uruguay, Gautemala and the Dominican Republic. U. S. *Senate Document*, No. 40, *op. cit.*, pp. 6–13.

[51] See Julius Goebel, Jr., *Recognition Policy of the United States*, pp. 44–68, for an excellent philosophical treatise on the theory of recognition.

[52] Article II, sec. 2, cl. 2.

but this enumeration is indicative of the nature of the powers, rather than all-inclusive.[53] Historically and judicially recognition has been and is considered as an executive function.[54]

Yet it is not necessary to resort to implication alone. In the recital of some of the presidential powers, the constitution provides that he " shall have power, by and with the advice and consent of the Senate, to make treaties, provided two-thirds of the senators present concur; and he shall nominate and by the advice and consent of the Senate shall appoint, ambassadors, other public ministers and consuls. . . ." [55] Thus recognition through the negotiation of a treaty or the appointment of a diplomatic or consular officer vests in the President. Certainly we may say that the initiative rests with him.

Further enumeration confers on the President the power to "receive ambassadors and other public ministers." [56] The reception of diplomatic agents vests in the President alone. It follows that recognition through the reception of diplomatic agents is an executive function. This method of recognition was inaugurated by President Washington in the reception of M. Genêt, May 17, 1793, as the Minister of the French Republic.[57] This method was followed in the recognition of Columbia, Brazil, and the Central American Federation of 1825. It was also used by the United States in the cases of Costa Rica, Nicaragua, and Panama.[58] It is the usual method of according recognition.

---

[53] Corwin, *President's Control of Foreign Relations, passim.* See also Matthews, *Conduct of American Foreign Relations, passim.*

[54] *Recognition of a New State: Is it an Executive Function?*, W. L. Penfield, 32 Amer. Law Rev. 1898, pp. 390–408, where the author goes into minute examination of the authorities such as Montesquieu, Blackstone, and the Constitutional Debates, in order to determine whether, at the time the Constitution was formed, the conduct of foreign relations was regarded by the framers as properly belonging to the Executive, and whether the conduct of such relations is implicit in the grant of executive powers to the President.

[55] Art. II, sec. 2.

[56] *Ibid.*, sec. 3.

[57] Jefferson's *Writings*, Ford Edition, v. VI, p. 217.

[58] U. S. *Senate Document*, No. 40, *op. cit.*, pp. 1–12.

The constitutional phrase "to receive ambassadors and other public ministers" means exactly what it says. It should not be interpreted in a narrow sense. It should be interpreted to include "all possible diplomatic agents, which any power may accredit to the United States."[59] Professor Corwin feels that the term "public ministers" includes "all foreign consular agents" as well as "diplomatic agents."[60]

In cases of recognition by the reception of diplomatic and consular officers, the president acts alone. Not so with the despatch of such agents to a foreign government. Here the constitution requires that another arm of the government, the Senate, be brought into play. Yet in this method the initiative remains with the Chief Executive. Until the President makes the nomination, the Senate can take no action.[61]

Also, in the granting of recognition by the negotiation of treaties the Senate has a share, inasmuch as their ratification requires the consent of that body. But here, as in the case of the despatch of diplomatic and consular officers, the initial step must be taken by the President. The President alone is responsible for the conduct of negotiations. Neither the constitution nor practice requires that he submit the names of commissioners to negotiate treaties to the Senate for confirmation. They are agents of the Chief Executive rather than "officers of the United states."[62] President Washington conferred with the Senate relative to the negotiation of certain treaties. He requested the confirmation of his appointees for that purpose. The arrangement prevailed as late as 1815. However, if we may judge by the experiences of Washington, Adams, and Jefferson, the arrangement was unsatisfactory.

---

[59] Opinion of Attorney-General Cushing, *Opinions of the Attorney-Generals*, v. 7, p. 209.

[60] *President's Control of Foreign Relations*, p. 46.

[61] For illustrations of this method of recognition in the cases of Bolivia, Haiti, Honduras, and Peru, see U. S. *Senate Document*, No. 40, *op. cit.*, pp. 4–13.

[62] Crandall, *Treaties: their Making and Enforcement*, pp. 75–76.

Since 1815 the practice has been otherwise. Only in exceptional cases have the names of such commissioners been submitted to the Senate for confirmation.[63] By this method the President is able to extend recognition on his own authority to an independent state by merely entering into treaty negotiations with such a power. This method was used in 1826 in according recognition to the government of Hawaii. A special representative was sent by the President to negotiate a treaty with the King of Hawaii. Similar recognition was subsequently accorded to the provisional Hawaiian government in 1893 through the negotiation of an annexation treaty. This method has been followed in the recognition of other states and governments.[64]

Once a state is recognized, subsequent governments within the state are generally recognized by the issuance of *Letters of Credence* to the diplomatic representative accorded to the prior government. These letters are issued by the President. Thus the President has it within his power to determine the legitimacy of a new government. He may determine the proper time to extend recognition. Nowhere are these principles more perspicuously illustrated than in our relations with France from 1793 to 1870.[65] Perhaps the most recent example of this method was the late recognition accorded to the Provisional Government in Russia. On March 22, 1917, Ambassador Francis,[66] in an address to the Council of Ministers, stated that he had the honor, as the Ambassador and Representative of the Government of the United States accredited to Russia, to say that the Government of the United States had recognized the new Government of Russia, and that he would "be pleased to continue intercourse with Russia through the medium of the new government." [67]

---

[63] Hyde, v. II, pp. 12–13 and authorities there cited.

[64] U. S. *Senate Document*, No. 40, *op. cit.*, pp. 1–12.

[65] Goebel, *Recognition Policy of the United States*, chapter 4, pp. 97–115.

[66] The United States' Ambassador accredited to the former Czar's government.

[67] *New York Times, Current History Magazine*, v. I, p. 293.

In addition to the aforementioned powers, the President is, by the constitution, made commander-in-chief of the armed forces of the country.[68] It appears that recognition has been granted in several instances through the use of this power. This was done as a matter of military and political strategy.[69] It was by virtue of this authority that President Wilson accorded recognition to Czecho-Slovakia during the World War. On September 2, 1918, Secretary Lansing, issued a statement which declared, *inter alia,* that the Government of the United States recognized a state of belligerency "between the Czecho-Slovaks . . . and the German and Austro-Hungarian Empires." It also recognized the Czecho-Slovak National Council as a *de facto* belligerent government, "clothed with proper authority to direct the military and political affairs of the Czecho-Slovaks." The Government of the United States further declared that it was prepared "to enter formally into relations with the *de facto* government thus recognized for the purpose of prosecuting the war against the common enemy, the Empires of Germany and Austro-Hungary."[70] Recognition of Poland[71] and Jugo-Slavia[72] was accorded in a similar manner.

Practice, the mother of things diplomatic, reveals recognition as the function of the Chief Executive. The President, acting alone, may accord recognition of a state of insurgency, of belligerency, or of independence. He is authorized by the constitution to grant such recognition by any of the forms known to International Law, except in the form of a treaty or by accrediting a representative to such new state.[73]

---

[68] Art. II, sec. 2.

[69] Comment, 12 *American Political Science Review,* p. 715.

[70] *Official Bulletin of the United States,* Sept. 3, 1918.

[71] January 26, 1919.

[72] February 7, 1919; *Political Science Review,* Supplement No. 70, September, 1919.

[73] Corwin, *President's Control of Foreign Relations,* p. 71. This means two-thirds of a quorum and not two-thirds of the elected members. A weighty opinion on a similar point was delivered by Mr. Chief Justice White in *Missouri Pacific Railway Co. vs. Kansas,* 248 U. S., 1919, 276.

This does not mean that the Senate, or even Congress, has not claimed the function as one of its own. Indeed some senators have declared that " recognition by this government of any people as a free and independent nation is one exclusively for the determination of Congress in its capacity as the law-making power " and that " this prerogative does not appertain to the Executive except so far as the President is, under the Constitution, by the exercise of the veto, made a part of the law-making power of the government." [74]

Usually, however, the Senate is not aggressive. Yet in at least five instances they have sought to influence the recognition policy of the Chief Executive.[75] In general, however, the President has accorded little, if any, weight to their recommendations. Recognition is primarily the function of the President.

In summary we find that recognition is the acknowledgment of the existence of a state or government by other states or governments. State life is a condition precedent to the extension of recognition. Recognition does not create the state. However recognition is necessary before a state or government can assert its fundamental rights of existence and independence. Such has been the development of the Family of Nations. Recognition may be *de jure* or *de facto*. Internationally the difference is important, but so far as the courts of the recognizant state are concerned, it is of little moment. In the United States the recognition function is vested in the national government by virtue of its complete control of foreign affairs. It is placed in the hands of the Executive Department where it logically belongs.

---

[74] Resolution introduced by Senator Bacon of Georgia, 1898, and reported in 32 *American Law Review*, 1898, 390.

[75] The Latin American republics, Texas, Mexico, Cuba and Russia. A brief summary is given by G. S. Moyer in his *Attitude of the United States toward the Recognition of the Soviet Republic*, especially pages 133–140 on Congressional attitude. A more detailed statement of Congressional interference will be found in Moore, *Digest*, v. I, sections 35, 36, and 37. The best discussion of the Russian situation is to be found in Ernest La Garde's, *La Reconnaissance du Gouvernement Des Soviets.* See also *Die de facto-Regierung im Volkerrecht*, von J. Spiropoulos.

CHAPTER III

Recognition by the Political Departments

A difficult situation faces any court which is called upon to determine the validity of an act done under the authority of a foreign state. This has been especially true in the United States and England in controversies before the courts involving the legality of acts performed under the authority of the unrecognized Soviet regime. The cases on this point fall into two general classes. First, those in which the political departments of the recognizant state have assumed a definite attitude toward the government in question. Second, those in which no definite position has been taken. This chapter is devoted to a consideration of those cases in which a definite attitude has been assumed by the legislative or the executive branches of the recognizant state.

In those cases involving a fixed attitude on the part of the political departments two factors have proved important. These have been the nature of the position, that is whether recognition has been expressly or impliedly granted or denied, and the time of the recognition, that is whether recognition antedated the act the validity of which is in litigation, or was granted subsequent to the commission of the acts in question but prior to the adjudication of the court.

Where recognition of belligerency, insurgency or independence has been accorded by the political departments prior to, or at the time the controversies have arisen, the courts have regarded such determination as binding upon the judiciary. They have consistently refused to enter into an examination to determine for themselves which government is the lawfully instituted authority in a designated state. Also, in cases where the political departments have positively refused to accord recognition the courts have regarded themselves as bound by such determination. They have refused to question the wisdom of the action of the political departments, or to put themselves at variance with their determination.

In those cases in which recognition has been granted between the time of the act in question and the time of the litigation, the courts have created the fiction of retroactivity; under what conditions and with what results will be seen when the question is examined in a later chapter.

With reference to those cases in which no position, either affirmative or negative, has been assumed by the political departments, but where it is a matter of world notoriety that a change has taken place, such as in Russia, the decisions are not uniform. Some of the courts have felt that they were bound to regard the old order of things as continuing until cognizance of the change was taken by the political departments, while other courts have felt that they were competent to judge the situation in question and independently to determine the status of the state. The succeeding chapter will be devoted to a consideration of this class of cases.

The writer feels that the above distinctions are warranted from an examination of the cases, although conscious that neither the courts, the lawyers, nor those few who have dared to write upon the subject, have always observed such a differentiation. While it may be said that conflicting expressions are to be found in some of the decisions, the writer defends the position that they are excerpts and not decisions, and that when the so-called conflicting expressions are considered with reference to the concrete facts of each case, keeping in mind the nature of the judicial function, they are entirely in harmony with and support the general classification as made.

Practically all of the recent cases rely upon the early precedents. These flowed from the political turnovers revolving around the French Revolution, the revolution in Santo Domingo and Haiti, the severance by the Latin American republics of relations with Spain and Portugal, and our own Civil War. Such precedents have exerted a profound influence upon the recent development of the judicial doctrine. It will be necessary to scrutinize the early decisions most carefully.

The first case in point presented to the American courts was *Clark vs. United States.* This case arose out of the non-importation act of 1809 and was decided in the circuit court.[1] The act in question forbade the importation of

[1] 3 Wash. C. C. 101, Federal Case No. 2, 838. The courts have regarded the determination of an attitude as a political question. On such questions the courts follow the political departments of the government. The following have been held to be political questions: the recognition of a government, *The Neredie,* 9 Cranch, 1815, 388; recognition of diplomatic and consular representatives, *The Rogdai,* 279 Federal, 1920, 130; recognition of belligerency, *The Itata,* 56 Federal, 1893, 505 recognition of insurgency, *United States vs. Three Friends,* 166 U. S., 1897, 1, see also 11 *A. J.,* 883, where an attempt was made before a Wisconsin Circuit Court to enjoin the shipment of arms to the allies during the world war; the status of an Indian tribe, *Cherokee Nation vs. Georgia,* 5 Peters, 1831, 1 and *United States vs. Holliday,* 3 Wallace, 1865, 407; *in re* the status of Indian tribes see also, *United States vs. Boyd,* 68 Federal, 1895, 577, where the court said: "In determing the attitude of the government toward the Indians,—all Indians,—the courts follow the action of the executive and other political departments of the government, whose more special duty it is to determine such affairs." The guaranty of a republican form of government, *Luther vs. Borden,* 7 Howard, 1849,1 and *Texas vs. White,* 7 Wallace, 1868, 700; jurisdiction over territory, *Wilson vs. Shaw,* 204 U. S., 1907, 24, where the court rejected the argument that the executive branch had exceeded its power in acquiring the Panama Canal Zone; the admission and deportation of aliens, 2 *Corpus Juris* 1075, notes and cases there cited; the beginning of a war, *The Protector,* 12 Wallace, 1871, 700, and *United States vs. One Hundred and Twenty Nine Packages,* 1862, Federal Case No. 15, 941; the termination of a war, *United States vs. Wall,* 278 Federal, 1921, 838, *The Commercial Trust Co. vs. Miller,* 281 Federal, 1922, 804; but see *United States vs. Hicks,* 256 Federal, 1919, 707 where one circuit court construed the President's message to Congress, on the cessation of hostilities wherein he said "the war thus comes to an end," as evidence that the President regarded the war as ended; the negotiation of treaties, *Fellows vs. Blacksmith,* 19 Howard, 1856, 366; the violation of a treaty, *Ware vs. Hylton,* 3 Dallas, 1796, 260, wherein Mr. Justice Iredell said: "These are considerations of policy, considerations of extreme magnitude, and certainly incompetent to the examination and decision of a court of Justice"; and the termination of treaties, *Terlinden vs. Ames,* 184 U. S., 1901, 270, which involved an interpretation of our extradition treaty of 1854 with Prussia.

goods into the United States " from any port or place situated in France, or its colonies or dependencies." The goods in question in this case had been imported from Santo Domingo, a former French Colony which, at the time, was under the control of revolutionists. In the prosecution it became important to know whether Santo Domingo was to be considered as a colony within the meaning of the non-importation statute. Clark defended that the *de facto* independence of Santo Domingo took the acts in question from under the statute, but the court adopted the opposite view. Mr. Justice Washington, who delivered the opinion, said, with reference to Clark's defense: " These arguments . . . had great weight with us. . . . But they seem to be so completely borne down by the opinion of the Supreme Court, pronounced in the case of *Rose vs. Himely,* that it is impossible, we think, to sustain them, without disregarding principles most clearly expressed in that opinion." [2]

This leads one to inquire as to the " principles most clearly expressed " in *Rose vs. Himely.*[3] An American vessel had also taken cargo at ports in control of the insurgents in Santo Domingo. Subsequently, it was seized on the high seas and carried into a Spanish port in Cuba where both the vessel and cargo were condemned and sold under the authority of a purported agent of the French government of Santo Domingo. Afterwards the goods were brought to the United States where they were claimed by the original American owner, but prior to the trial both the vessel and the cargo were condemned by a French court in Santo Domingo on the ground that the vessel had violated a French decree prohibiting trade with the insurgents.

On appeal to the Supreme Court Mr. Chief Justice Marshall sought to determine whether the sentence of the French tribunal was that of a prize court or a court enforcing a

[2] *Clark vs. United States,* Federal case No. 2,838, 3 Wash. C. C. 101 at 102.
[3] 4 Cranch, 1808, 241.

municipal regulation. He felt that it was necessary to determine this in order better to determine the jurisdiction of the French tribunal.[4] He proceeded to examine the acts and decrees of the French government in order to determine the exact nature of the judgment. He concluded that the vessel and cargo had been condemned for violation of the French municipal regulation. Inasmuch as the vessel had been seized on the high sea and never carried within the jurisdiction of the court, the learned Chief Justice held that the condemnation by the French court was ineffective and gave judgment in favor of the American claimants.

The attorneys had argued that the court should not stop there. They had argued that Santo Domingo, "having declared itself a sovereign state, and having maintained its sovereignty . . . by arms, must be considered and treated by" the courts of the United States "as sovereign in fact, and as being entitled to maintain the same intercourse with the world that is maintained by other belligerent nations." It was in answer to this contention that Mr. Chief Justice Marshall said that "it is for governments to decide whether they will consider Santo Domingo as an independent nation."[5] No cases are cited on the point. The only reference made is to Vattel on what he deemed the law to be. "But the language of that writer," said Marshall, "is obviously addressed to sovereigns, not to courts."

Examination of *Rose vs. Himely* reveals that Mr. Chief Justice Marshall's statement was obiter dictum. It appears to have been only a passing comment on the argument of the attorneys. However, it was considered the ruling principle in *Clark vs. United States* and subsequent cases.[6]

[4] "In making this inquiry the relative situation of France and Santo Domingo must necessarily be considered. The colony of Santo Domingo, originally belonging to France, had broken the bond which connected her with the parent state, had declared herself independent, and was endeavoring to support that independence by arms. France still asserted her claim of sovereignty, and had employed a military force in support of that claim. A war *de facto* then unquestionably existed between France and Santo Domingo." 4 Cranch, 1808, 241 at 272.

[5] *Ibid.* at 272.

[6] *Rose vs. Himely* was modified, if not reversed, in *Hudson vs. Guestier*, 4 Cranch, 1808, 293, and 6 Cranch, 1810, 281.

Nevertheless, Mr. Justice Washington had good reason for adopting the position which he assumed in *Clark vs. United States,* although Marshall's dictum did not apply. The non-importation act expressly stipulated that it should apply to French "colonies and dependencies." France still claimed Santo Domingo as a possession. Prior and subsequent events showed that her claim was recognized by the United States. The political departments of our government had dealt with the French government as having authority over the colony in question. It would have embarrassed the political departments for the court to have permitted the "*de facto* situation to take Santo Domingo out of the operation of the statue." The true reason back of the court's decision appears to have been the assumption of a fixed attitude on the part of the political departments, rather than reverent regard for the dictum in *Rose vs. Himely.*

The exact issue was first presented to the United States Supreme Court for determination in 1818 in *Gelston vs. Hoyt.*[7] The case arose out of an act of 1794[8] which imposed a forfeiture of any ship fitted out with the intent that it be employed "in the service of any foreign prince or state," to commit hostilities upon the subjects or property of "another foreign prince or state" with whom the United States were at peace. The Collector of Customs of New York had seized the vessel in question, on the ground that it was being used in violation of the neutrality laws of the United States.

The plaintiffs brought action to recover the vessel. They contended that the neutrality laws had not been violated inasmuch as the vessel was fitted out for the use of that part of Santo Domingo under the *de facto* control of *Petion,* against that part of Santo Domingo under the *de facto* control of *Christophe,* which, being unrecognized, were not

[7] 3 Wheaton, 1818, 246.
[8] Ch. 50, Sec. 3.

foreign states or princes, within the meaning of the neutrality laws. The defendants, public officers, had offered to prove the *de facto* status of the Petion government, but the evidence was rejected by the lower court. The Supreme Court held that it was properly rejected.

"If the court was bound to admit the evidence . . . it must have been upon the ground that it was bound to take judicial notice of the relations of the country with foreign states, and to decide affirmatively, that *Petion* and *Christophe* were foreign princes, within the purview of the statute." Mr. Justice Story added: "No doctrine is better established than that it belongs exclusively to governments to recognize new states in the revolutions which occur in the world." The Justice felt that "until such recognition, either by our own government or the government to which the new state belonged, courts of justice . . . are bound to consider the ancient state of things as remaining unaltered."[9] Express reference is made to *Rose vs. Himely,* 4 Cranch 241.[10]

The cases cited in *Gelston vs. Hoyt* appear to sustain the decision more than in *Clark vs. United States.* The Act of 1794 expressly stated that it should apply only where a "foreign prince or state" was involved. If the court had acknowledged either the *Petion* government or the *Christophe* government as a "foreign prince or state" it would have put them at variance with Congress which anticipated that the Act of 1794 should apply only to recognized governments.

At the same session of the court, fifteen days later, Mr. Chief Justice Marshall had occasion to comment on the delicacy and difficulty of this question. In the course of his argument to the court in *United States vs. Palmer,*[11] one

---

[9] *Gelston vs. Hoyt,* 3 Wheaton, 1818, 246 at 324.

[10] See also, *In the Manila,* 1 Edwards, 1808, 1, 165 English Reprints, 1011; *City of Berne vs. Bank of England,* 9 Ves. Jun., 1804, 347, 32 English Reprints, 636; *Dolder vs. Bank of England,* 10 Ves. Jun., 1804, 284, 32 English Reprints, 853; ibid., 10 Ves. Jun., 1804, 352, 32 English Reprints, 881; ibid., 11 Ves. Jun., 1805, 283, 32 English Reprints, 1097.

[11] 3 Wheaton, 1818, 610.

Blake had insisted, on this point, that "nothing but the most explicit, public and notorious acts of the government should be noticed by courts of justice. Nothing should be left to inference or conjecture; because, such a course might lead to a usurpation by the courts of the high prerogative of making war and peace, and the whole nation would become responsible to other nations for the error of judgment in a department with which it had not entrusted the care of its foreign affairs. In the infinite variety and complication of these affairs, the language and conduct of the executive may be misunderstood; and, therefore, nothing short of an act of the whole legislature, a treaty, a proclamation of the President, or the public reception of an ambassador from the new state, ought to be considered as a recognition of its independence." [12]

The court did not concur in the argument. The Chief Justice "observed that such questions are generally rather political than legal in their character. They belong more properly to those who can declare what the law shall be; who can place the nation in such a position with respect to foreign powers as to their own judgment shall appear wise; to whom are entrusted all its foreign relations; than to that tribunal whose power as well as duty is confined to the application of the rule which the legislature may prescribe for it."

In the war between France and Santo Domingo, the United States could have engaged itself with the one party or the other, or observed absolute neutrality, or recognized the new state absolutely, or else have made a limited recognition of it. But if the United States remained neutral, as it did, and recognized the existence of a civil war, "its courts cannot consider as criminal those acts of hostility which war authorizes, and which the new government may direct against its enemy. To decide otherwise, would be to determine that the war prosecuted by one of the parties was unlawful, and would be to arraign the nation to which the court belongs

[12] 3 Wheaton, 1818, 610 at pp. 623–625.

against that party. This would transcend the limits prescribed to the judicial department."[13] The courts of the Union must view newly constituted governments "as they are viewed by the legislative and executive department of the government."[14] For the first time the court intimates that recognition is a legislative, as well as an executive, function.

Again, the President had adopted a course, neutrality, and the courts felt bound by the decision of the Executive. The court observed that a different course might have been taken by the Executive, but that the judiciary must follow once a decision had been made.

Mr. Justice Johnson, in *United States vs. Palmer,*[15] agreed with the majority of the court, but insisted upon writing a separate opinion. The following year, while on circuit duty, the precise question was raised before him in *The Consul of Spain vs. La Conception.*[16] A Spanish owned vessel was seized by a cruiser of the revolted provinces of Buenos Ayres. When it was brought into an American port the owners libelled it, and the District Court ordered restoration, *inter alia,* on the ground that the commission issued by the Buenos Ayres government, then unrecognized, could not be recognized as valid. On appeal to the Circuit Court, Justice Johnson reversed the determination of the District Court. He held that the commission issued to the cruiser could be recognized because of the existence of war, the acknowledgment of which had been made by the political departments of our government.

It was argued, and cases and opinions were cited to show,

---

[13] *U. S. vs. Palmer,* 3 Wheaton, 1818, 610, at 634–635. This was a prosecution for robbery committed on the high seas. The circuit court of the United States, for the District of Mass., was divided in opinion and certified ten questions to the Supreme Court, seven of which involved the rights of a colony or portion of an established empire which has proclaimed itself an independent nation, and was asserting and maintaining its claim to independence by arms.

[14] 3 Wheaton, 1818, 610 at 643.

[15] *Ibid.*

[16] Federal Cases No. 3,137, 2 Wheeler Cr. Case, 1819, 597.

that the Circuit Court could not recognize the independence of a revolted colony until full recognition had proceeded from our government. The court refused to agree entirely with the argument. On the point the court observed that "recognition by our own government, whatever be the state of fact, removes all question of doubt and our courts must consider the governments thus recognized as independent. . . ."[17] However, the court felt that there exist certain *de facto* situations of which cognizance must be taken by the courts in the course of adjudications.

Mr. Justice Johnson made certain observations which too often have been misunderstood and misconstrued by courts and writers who overlook the fact that this decision was reversed on appeal to the Supreme Court. New proofs were taken which showed that the vessel was originally built, equipped, manned and armed in the United States for a cruise against Spain, and that there had never been a bona fide sale at Buenos Ayres. Such evidence showed conclusively that the American neutrality laws had been violated. Therefore, it was unnecessary for the court to consider the point pressed before the District and Circuit Courts.

The court examined and reaffirmed the doctrine that recognition by the political departments binds the judiciary, the following year, 1819, when it was put in issue, in *The Divina Pastora.*[18] Mr. Chief Justice Marshall said: "The decision at the last term, (referring to *United States vs. Palmer*), establishes the principle, that the government of the United States, having recognized the existence of a civil war between Spain and her colonies, but remaining neutral, the courts of the Union are bound to consider as lawful those acts which war authorizes, and which the new governments in South America may direct against their enemy."[19]

[17] Federal Case No. No. 3, 137, 2 Wheeler Cr. Case, 1819, 597. 6 Federal Cases 360.
[18] 4 Wheaton, 1819, 52.
[19] *Ibid.*, pp. 63–64.

Ten years later, in an argument to the court, in answer to the proposition that the courts could examine political questions, one Jones[20] asserted that the principle is too obviously a necessary corollary of the connection of courts of justice with the government under which they are established, to require illustration. "This court," said he, referring to the Supreme Court, "is precluded from entertaining any other opinion, than that which has already been expressed by the government and all its citizens, except those few whose private interests induce them to cling to an exploded fallacy." This was the view taken by the court.[21]

Equally strong language issued from the court itself in *Charles L. Williams vs. Suffolk Insurance Company.*[22] The Suffolk Insurance Company had issued marine insurance policies on two vessels, the *Harriet* and the *Breakwater,* to sail on a sealing voyage, to the Southern hemisphere "with liberty . . . to touch at all islands, ports and places, for the purpose of taking seals, and for information and refreshments. . . ."[23] The *Harriet* had proceeded on its voyage when it was ordered by the government of Buenos Ayres not to catch seals off the Falkland Islands. The master of the vessel disregarded the orders. The vessel was seized and condemned under the authority of the government of Buenos Ayres.

In two actions of assumpsit, on the policies, the Suffolk Insurance Company defended that they were relieved of

---

[20] See *Foster vs. Neilson,* 2 Peters, 1829, 253 at 283.

[21] *Ibid.* 306–309 *passim.* The determination of a boundary line is a political question, the determination of which, by the political departments, the courts are bound to respect. *Foster vs. Neilson* 2 Peters, 1829, 253; *U. S. vs. Arredondo,* 6 Peters, 1832, 711; *Garcia vs. Lee,* 12 Peters, 1838, 511; *U. S. vs. Yorba,* 1 Wallace, 1863, 412 at 423; *U. S. Lynde,* 11 Wallace, 1870, 632 at 638. In the last case the court says that it is not aware of any case in which the principle has been doubted by the courts. However, expressions may perhaps be found in some opinions, which, "detached from the case under consideration, might create some doubt on the subject. But these expressions must always be taken with reference to the particular subject matter in the mind of the court." *Garcia vs. Lee,* 12 Peters, 1838, 511 at 520.

[22] 13 Peters, 1839, 415.

[23] 14 *Transcript of the Record,* United States Supreme Court, 1050.

liability inasmuch as the master of the *Harriet* had disregarded the orders of the Buenos Ayres government. The plaintiffs responded that they were not bound by the orders of the Buenos Ayres government, because it had no jurisdiction over the Falkland Islands; the government of the United States not having acknowledged, but having expressly denied its claims. The defendants replied that the islands were the property of the Buenos Ayres government and contended that the court should determine for itself whether such were the facts of the case.

When the case came before Mr. Justice Story in the Circuit Court,[24] he recognized that the American government "insists that the Falkland Islands do not constitute any part of the dominions within the sovereignty of Buenos Ayres," while Buenos Ayres maintained exactly the opposite position. Mr. Justice Story said that "in this state of the diplomacy between the two countries . . . the question is whether it is competent for this court to reexamine and decide . . . and thus to interpose its positive umpirage to settle the matters in dispute . . . ."[25] He answered his question by saying that the court was "bound up by the doctrines and claims insisted on by its own government, and that it must take them to be rightful, until the contrary" was established by some formal and authorized action of that government.[26] He said: "This court is bound, so far as its own functions are concerned, to act upon the ground that the claims of our government, and its assertions of its rights in this respect, are correct. *Omnia rita acta.*"[27]

The court regarded the argument as more than the rejection of an exploded theory. It was regarded as a basic principle underlying our governmental structure for "it might otherwise happen that the extra-ordinary spectacle

[24] Federal Case No. 17,738, 1838; 29 Federal Cases, p. 1402; 3 Sumner 270.
[25] *Ibid.*, p. 1403.
[26] *Ibid.*, p. 1404.
[27] *Ibid.*

might be presented of the courts of a country disavowing and annulling the acts of its own government in matters of state and political diplomacy." [28]

On appeal to the Supreme Court, Mr. Justice McLean expressed surprise that there should have been any doubt on the point.[29] He stressed the point that it is not within the province of the courts to pass upon the wisdom of the action of the Chief Executive. "It is enough to know, that in the exercise of his constitutional functions, he has decided the question. Having done this under the responsibilities which belong to him, it is obligatory on the people and government of the Union." And, the court ordered its decision to be certified back to the Circuit Court: "That, inasmuch as the American Government has insisted and does still insist, through its regular executive authority, that the Falkland Islands do not constitute any part of the dominions within the sovereignty of the government of Buenos Ayres, the action of the American Government on this subject is conclusive on the said Circuit Court." [30]

The court decided that the vessel was not bound to abandon the voyage, under the threat of illegal capture. It held that the insurers were liable to pay for the loss of the vessel and cargo, inasmuch as the master of the vessel in refusing to obey the orders to leave the islands, had acted under a belief that he was bound so to do, as a matter of duty to the owners, and all interested in the voyage, and "in vindication of the right claimed by the American Government." [31]

It has been argued that this part of *Williams vs. Suffolk Insurance Company* was *obiter dictum:* that the court did not have to decide between conflicting claims of the right of recognition by the two departments of government. Such

[28] 14 *Transcript of the Record,* United States Supreme Court Reports, 1052.
[29] 13 Peters, 1839, 415.
[30] *Williams vs. Suffolk Insurance Company,* 13 Peters, 1839, 415 at pp. 419–420.
[31] *Ibid.,* 421.

may be true, but it does not abrogate the fact that the court had to decide whether the seizure was valid in order to determine liability. The alleged ground of invalidity was the act of the President recognizing the independence of Buenos Ayres while at the same time expressly denying its sovereignty over the Falkland Islands. Under these circumstances the court held that the Falkland Islands must be deemed to belong to Spain until the title of Buenos Ayres had been admitted by our government. It determined liability accordingly. The court felt bound by the determination of the Chief Executive, and resolved to abide by such determination until it should be changed by the President.

The decision came under review by the Supreme Court in *Jones vs. United States.*[32] By an act of Congress of 1856, the President had been authorized to extend, by proclamation, the jurisdiction of the United States over any unoccupied island having a deposit of phosphate, or guano, which might be discovered and occupied by any citizen of the United States, the usual rules of International Law governing discovery having been complied with. The United States acquired jurisdiction over the Navassa Island by virtue of such discovery and occupation. Jones had been convicted of the murder of one Foster on Navassa Island. On appeal he raised a question as to the jurisdiction of the court, but the Supreme Court affirmed the conviction.

Mr. Justice Gray, who delivered the opinion of the court, said that who is the sovereign, *de jure* or *de facto,* of a territory is not a judicial, but a political question, the determination of which by the legislative and executive departments of any government "conclusively binds the judges, as well as all other officers, citizens and subjects of that government." Then he added: "This principle has always been upheld by this court, and has been affirmed under a great variety of circumstances." [33]

---

[32] 137 U. S., 1890, 202.
[33] *Ibid.,* 212.

The court held that it was bound to take judicial notice of the recognition or denial of the sovereignty of a foreign power by the government whose laws it administers. Such notice could be had from the acts of the legislature and executive, " even though those acts were not formally put in evidence, nor in accord with the pleadings." [34]

After having stated the above premise, the court noted that in the ascertainment of facts of which the court was bound to take judicial notice, the judges may refresh their memory and inform their conscience from such sources as they deem most trustworthy.[35] As to international affairs, such as the recognition of a foreign government, or of the diplomatic character of a person claiming to be its representative, they may inquire of the Foreign Office or the Department of State.[36]

In the instant case the court proceeded to examine the acts of Congress, the documents on file in the State Department, and the proclamations of the President. In these official instruments and documents Navassa Island had been regarded as a part of the United States. The United States had jurisdiction over it for purposes of enforcement of the law in question.[37] The case is unique in that it did not in-

[34] *U. S. vs. Reynes,* 9 Howard, 1850, 127; *Kennett vs. Chambers,* 14 Howard, 1852, 38; *Hoyt vs. Russell,* 117 U. S., 1885, 401; *Coffee vs. Grover,* 123 U. S., 1887, 1; *State vs. Dunwell,* 3 R. I., 1855, 127; *State vs. Wagner,* 61 Maine 1873, 178. In *Coffee vs. Grover,* involving conflicting titles to land, where the title depended upon a disputed boundary between Georgia and Florida, the court determined the true boundary by consulting public documents, some of which had not been given in evidence at the trial, nor referred to in the opinion of the Supreme Court of Florida.

[35] *Fremont vs. U. S.,* 17 Howard, 1854, 542 at 557; *Brown vs. Piper,* 91 U. S., 1875, 37.

[36] *Ex parte Hitz,* 111 U. S., 1883, 766, where the court made inquiry of the State Department to determine the relations of a Mr. Hitz as Political Agent of the Swiss Confederation. See also *In Re Baiz,* 135 U. S., 1890, 403, where the question was raised, in 1890, regarding status of three Central American countries.

[37] *Jones vs. United States,* 137 U. S., 1890, 202. The court gave special attention to the memorial sworn to by Peter Duncan, the discoverer of the island, on Nov. 18, 1857 and to the Proclamation of the Secretary of State of December 8, 1859, and other papers of intermediate dates filed in the Department of State. These had been communicated by the President to the Senate on April 12, 1860. *Ibid.,* 217–224.

volve a state of belligerency, insurgency, or independence. The sole question was one of jurisdiction. The case turned upon internal recognition and the exercise of internal sovereignty.

Thus far we find that recognition involves the determination of political questions, which belong to the departments of our government which have charge of our foreign relations: the legislative and executive departments. Once such questions are answered by those departments, the courts are bound to follow their decision. If such were not the established rule, cases could arise in which the executive department might consider a foreign government as at war with the United States, while the judiciary would consider it in a state of peace, and at the same time the legislative department would regard it an non-existent.[38]

Examination reveals a second class of cases where the same principle of law has been applied. This class includes those cases in the examination of which the courts have found that recognition has been expressly refused, or withheld, by the political departments. It may be that the government or state under consideration has been so treated by the political departments of the government as to presume the existence of the old order. The courts in their decisions do not appear to have been conscious of the precise difference in facts, although they appear to have reached the proper conclusions. It matters not save in so far as it has led to confusion in subsequent cases.

This type of case was presented first to the English courts. Early in the nineteenth century, 1804 and 1805, three cases [39] came before the British High Court of Chancery. The city

[38] Even the courts might not be able to agree. It is conceivable that each court might recognize a distinct faction and there would be as many factions recognized as there are recognizing courts. The courts will not render what they consider to be a vain decision.

[39] *City of Berne vs. Bank of England,* 9 Ves. Jun., 1804, 347; *Dolder vs. Bank of England,* 10 Ves. Jun., 1804, 352; *Dolder vs. Lord Huntingfield,* 11 Ves. Jun., 1805, 283.

of Berne, Switzerland,[40] sought to restrain the Bank of England and the South Sea Company from transferring certain funds which had been purchased by the municipality prior to the French revolution. The respondents defended on the ground that the then existing government of Switzerland, being unrecognized by the government of England, could not be noticed by the court. Lord Chancellor Eldon was "much struck with the objection." He said that "it was extremely difficult to say, a judicial court can take notice of a Government, never authorized by the Government of the Country, in which that Court sits." It appears that a negative position, a denial of the new government, had been taken by the English government and the judiciary felt bound by their determination.

At about the same time, a British court sitting at Halifax condemned an American vessel [41] for carrying goods to the insurgents in Haiti and Santo Domingo. The court condemned *The Happy Couple* on the ground that England had not recognized a condition of insurgency, but had expressly regarded the island as a French colony. The political departments had denied the existence of a state of insurgency. Three years later, in 1808, other British courts held that colonial ports dominated by insurgents should not be regarded as colonial ports of France within the meaning of the orders in council subjecting neutral ships to condemnation for trading from colonial ports of the enemy, under which the condemnation of *The Happy Couple* had been made.[42]

The courts did not thereby overrule the decision in *The Happy Couple*. The courts construed subsequent orders in council as amounting to an acknowledgment of a state of insurgency. This led the court, in the case of *The Pelican*,[43] to declare that "it always belongs to the government of the

---

[40] *City of Berne vs. Bank of England*, 9 Ves. Jun., 1804, 347.
[41] *The Happy Couple*, Stewarts Reports, 1805, 65.
[42] *The Manilla*, Edw. Adm., 1808, 1; *The Pelican*, Edw. Adm., App. 1809.
[43] *The Pelican, supra*.

country to determine in what relation any other country stands toward it." Then the court added: "That is a point upon which courts of justice cannot decide." At the time the court made these observations the judges were conscious of the change in the attitude taken by the British government in its orders in council. The three cases must be read in that light.

In the United States the point was first raised in *Kennett vs. Chambers,*[44] which involved the independence of Texas. A contract had been executed in Cincinnati, September 16, 1836, whereby a general in the Texas army, was to convey certain lands in Texas to Kennett and others in consideration for which the latter were to equip the said General Chambers' army. Texas had declared herself independent but, at the time of the making of the contract, had not been recognized by the United States. Subsequently the plaintiffs sought to compel performance of the contract. Chambers defended that the contract violated the neutrality laws of the United States. The District Court held that the contract was for an illegal purpose, and therefore took the position that it was void *ab initio*.

It was urged by the plaintiffs, on appeal, before the Supreme Court,[45] that Texas, on September 16, 1836, was an independent state; therefore, the contract in question did not transgress the neutrality laws of the United States. The court refused to agree. Able Chief Justice Taney wrote the opinion. He declared that it was a sufficient answer to the argument to say that the question whether Texas had, or had not, at that time become an independent state, "was a question for that department of our government exclusively which is charged with our foreign affairs." If the courts undertook to inquire whether Texas had not in fact become an independent sovereign state before she was recognized as

[44] 14 Howard, 1852, 38.

[45] *Kennett vs. Chambers,* 14 Howard, 1852, 38.

such by the treaty-making power, the courts would take upon themselves the exercise of political authority, " for which a judicial tribunal is wholly unfit, and which the Constitution has conferred exclusively upon another department." [46]

The court found that a negative attitude had been consciously assumed by the political departments of the government. Both Congress and the President denied the existence of Texas as an independent state. The court examined the messages of the President of the United States to the Senate on the subject. It also construed a letter, in point, from the President to the Governor of Tennessee, and a note from the Secretary of State to the Mexican Minister, even though none of these documents had been put in evidence in the case. It was with these facts in mind that the learned justice stated that until Texas was recognized by our government it must be considered as belonging to Mexico.

The point was again raised in the second case of *United States vs. Trumbull.*[47] In a prosecution for violation of the neutrality laws of the United States one Catton was subpoenaed by the prosecution. He appeared in answer to the subpoena, and presented to the court his *exequatur,* issued by President Cleveland.[48] The *exequatur* showed that he had been duly recognized by the Chief Executive as the duly appointed vice-consul of Chile at San Francisco. It declared him to be " free to enjoy and exercise such functions, powers and privileges as are allowed to the vice-consuls of the most favored nations in the United States." He also presented to the court his consular instructions which he had received from the Chilean government, and asked to be relieved from further attendance as a witness. He based his request upon his consular immunity.

The counsel for the United States denied that the immunity asserted by Mr. Catton existed. They offered to prove that

---

[46] *Kennett vs. Chambers,* 14 Howard, 1852, 38 at pp. 50–51.
[47] 48 Federal, 1891, 94. This was not the initial case.
[48] The *exequatur* bore the date of January 26, 1888.

the government which he represented had been overthrown. The court found itself "unable to take that view of the matter." The court declared that it could not "say that the person who holds the unrevoked *exequatur* issued by the President . . . is in fact not such officer. The recognition of representatives of foreign countries is a matter for the executive department of the government, whose action in the premises is accepted and followed by the judicial department."[49] The political department of the government had in effect denied the existence of the revolutionary government in Chile. The court rightly regarded itself bound by such decision.

More recently the cases arising out of the non-recognition of Russia have presented the identical question to the lower federal courts. In at least two instances one Ludwig Martens, the Soviet representative to the United States, instituted proceedings in admiralty in the District Courts[50] to recover possession of three Russian public vessels which at the time, were under the control of the duly accredited representatives of the Kerensky government. The courts dismissed the suits in both instances.

Martens insisted that he represented and spoke for the Russian sovereignty, regardless of whom the State Department in Washington received, and that the courts should hand over the vessels to him and to the organization back of him. The courts said that this was a question of state, which involved international relations and was "primarily for the State Department." It involved "considerations of national policy which are justiciable and touching it the view of the Chief Executive is the view, not of a branch of the government, but of the national sovereignty, equally binding upon all departments."[51] The court held that it could not

---

[49] Wharton, *International Law Digest*, p. 552.

[50] *The Rogdai*, 278 Federal, 1920, 294; *Ibid.*, 279 Federal, 1920, 130; *The Penza and the Tobolsk*, 277 Federal, 1921, 91.

[51] *The Rogdai*, 278 Federal, 1920, 294 at 296.

"make an independent inquiry, for to do so . . . would be to recognize Martens, while the State Department" denied his existence as well as the existence of the purported organization back of him.[52] A definite attitude had been taken by the political departments and the court felt bound by their determination.

One of the few cases in point in the state courts was before the New Jersey Court of Errors and Appeals in *O'Neill vs. Central Leather Company*.[53] This court acknowledged that it was bound to follow the determination of the political branches of the national government. They examined these and found that the official communications of the President to Congress left no doubt, or room for a contrary inference, that in November 1913, and January 1914, the Carranza and Villa forces in Mexico were recognized by our government as engaged in actual war, and that the courts should govern themselves accordingly.

The New York[54] courts likewise recognize, that, as to them, the negative decision of the President on the question of whether a particular government has been established is conclusive regardless of whether it be right or wrong. They concede that it is not for the judiciary to question the wisdom of action on the part of the other branches of the government.

The cases which have elicited the most discussion and criticism have been those in which recognition was accorded between the time of the commission of the acts in question and the litigation. In the adjudication of these cases the courts have created the fiction of retroactivity. The cases have centered around the belated recognition of Mexico by the United States, and the recognition of the Soviets by the

---

52 *The Penza, the Tobolsk,* 277 Federal, 1921, 91 at 93.

53 94 Atlantic, 1915, 789.

54 *State of Yucatan vs. Argumedo,* 92 Misc. Rep., 1915, 547; 157 N. Y. Supp. 219; and see also 179 N. Y. Supp. 713, 109 Misc. 306; 181 N. Y. Supp. 958.

English government. They have involved the assumption of an attitude by the political departments of the government which bound the courts equally as much as in the cases previously considered. Special attention will be given to the retroactivity problem at a later point.[55]

It is next in order to inquire how the courts are to know whether the political departments have assumed a definite attitude toward a particular government. The courts have followed the well-established rule by saying that judicial notice may be taken of the determination of political questions by the political departments of the government. The courts have examined the acts and proclamations of these departments in order to determine the juristic status of the government under consideration. This method has been followed both in the United States and England.

One of the most interesting cases in point is *Yrissari vs. Clement*,[56] which came before the English courts in 1826. An action for libel was brought by the plaintiff as the representative of the Republic of Chile. The defendants objected that the plaintiff had not proved that Chile was a state inasmuch as the English government had not recognized it. In the course of his opinion Lord Chief Justice Best observed that there are three sorts of foreign states: first, states that are merely acknowledged as sovereign independent states; secondly, states in connection, or such as are connected with England by existing treaties; and thirdly, sovereign states unacknowledged by the English government such as Japan, Siam, and many other states which commerce had made her acquainted with.

In cases relative to the first two mentioned classes it is only necessary to prove that the recognizant government has ac-

[55] A chapter is devoted to this problem. See, however, *Murray vs. Vanderbilt*, 39 Barbour, 1863, 140 and *Underhill vs. Hernandez*, 168 U. S., 1897, 250 for *dicta* in two early cases. See also *Kennett vs. Chambers*, 14 Howard, 1852, 38, often cited as contra.

[56] *Yrissari vs. Clement*, 3 Bing., 1826, 432; 130 English Reprints, 579.

knowledged them or treated them as sovereign independent states. "In many cases," said the court, "it would be unnecessary even to adduce this proof for the great states of the world are taken notice of in acts of Parliament made for confirming treaties and regulating the intercourse with them and of such states the Courts of Law take judicial notice." [57]

The rule is not uniform as to the method by which the courts inform themselves of the views of the political departments. In a case such as that of France or of Brazil where the sovereignty is notorious the Court will act *mero motu*.[58] Also, the court may direct its appropriate officer to make inquiry of the appropriate government department.[59] Sometimes the government in question has addressed a plea for immunity to the Foreign Office of the recognizant state and this has been endorsed and communicated to the court.[60] Also, the court will allow letters from the Foreign Office of the recognizant state concerning the status of the state, or government, in question to be read. It may be that the Law Officers of the Crown, as in the *Parlement Belge*,[61] or the officials of the Attorney General's office, will initiate proceedings to raise the question of the immunity of the foreign state or its property and will appear in support of the claim. Finally, the court will, on its own initiative, invite the Law Officers to appear and address the court upon the status of the foreign state, and to communicate the view of the government. Such a statement is considered the equivalent of a certificate from a Government Department.[62]

In a number of instances the actions of the political departments have not been clear. In such cases the courts have

---

[57] *Yrissari vs. Clement,* 3 Bing., 1826, 432 at 437.

[58] *Mighell vs. Sultan of Johore,* 1894, L. R. 1 Q. B. 149 at 161.

[59] *Statham vs. Statham and the Gaekwar of Baroda,* L. R. (1912) Prob. Div. 92.

[60] *Porto Alexandre,* 89 L. J. P. (1919) 97; 1920, P. 30.

[61] 1878, L. R., 5 Pro. Div., 197.

[62] *The Gagra* 88 L. J. P., 1919, 101.

found it necessary to construe them. This was done by the Supreme Court of the United States in the famous case of *Cherokee Nation vs. Georgia.*[63] The Cherokee Nation claimed the right as a *foreign nation* to institute a suit in the Supreme Court of the United States to restrain the state of Georgia from enforcing certain objectionable legislation. The question of jurisdiction became important and the court was forced to interpret acts of Congress and of the President. The judges did not agree upon the interpretation. A majority of the court felt that the Cherokee Nation was not a *foreign state* and could not institute the suit in question, while a minority felt that the Cherokee Nation had been treated as a *foreign state* by the political departments of the government and was capable of bringing the suit in question.[64]

The English courts have had occasion to construe acts of the political departments in at least three instances involving the recognition of Russia. The first arose in 1919 in the case of *The Annette and the Dora.*[65] A libel had been filed against certain vessels which in turn claimed immunity on the ground that they had been requisitioned by the Provisional Government of Northern Russia. Thereupon the Admiralty Court addressed an inquiry to the British Foreign Office. It was informed that the government in question had not been recognized.

The court denied the immunity asked for saying that immunity depended on recognition. The judge said: "I have here a negative statement that the Provisional Government of Northern Russia has not been formally recognized by His Majesty's government. I am asked to infer from that that it has been informally recognized as a sovereign state. I do not think that I ought to draw that conclusion. I must be satisfied before I can recognize the Provisional Govern-

[63] 5 Peters, 1831, 1.
[64] A weighty dissenting opinion was written by Mr. Justice Johnson.
[65] Admiralty, 88 L. J. P., 1919, 107.

ment of Northern Russia as a sovereign state for the purposes of this case that the British Government so recognizes it. I am not satisfied." [66]

In the initial case of *Luther vs. Sagor,*[67] in speaking of the materials from the Foreign Office on the legal status of the Soviet Republic, Judge Roche said: " On these materials I am not satisfied that His Majesty's government has recognized the Soviet Government as the government of a Russian confederative republic or of any sovereign state or power." He was therefore unable to recognize it, or to hold it as sovereign, or as able by the decree in question to deprive the plaintiff company of its property.[68] At the time the case went up on appeal Great Britain had accorded *de facto* recognition to the Soviets and the court stated that the note of the Foreign Office which declared that it recognized the Soviet Government " as from " a certain date was intended to mean " as on " June 1918. Such was the date of the confiscatory decrees in question in the case.[69]

The next year, 1922, the Court of Appeal again had occasion to interpret communications from the Foreign Office. In an initial suit on an insurance policy,[70] it became important to know whether certain acts of confiscation of the Provisional Worker and Peasant Government were to be considered the acts of the Russian Socialist Federated Soviet Republic. The latter government had been recognized by Great Britain. The insurance policy covered loss by " riot, revolution, and war " but did not cover destruction or confiscation by the government of the country in which the property was situated. Judge Roche of the lower court, who had delivered the initial opinion in *Luther vs. Sagor,*[71] held that the acts causing the loss, by their nature and by the man-

[66] *The Annette and the Dora, supra,* p. 111.
[67] 1821, L. R. 1 K. B. 456.
[68] *Ibid.*, p. 477.
[69] *Luther vs. Sagor* 1921, L. R. 3 K. B. 532.
[70] *White, Child and Beney, Ltd. vs. Simmons,* 127 L. T. R., 1922, 571.
[71] 1921, L. R. 1 K. B. 456.

ner and occasion of their execution, " had all the appearance of acts of 'revolution' and of 'military and usurped power' and not being satisfied " on the materials before him that the exception as to the action of the recognized government applied, held " that the acts were what they " appeared to be. He allowed a recovery.

This determination was reversed by the Court of Appeal. The appellate court held that the government referred to in the exception was not the government existing when the policy was issued, but " the government existing at the time the acts in question took place," and held that the Soviet government came into existence on or about November 14, 1917. Lord Justice Bankes felt "that the sources of information with regard to the time when a particular Foreign government came into existence as a government " was not a matter for the Foreign Office to determine. The exact date must depend on the particular facts before the court from which the court draws its own conclusions. It appeared to him " that the Soviet Government recognized by His Majesty's Government as the *de facto* government of Russia, was in existence as a government in Russia on the 27th of December, 1917." [72]

Lord Justice Atkin, of the Court of Appeal, in the course of his judgment, pointed out that Judge Roche had " sought to obtain from the Foreign Office a statement with regard to the precise date at which the existing Soviet authority came into being as a government. But the Foreign Office did not answer that question." [73] On the evidence before the court it appeared to be plain that the government which had been recognized by the British government was exercising the functions of government over the country in which the insured property was situated at the material dates in the

---

[72] *White, Child, and Beney, Ltd., vs. Simmons,* 127 L. T. R., 1922, 571 at pp. 582–583.

[73] *Ibid.,* p. 584.

case. The court made its own interpretation of the materials submitted by the Foreign Office.

We note that in the two preceding cases the Court of Appeal made direct inquiry of the executive. In the United States this point was raised and modified in the case of *The Russian Government vs. Lehigh Valley Railway.*[74] An action was brought prior the fall of the Provisional Government to recover damages for a property loss sustained in the famous Black Tom explosion. The defendant moved to dismiss the suit on the ground that there was no Provisional Government and hence no plaintiff. Thereupon the plaintiff produced a certificate from the Secretary of State to the effect that the Kerensky government had been recognized and that Mr. Bakhmeteff was its duly accredited ambassador to the United States. The attorneys also produced a statement from Mr. Bakhmeteff that the action had been instituted by proper authority.[75]

At this juncture the defendants asked the court to address an independent inquiry to the State Department concerning the status of the Kerensky Government at that time. The court refused to make the inquiry. It held that the certificates from the State Department were conclusive. However, the court admitted that there may " arise situations of a character which would suggest to the courts an inquiry of this nature, but the court will make official inquiry only for reasons of an impelling character, especially where such inquiry may involve pending questions of the greatest delicacy." [76] However, in this case the courts regarded the certificates from the State Department as conclusive.[77]

In concluding the discussion of this group of cases we find that where an attitude toward a government or state has

---

[74] 293 Federal, 1919, 133, and 293 Federal, 1923, 135.

[75] These are reproduced in full in the case.

[76] *Russian Government vs. Lehigh Valley Railway, supra,* p. 133.

[77] For the ultimate disposition of this case, discussed *infra* see *United States Daily,* December 13, 1927.

been taken by the executive or legislative departments of the recognizant government, or both, the courts regard the decision as binding upon the judiciary. In such cases the sole function of the courts is to interpret the communications solicited from the political departments of the government.

The cases indicate three reasons back of this rule. In the first place, sound reasoning, as well as policy, demands that the judiciary act in unison with the political departments in matters involving foreign relations.[78] In the second place, the conduct of foreign affairs of which recognition forms a part is, by the Constitution, vested exclusively in the political departments of the government.[79] Finally, the courts are not equipped to decided such questions. They are political in nature.[80] The courts themselves have given the foregoing as the reasons why they should not enter into an examination of the facts to determine for themselves which is the lawfully instituted government in a designated state where a previous decision has been made by the political departments. An additional reason, unmentioned in the decisions, is that in the absence of recognition, in cases of adverse judgment, the courts would have no means of enforcing their decisions.

The rule is the same, whether it be the recognition of a state of insurgency,[81] or of belligerency,[82] or of complete independence [83] of a foreign community. The legal consequences are the same regardless of whether the attitude is favorable or unfavorable, and regardless of whether recog-

---

[78] *The Rogdai*, 278 Federal 294; *Ibid.*, 279 Federal, 1920, 130; *The Hornet, supra; Foster vs. Globe Venture Syndicate*, 69 L. J. Ch., 1900, 375.

[79] *Oetjen vs. Central Leather Co., supra; Ricaud vs. American Metal Co., supra* and the cases there cited.

[80] *Kennett vs. Chambers, supra; Republic of Peru vs. Peruvian Guano Co., supra.*

[81] *The Three Friends*, 116 U. S., 1890, 1; *The Pelican*, 1809, Edw. Adm., App. D.

[82] *The United States vs. Palmer*, 3 Wheaton, 1818, 610 at 634; *The Divina Pastora*, 4 *Wheaton*, 1819, 52 at 63; *The Nueva Anna*, 6 Wheaton, 1821, 193.

[83] *Thompson vs. Powles*, 2 Sim., 1828, 194 at 212; *Taylor vs. Barclay*, 2 Sim., 1828, 213; *Republic of Peru vs. Dreyfus Brothers*, L. R. 38 Ch. D., 1888, 348.

nition is made prior to, at the time, or subsequent to the rise of the controversy under adjudication. In all cases the courts take judicial notice of the actions of the political branches of the government.

There remain to be considered those cases in which, at the time of the litigation, no position has been taken by either the legislative or the executive departments of the government. It is this type of case which has given the courts their greatest concern, and to which attention will be given in the succeeding chapter.

CHAPTER IV

JURISTIC STATUS OF UNRECOGNIZED GOVERNMENTS

In the preceding chapters we found that recognition is merely the admission of the facts of state life and that these facts may exist independent of their recognition or admission. This is just as true in international life as it is in national or municipal life. Since the act of admission is essentially one of discretion or policy, it belongs naturally to the political departments of the government and particularly to the department in charge of foreign affairs. Once the political departments have declared their policy such decision is conclusive and binding upon the judicial branch of the government.

On the other hand if the political departments have not declared in favor of a *de facto* situation, whether it be a condition of insurgency, belligerency or independence, or if by their actions the political departments neither expressly nor impliedly deny the existence of the *de facto* situation, but merely hold aloof and withhold recognition, a very different situation is encountered. It can scarcely be said that the mere withholding of recognition is a denial of the existence of state life. It is not: at most, it is only a failure to admit it.[1]

The political departments may be in doubt, or they may keep silent awaiting further developments. Meanwhile the facts of state life move on: the state embryo develops to normal statehood. It thrives and functions. Other states notice it and accord it recognition. Encouraged by such admissions on the part of older states, the new state launches

[1] See the award of Mr. Chief Justice Taft as sole arbitrator in the controversy between Great Britain and Costa Rica, *supra*.

into a policy of anti-capitalism and attempts to convert all people to the wisdom of its policy. At this juncture the acts of the *de facto* state, or the facts of state life, are put in evidence in the courts of non-recognizant states. A suit is instituted against an unrecognized state or government, or the recognized government itself institutes the suit, or a suit is instituted by a corporation created by the unrecognized government, or such a corporation sets up non-recognition as a bar to a suit, or it may be that the acts of the non-recognized government are set up as a defense in a suit in the courts of a non-recognizant state. Such cases involve points of recognition: individual rights hinge upon them, and the courts cannot escape them in their decisions. They are *de facto* situations.

Are the courts of non-recognizant states to treat the silence of their coordinate political departments as evidence either for or against the actual existence of the facts? May the courts take cognizance of the actual facts as they exist? It is this type of situations to which attention is invited in the present chapter.

The cases center around the *de facto* situations created by the unrecognized Latin American states in their early history, the War of 1812, the Civil War, and the present Soviet regime in Russia. In the cases under consideration in this section the issues before the courts turn upon the existence of *de facto* situations: recognition is only incidentally involved. In the cases considered in the preceding chapter the issues turned upon recognition: political considerations were involved and the courts rightly looked to the political departments for guidance. The instant cases involve such problems as the interpretation of a treaty, the duties of a non-recognizant state in cases of *de facto* war, the immunities of *de facto* governments and states or their foreign representatives, and the ability of such *de facto* states, governments and foreign agents to sue or be sued in the courts of a non-recognizant state: questions of fact, not policy.

The decisions of the courts in such situations are by no means uniform. Some of the courts have boasted of their ability to determine the juristic status of a state or government only to embarrass their successors on the bench, as well as the political departments.[2] Generally, however, the courts have been more conscious of a desire to avoid embarrassing the executive department in its control of foreign affairs.

An examination reveals three distinct types of treatment of these situations. In the first group of cases the courts have regarded the old order of things as continuing. This treatment is somewhat comparable to some of the cases which we have already considered, except, that in these cases, involving a continuation of the old order, the courts independently have enunciated the principle, rather than followed a predetermined policy of the President or Congress. This has been unfortunate in that in some of the early cases the judges appear to have been confused. One is not always able to determine with precision which of the two rules the courts pretend to have adopted.

The view that the courts will regard the old order as continuing was first injected into the American decisions by Mr. Chief Justice Marshall in his now classical dictum in *Rose vs. Himely*.[3] Here the learned judge observed that " courts of justice must consider the ancient state of things as remaining unaltered " and the sovereign power of France over Santo Domingo as still subsisting unless relinquished by France or recognized by the Government of the United States.

This dictum was accepted as conclusive by Mr. Justice

[2] The courts of the United States and England interpret and apply International Law as a part of their municipal law. *The Paquete Habana*, 175 U. S., 1900, 677; *Triquet vs. Bath*, 3 Burr., 1764, 1478. Contra, by implication, *West Rand Gold Mining Co., vs. Rex*, 1905, L. R. 2 K. B., 391.

[3] 4 Cranch, 1808, 241 at 272.

Story in *Gelston vs. Hoyt*,[4] where he took the position that until recognition of the *Petion* government in Santo Domingo by our government or the government to which the new state formerly belonged, "courts of justice are bound to consider the ancient state of things as remaining unaltered."[5] Although Mr. Chief Justice Marshall had in mind the refusal of the political departments to acknowledge the independence of Santo Domingo, yet his *dictum* formed the basis of subsequent decisions in which the courts themselves enunciated what they considered to be the same rule, but which was in fact quite different.

As early as 1811 Mr. Justice Washington[6] construed acts of our government, in relation to Santo Domingo, "in order to discover the light in which Congress viewed it." He found that our government had refused to acknowledge the independence of the island. On the other hand he found that it had "very plainly declared the contrary."[7]

In a subsequent case, *Kennett vs. Chambers*,[8] the court followed the set precedents. However, Mr. Chief Justice Taney, who delivered the opinion of the court, was conscious that he was following the decision already made by the President and Congress with reference to the independence of Texas. He pointed out that Texas, although seemingly independent, "had not been acknowledged by the United States; and the constituted authorities charged with our foreign relations, regarded the treaties we had made with Mexico as still in full force, and obligatory upon both nations."[9] The independence of Texas was not acknowledged by the Government of the United States until the beginning of March, 1837. Up to that time, it was regarded as a

[4] *Gelston vs. Hoyt*, 3 Wheaton, 1818, 246.
[5] *Ibid.*, at 324.
[6] *Clark vs. United States*, Federal Case No. 2,838, 5 Fed. Cas. 932.
[7] *Ibid.*, at 933 and 934.
[8] 14 Howard, 1852, 38. The case involved suit on a note which was void *ab initio* because in violation of our neutrality laws.
[9] *Ibid.*, p. 46.

part of the territory of Mexico. Such was the conscious position taken by the learned chief justice.

Mr. Chief Justice Taney attached great weight to the President's message of December 22, 1836, to the Senate in which he referred to the "delicacy and responsibility" of recognition and commented on the policy of the United States. He noted that the President had advised Congress against the acknowledgment of the independence of Texas at that time. He quoted at length from the President's message, and concluded that "the whole object of the message" appeared to have been "to impress upon Congress the impropriety of acknowledging the independence of Texas at that time; and the more especially as the American character of her population, and her known desire to become a State of this Union, might, if prematurely acknowledged, bring suspicion upon the motives by which we were governed."

The court quoted from the public documents not only to show that, in the judgment of our government, "Texas had not established its independence at the time[10] . . . but to show how anxiously the constituted authorities were endeavoring to maintain untarnished the honor of the country" and to place it above the suspicion of taking any part in the conflict. Later in its decision the court referred to this as the "open and avowed policy" of our government.[11]

For the purpose of the case the struggle between Mexico and Texas was not even recognized as a state of insurgency or belligerency and the court did not have to decide how far the courts would enforce a contract when two states, acknowledged to be independent, were at war and this country neutral. Until such recognition in this case the court regarded the old order as continuing, but in so doing it was consciously adhering to the "open and avowed policy" of the executive department. The cases of *Rose vs. Himely, Gelston vs.*

[10] That is, at the time the contract under consideration was executed, 1836.
[11] *Kennett vs. Chambers*, 14 Howard, 1852, 38 at 48.

Hoyt, and *De Wutz vs. Hendricks* were cited as being in accord.[12] The old order continued.

Prior to the rendition of the *Kennett vs. Chambers* decision [13] the Supreme Court had established a *dictum* on the point in the case of *Williams vs. The Suffolk Insurance Company*,[14] where Mr. Justice McLean found that the President in his message, and in his correspondence with the government of Buenos Ayres, had denied the jurisdiction which Buenos Ayres assumed to exercise over the Falkland Islands: facts which the court said " must be taken and acted on . . . as thus asserted and maintained." [15]

In taking cognizance of a *de facto* situation which involved an internal change, the state courts as early as 1847 regarded the former status as continuing.[16] In that year a case involving the point was decided in the Supreme Court of Louisiana. The voyage of an American vessel had been broken up and the cargo had been landed and sold under color of an insurgent military authority at Champeachy, in the Mexican province of Yucatan. The judges requested the counsel to furnish the court with information as to the course assumed by the Government of the United States toward the so-called insurgent government in Yucatan. The Louisiana court declared that the " proceedings of courts in cases of this kind depended entirely on the action of the general government." There was no evidence before the court that a state of insurgency had been recognized by the United States as existing between the insurgent power in Yucatan and the national government of Mexico. Under these circumstances the court denied the rights of the defendant, presumed the old order to continue, and gave judgment

[12] *Rose vs. Himely*, 4 Cranch, 1808, 272; *Gelston vs. Hoyt*, 3 Wheaton, 1818, 324; and *De Wutz vs. Hendricks*, 9 Moore's C. B. Reports, 1824, 586.

[13] 14 Howard, 1852, 38.

[14] *Williams vs. Suffolk Insurance Co.*, 13 Peters, 1839, 415.

[15] *Ibid.*, p. 420.

[16] *Dimond vs. Petit*, 2 La. Ann., 1847, 537.

for the plaintiffs.[17] The court itself took the initiative: it presumed that the old arrangement continued and decided the case accordingly.

The most positive language is found in the case of *The Hornet.*[18] A steamer had been seized upon a libel of information, founded upon a charge of violating the neutrality laws of the United States. One Morales Lemus, an agent of the so-called "Republic of Cuba," asked to be allowed to intervene, to interpose a claim for the property on behalf of his so-called government, and thereby contest the suit.

At the trial of the case in 1870 before District Judge Brooks the only question argued and decided was as to the propriety of allowing the claim of Senor Lemus. Judge Brooks confessed ambarrassment on being called upon to decide such an important question and intimated that he would appreciate a revision at the hands of the Supreme Court.[19] He considered the cases of *The United States vs. Palmer,*[20] *The Divina Pastora,*[21] and *Luther vs. Borden*[22] at length. He did not deem it necessary to refer to other cases and held that "it cannot be intended that such (recognition) power should be vested in the courts." He thought that "it would be a power dangerous to our government to be so vested, and one which judges could not so well exercise as Congress or the Executive."

The courts must give regard to the old *status quo,* for if the courts, before the political departments have spoken, have the right to take one step in this direction, Judge Brooks

[17] In this case the defendant, an American citizen, was one of the captors: "Indeed," said the court, "from the evidence, we should infer him to have been the leader of them," and he is sued for damages by the plaintiff, who was the owner of the vessel and one-half of the cargo.

[18] Federal Case No. 6,705, 12 Federal Cases 529.

[19] "Were I satisfied that my opinion would be revised by the supreme court, and be by that body corrected if wrong, I would announce the conclusion to which I have come with less reluctance than I do." 12 Federal Cases, 529 at 530.

[20] 4 Wheaton, 1818, 610.

[21] 4 Wheaton, 1819, 52.

[22] 7 Howard, 1849, 1.

could "not see any limit to their power, short of declaring perfect freedom and independence." The court endeavored to determine the attitude of the political departments: it inquired, "what act had been performed," what resolution, declaration or proclamation had been made by Congress or the Executive, "indicating an intention on their part to acknowledge, at any time or to any extent, the existence of the Republic of Cuba?" Nothing of that character had been shown. In the absence of such proof he held that he could "not know of the existence of such a government." The claims of the purported agent of the so-called "Republic of Cuba" were denied: the court assumed that the old order of things continued.

The issue had been raised under a slightly different set of facts as early as 1821.[23] The cargoes of two Spanish vessels had been captured and condemned by a pretended Mexican court of admiralty sitting at Galveston, under the alleged authority of the unrecognized Mexican republic. After the condemnation, the goods were brought into the port of New Orleans. There the goods were libelled in the federal District Court, by the Spanish consul on behalf of the original owners. The court decreed restitution.

The captors appealed to the Supreme Court where they contended that the cargoes had been seized and condemned by the Mexican state under its power to authorize captures in war. The Spanish consul defended that in the absence of recognition no power of capture should be admitted by the court. The court stated that it did not recognize the existence of any court of admiralty sitting at Galveston under Mexican authority with jurisdiction to adjudicate on captures. Furthermore, the Government of the United States had not hitherto acknowledged the existence of any Mexican republic or state, at war with Spain, so that the court could

---

[23] *The Nueva Anna and The Liebre: the Spanish Consul, Claimant,* 6 Wheaton, 1821, 193.

not consider as legal any acts done under the flag and commission of such republic or state. Every department of the national government denied the existence of the purported Mexican republic.[24] Each regarded Mexico as a Spanish possession.

On reflection it appears that it is a pure fiction for the courts to say that in such cases the prior status must be deemed to continue. Nevertheless, it furnishes a theory upon which the courts are able to operate. In the recent cases arising out of the belated recognition of the Carranza regime, and the non-recognition of the Soviet Republic, the fiction has mocked the truth, but no more so than the State Department's continued recognition of the Kerensky government. The unfortunate thing is that such situations possess latent dangers and may result in the miscarriage of justice.

Some of the courts have realized the absurdity of presuming a continuance of the old order, and have adopted a second alternative. In the absence of recognition, they regard a *de facto* government as non-existent, without regard for the old regime. This view is also open to attack, in that it evades the true facts of state life, yet it has received much consideration at the hands of the courts. Although this alternative is evasive of the truth, yet it forms the basis of a number of interesting decisions to which attention must be called.

In a comparatively recent case, 1922, an American citizen resident in Mexico had died intestate. The Mexican courts had appointed his widow administratrix, but the New York courts denied the capacity of such administratrix to sue on the executed notes of a domestic corporation.

When the suit was instituted the counsel for the corporation defended that an administratrix appointed by a foreign court could not maintain an action in any of the courts of the

[24] See also *The United States vs. the Pirates,* 5 Wheaton, 1820, 184, for a discussion of seven previously considered cases which involved a similar point.

United States so long as the foreign government remained unrecognized by the State Department in Washington.

Thereupon the defendant corporation moved for judgment on the pleadings. The Supreme Court of New York granted the motion. The court said: "The administratrix plaintiff is an officer of a foreign court. . . . It is syllogistically true that if the foreign court has no recognized power here she may not assert a right derived through her appointment therefrom. . . . The Mexican government is not *de facto* here, since recognition alone can make it so.

"It may have all the attributes of a ruling faction, a colony, a district of people, or maintain any other form of suzerainty in its established domain, but its power as a government remains nil without our patent of recognition. As the parent of the court it cannot have notice, either judicial or administrative, and surely the creature cannot be possessed of a power not given its creator. The duty to declare the legal incapacity to sue is paramount to a consideration of the evils attendant upon the failure of justice resultant upon this policy of international relations." [25]

[25] *The Unrecognized Government or State in English and American Law*, E. D. Dickinson, 22 Mich. Law Rev., 1922, 29 and 118 for discussion of the instant case. Contra, *Russian Socialist Federated Soviet Republic vs. Cibrario*, unreported opinion, in which Judge McAvoy, in allowing an action for an accounting on a trust, by an unrecognized government, said: "Whether the government be a *de facto* government or a society, colony, district of people, or a voluntary association capable of owning and disposing of money and property is not inherently germane to its right to succession to the former sovereignty of Russia, the reception and despatch of ambassadors, consuls and other governmental agents, the power to issue commissions of military or naval operations which would be recognized by neutrals, or the possession of other indicia of sovereign power. The question of its existence as the proprietor of this money and property is one of fact and justiciable in common courts unless the claim be suggested by a recognized authority of the former regime that the earlier order of government demands the fund or chose." However, this determination was unanimously reversed by the Appellate Division of the First Department, 198 App. Div., 1921, 869, 191 N. Y. Supp. 543. The case was then taken to the Court of Appeals which unanimously affirmed the reversal below. 235 N. Y., 1923, 255. Suit was then instituted by one Preobazhenski, as trustee. The court held that the right of action had been extinguished by the former suit. But the court said that even if it had not been terminated "the fact that the so-called Soviet Republic has been held not to have capacity to sue in the courts" of New York, "its individual members have no better or greater rights than their principal." *Preobazhenski* et al. *vs. Cibrario* et al., 192 N. Y. Supp., 1922, 275.

The widow, having failed in the initial suit, procured letters of administration in New York state; whereupon, she moved to amend her pleadings by asserting her status as administratrix under the New York law and dropping her status as administratrix under the Mexican law. The Supreme Court, at the special term, New York county, March, 1922, allowed the pleadings to be amended. Mr. Justice McAvoy, who delivered the former opinion, felt that a strict interpretation of the statute would "permit the court to allow this amendment or supplement to her complaint, and it would seem a purely technical exercise of power and discretion to refuse it." [26] "The local administratrix, gifted by the courts here with power, has the right of suit, and is thus always a proper party for instituting an action," said he.[27]

The motion to amend the pleadings was reversed [28] by the appellate division. It adopted the view [29] that the "motion was to permit the plaintiff to serve an amended complaint when there was nothing to amend." Having denied her access to the courts, it would be anomalous to entertain a motion to amend her complaint: [30] whereupon the appellate division denied the motion to amend the petition. The ultimate disposition of this case cannot be determined from the reports.

In this case much delay, if not injustice, and litigation costs were heaped upon the plaintiff. It does not appear from the pleadings that the defendants denied liability on the notes; the case turned upon the defense of non-recogni-

---

[26] Civil Practice Act, sec., 192.

[27] *Pelzer vs. United Dredging Company*, 118 Misc. Rep. 210, 193 N. Y. Supp. 675.

[28] *Ibid.*, 200 App. Div. 646, 193 N. Y. Supp. 676.

[29] First Department, Appellate Division, Supreme Court, Apr. 7, 1922.

[30] Other citations for subsequent trials are: *Pelzer vs. Perry*, 194 N. Y. Supp., 965; *Pelzer vs. United Dredging Co.*, 194 N. Y. Supp., 965; *Pelzer vs. Perry, Pelzer vs. United Dredging Co.*, 196 N. Y. Supp. 342, 202 App. Div. 58. One cannot ascertain from the cases reported what disposition of the case was ultimately made.

tion. In the case of Mexico considerations of diplomacy restrained an expression of recognition until long after the Carranza faction was in *de facto* control. The silence of the political departments did not necessarily connote that a government did not exist; that a state of anarchy prevailed south of the Rio Grande. Nevertheless, the courts took the position that in the absence of recognition cognizance of the situation could not be taken.[31] It would appear that the court should have recognized the *de facto* situation and allowed a recovery, inasmuch as both parties were within the jurisdiction of the court and the defendants did not deny liability.

Two years later, 1924, the same department of the appellate division of the New York Supreme Court had occasion to reconsider the point. An application had been made by the Salamandra Insurance Company,[32] a Russian private corporation, for an order of mandamus to compel the New York Commissioner of Insurance to deliver up certain securities which had been deposited to guarantee the performance of insurance contracts made by the company within the state of New York. The State Superintendent of Insurance opposed the application upon the ground that the petitioner had been destroyed by the decree of the Soviet Government, hence it was not entitled to the property. The application was granted and the determination was unanimously affirmed, without opinion. Thus it does not appear whether the court regarded the decision as a modification of the principle enunciated in *Pelzer vs. United Dredging Company*. However, a pertinent difference in the cases makes it possible to square the decisions.[33]

---

[31] 193 N. Y. Supp. 675.

[32] *Salamandra Insurance Company vs. Stoddard,* 209 App. Div. (N. Y.), 1924, 871.

[33] The difference is in the facts of the two cases. *In Pelzer vs. United Dredging Company* it appears that the plaintiff claimed as administratrix by appointment from a Mexican court at which time Mexico stood unrecognized. While in the *Salamandra Insurance case* the plaintiff was incorporated under the former Czar's government, which at the time was recognized by the United States.

In those jurisdictions in which retroactivity is the established rule,[34] if the courts insist that until affirmative action is taken by the political departments of the government, the *de facto* government may be regarded as non-existent, or the prior status may be deemed to continue, their insistence creates an arbitrary distinction. In a suit brought prior to such recognition the action of the *de facto* foreign government would be regarded as void, while in the same suit brought subsequent to recognition the same acts would be regarded as valid, or if recognition is accorded while the case is in litigation the acts would be regarded as valid. This was the identical situation presented in the *Luther vs. Sagor* cases.[35]

A dictum to this effect was enunciated in *Yucatan vs. Argumedo.*[36] An action was brought in the New York courts by the Mexican state of Yucatan against a former governor for alleged mismanagement of the funds of the plaintiff state. The action was instituted October 1, 1915, by authorities acting under the Carranza government which had driven the defendant from the country. Eighteen days later the United States accorded *de facto* recognition to the Carranza government. At the trial Argumedo denied the ability of the state of Yucatan to prosecute the suit because the Carranza faction stood unrecognized at the time the suit was instituted. The court upheld the right of the plaintiff to sue inasmuch as recognition was retroactive in effect and validated the plaintiff's claim.

However, the court said that if this had been a controversy between two factions, each claiming to constitute the *de facto* government of a foreign state and in order to render an

---

[34] In cases involving recognition between the time of the commission of the act and the litigation.

[35] 1921 L. R. 1 K. B., 456 for the initial case. 1921 L. R. 3 K. B., 532 on appeal. Discussion of the point is reserved for treatment in a subsequent chapter dealing with retroactivity.

[36] 92 Misc. Rep., N. Y., 1915, 547. The doctrine of retroactivity should not have been applied in this case since no act done within the jurisdiction of the recognized government was in question in the case.

effective judgment the court had to determine which faction did constitute the *de facto* government, the court would have declined jurisdiction.[37] By its attitude the court implied that in the absence of recognition recovery could not be had: in its absence the court would regard the *de facto* government as a non-entity.

In 1923, the Court of Claims adopted the same view and, seemingly, conclusively determined that an unrecognized government can not be proved before that court, regardless of how meritorious it regards the claim.[38] It appears in this case that a private Russian insurance company, incorporated under the Russian laws prior to 1918, with its home office at Petrograd, had moved its central office to Paris and continued to do business from that office. Prior to and subsequent to the removal of the head office the insurance company had sold fire and marine insurance in the United States.

In an action brought in the United States Court of Claims to recover certain back taxes, the government moved to dismiss the suit on the ground that the court had no jurisdiction, because Russia remained unrecognized. The Court of Claims so held and dismissed the suit. The court found that the case itself was meritorious, but the jurisdictional issue barred relief. The court felt that it could not enter into a review of political and social conditions to ascertain what is an apparent, open and notorious fact.

The plaintiff then argued that in the absence of recognition the court should presume the continuance of the Provisional Government which preceded the Soviet Republic. The court conceded that such a view was interesting and inviting, but refused to concur in it, because the plaintiff company itself " was compelled to flee in haste to a foreign country in order to preserve its assets and conduct its ordinary business, free from the dangers of a successful revolution " " The case it-

---

[37] *Yucatan vs. Argumedo,* 92 Misc. Rep. (N. Y.), 1915, 547, at 552.
[38] *Rossia Insurance Co., vs. United States,* 58 Ct. of Cl., 1923, 180.

self," said the court, "is manifestly meritorious and but for the lack of jurisdiction would undoubtedly result in substantial relief to the plaintiff company." [39] The contentions might with more propriety be addressed to Congress, "the only tribunal with jurisdiction to entertain them."

Syllogistically this view means that where a *de facto* government fails, recognition not having been accorded, all of its acts are void. It does not seem logical to say that a *de facto* government must maintain its position until recognition is accorded in order to validate its governmental acts. It was to escape this dilemma that some of the courts early searched for a third alternative.

This alternative has been to allow the court to investigate the *de facto* situation, and independently to determine the exact status of the government in question. Obviously this method should not be resorted to save in those cases wherein no definite attitude has been taken by the political departments. In such cases the method has a considerable degree of justification.

In the United States, Mr. Chief Justice Marshall took cognizance of a *de facto* situation for the first time in the celebrated case of *Rose vs. Himely*. Consideration was given to this case in the preceding chapter. The next instance was in 1819 in a case arising out of the War of 1812.[40]

The collector of customs at Castine, Maine, after the termination of the war, instituted suit to collect the duty on goods brought in through the port at the time it was under the *de facto* control of the British. The importers defended that they had paid all duties levied by the British officials, the authorities in control of the port at the time the goods were brought in, and that they were *ipso facto* relieved of further liability. The Supreme Court so held. It refused to sustain our government's claim. In so doing Mr. Justice Story

[39] *Rossia Insurance Co., vs. United States,* 58 Ct., of Cl., 1923, 180 at 181.
[40] *United States vs. Rice,* 4 Wheaton, 1819, 246.

was thereby forced to acknowledge and judge the *de facto* situation, which the importers had set up as a defense.[41] This case did not involve an act of Congress or a proclamation of the President. The only issue was the existence of a *de facto* situation of which the Supreme Court of the United States took cognizance.

A dictum to this effect was announced by Mr. Chief Justice Marshall in 1818 in the case of *United States vs. Palmer*,[42] where the learned justice said that persons or vessels " employed in the service of a self-declared government " acknowledged to be maintaining its separate existence by war " must be permitted to prove the fact of their being actually employed in such service, by the same testimony which would be sufficient to prove that such vessel or person was employed in the service of an acknowledged state. . . . Such unacknowledged state . . . may be proved by such testimony as the nature of the case admits. . . ." [43]

In 1820, Mr. Justice Livingston, in a case involving the legal status of Venezuela, found it necessary to remark that " this republic is composed of the inhabitants of a portion of the dominions of Spain in South America, who have been for sometime past, and still are, maintaining a contest for inde-

---

[41] " By the conquest and military occupation of Castine, the enemy acquired that firm possession which enabled him to exercise the fullest rights of sovereignty over that place. The sovereignty of the United States over the territory was . . . suspended, and the laws of the United States could no longer be rightfully enforced there, or be obligatory upon the inhabitants who remained and submitted to the conquerors. By the surrender the inhabitants passed under a temporary allegiance to the British government, and were bound by such laws, and such only, as it chose to recognize and impose. From the nature of the case no other law could be obligatory upon them, for where there is no protection or allegiance of sovereignty, there can be no claim to obedience. Castine was, therefore, during this period, so far as respected our revenue laws, to be deemed a foreign port; and goods imported into it by the inhabitants, were subject to such duties only as the British government choose to require," said the court. *United States vs. Rice*, 4 Wheaton 246 at page 254. Mr. Justice Story delivered the opinion. The courts of the United States have applied the same principle where duties are paid to insurgents in *de facto* control of a foreign port. See on this point: *Fleming vs. Page*, 9 Howard, 1850, 603; *MacCleod vs. The United States*, 229 U. S., 1913, 416.

[42] 3 Wheaton, 1818, 610.

[43] *Ibid.*, p. 635.

pendence with the mother country." Although not acknowledged by our government as an independent nation "this nation cannot but respect the belligerent rights of both parties; and does not treat as pirates the cruisers of either, so long as they act under, and within the scope of their respective commissions."

In the case of *The Consul of Spain vs. La Conception,* Mr. Justice Johnson, while on circuit duty, had occasion to observe that courts exercising jurisdiction of International Law may often be called upon to deduce the fact of national independence "from history, evidence, or public notoriety where there has been no formal public recognition. The actual possession and long exercise of all the attributes of a state of independence may be legally resorted to, without giving just cause of umbrage to a nation that does not possess the power to subjugate a revolted colony. There exist many nations at this day which may claim of courts of International Law all the rights of independent nations and may be judicially recognized as such, notwithstanding no act of government has acknowledged them in that capacity."[44] This statement of the learned justice is most interesting in view of the recent cases involving the non-recognition of Russia and the belated recognition of Mexico, in the course of which the courts refused to accord the *de facto* governments any status in the absence of recognition.[45]

At about the same date the English courts declared in favor of the same view. Lord Justice Best, on one occasion, said that the "existence of unacknowledged states must be proved by evidence." He felt that the proof necessary to establish the existence of the governments under consideration, Chile and Buenos Ayres, was that they were associations formed for mutual defense, which acknowledged no authority

---

[44] Federal Case No. 3,137, 6 Federal Cases 360, 2 Wh. Cr. Cases, 597.

[45] *Rossia Insurance Co., vs. United States, supra; Pelzer vs. The United Dredging Co., supra;* see especially *R. S. F. S. R. vs. Cibrario, supra* and *Preobazhenski vs. Cibrario et al supra.*

other than that of their own government, observed the rules of justice to the subjects of other states, lived generally under their own laws and maintained their independence by their own force. He felt that it made no difference "that the new state formed part of another acknowledged state: states may be legitimately divided. The states of Holland and America were treated as sovereign states by the nations of Europe before their independence was acknowledged by Spain and Great Britain." [46]

The point was reserved for the subsequent consideration of the court, and when the defendants pressed their point on a new motion, Lord Justice Best said: "I decided at the trial that the existence of these states (referring to Chile and Buenos Ayres) was proved and I have now the satisfaction to state that all my learned brothers fully concur with me in thinking that there is no foundation for the objection which has been raised. . . ." [47]

The defendants pressed their argument for a non-suit on their new motion, but the court held that calling Chile a state in the alleged libel made further proof unnecessary: it was an admission of the very fact on the part of the defendant which he was attempting to disprove. On principle it would seem that proof of the existence of the *de facto* gov-

---

[46] *Yrissari vs. Clement,* 3 Bing., 1826, 432 at 437. This case involved an action for libel. The plaintiff claimed to be the duly appointed representative of Chile, for which he was attempting to float a loan in England. Plaintiff alleged that defamatory matter had been published concerning his actions in connection with the loan. At the trial before the English Court of Common Pleas he offered evidence that Chile was a state. It was objected that the court should take judicial notice that Chile belonged to Spain. The court was asked to regard the old order as continuing. The court refused. The justice said: "I take the rule to be this—if a body of persons assemble together to protect themselves, and support their own independence, and make laws, and have Courts of Justice, that is evidence of their being a state. We have had, certainly, some evidence here today that these provinces formerly belonged to Spain; but it would be a strong thing to say, that because they once belonged, therefore they must always belong. . . . It makes no difference whether they formerly belonged to Spain, if they do not continue to acknowledge it, and are in possession of a force sufficient to support themselves in opposition to it."

[47] *Ibid.,* 100 Eng. Rep. 579.

ernment in Chile should have been sufficient, without the defendant's admission. In fact, the suit did not require a decision on the point of recognition, inasmuch as libel is as injurious to the representative of a *de facto* government as to anyone else. The case turned primarily upon the proof of the *de facto* government in Chile, although recognition was incidentally involved.

Eight years later another *de facto* situation was presented to the United States Supreme Court in the case of *Keene vs. McDonough.*[48] The case involved the title to certain lands in Louisiana. The defendant relied for title upon a decree of a Spanish court, which decree was made subsequent to the cession to, but antedated the actual possession by the United States. The plaintiff denied the jurisdiction of such a tribunal to confirm the title in question. The court gave judgment for the defendants inasmuch as the adjudication, having been made by the Spanish tribunal after the cession, did not make such a determination void. The court said that it knew historically "that the actual possession of the territory was not surrendered until some time after these proceedings took place. It was the judgment, therefore, of a competent Spanish tribunal, having jurisdiction of the case, and rendered whilst the country, although ceded, was, *de facto,* in the possession of Spain, and subject to Spanish laws. Such judgments, so far as they affect the private rights of the parties thereto, must be deemed valid."[49] The court allowed the *de facto* situation to be proved by evidence.

Reference has already been made to the status of the Southern Confederacy. Numerous cases arose[50] in which

---

[48] 8 Peters, 1834, 308.

[49] *Keene vs. McDonough,* 8 Peters, 1834, 308 at 310.

[50] Perhaps the case most often cited is *Thorington vs. Smith,* 8 Wallace, 1868, 1, which involved the effect to be given to a realty contract between two residents of Alabama, where the agreement was entered into during the rebellion and the purchase price was to be paid in Confederate currency. The court felt that the facts came within the rule laid down in *United States vs.* Rice, *supra,* which involved the *de facto* situation in Castine, Maine, during the War of 1812, and decided accordingly.

its juristic status was involved, especially as regards the effect of acts which bore the sanction or approval of the *de facto* government or governments.[51] In these decisions the courts discussed the *de facto* character of the Confederacy. They described it as a government of paramount force. A number of these cases are listed in the note.

One of the most important cases was that of *The Home Insurance Company*.[52] A suit was brought by a Georgia insurance company, incorporated under the laws of that state during the rebellion, in the United States Court of Claims, for the recovery of the proceeds from the sale of cotton captured by the military forces of the Union during the war. The government attacked the validity of the incorporation, but the court held that it had a sufficiently valid existence to enable it to maintain the suit in question.

The court felt that " whatever act of the legislature of a rebel state did not tend to further or support the rebellion," or to defeat the just rights of citizens, " but related merely to the domestic affairs of the people of the state as a community," aside from the connection of that people with the rebellion, was a valid act by a *de facto,* though unlawful, government, which must be sustained in the courts of the United States.[53]

On appeal the Supreme Court affirmed the decision of the Court of Claims. It observed that any other doctrine would " work great and unnecessary hardship upon the people of those states, without any corresponding benefit to the citizens of other states, and without any advantage to the national government." [54] In the instant case the court regarded the

---

[51] *United States vs. Insurance Co.,* 22 Wallace, 1875, 99; *Mauran vs. Insurance Co.,* 6 Wallace, 1867, 1; *Delmas vs. Insurance Co.,* 14 Wallace, 1871, 661.

[52] 8 Ct. of Cl., 1872, 449.

[53] *Ibid.,* 450

[54] *U. S. vs. Insurance Co.,* 22 Wall., 1875, 99. Other cases are: *Ford vs. Surget,* 97 U. S., 1878, 594; *Ketchum vs. Buckley,* 99 U. S., 1878, 188; and *Baldy vs. Hunter,* 171 U. S., 1898, 388.

de facto government as one of paramount force. The court held that the acts in question were valid. The attitude of the Court of Claims in this case appears to have been in accord with the position taken by the Supreme Court. The case can hardly be squared with its recent decision in *Rossia Insurance Company vs. United States,* discussed *supra.*

It has been remarked that this alternative has much merit in it. However, Sir Robert Phillimore in the case of *The Charkieh* put this alternative in bad repute.[55] This was an action instituted on behalf of the Netherlands Steamship Company against the steamship *Charkieh* for damages arising out of a collision in the river Thames. Subsequent to the arrest of the vessel His Highness, Ishmail Pacha, Khedive of Egypt, filed an application to restrain further proceedings in the suit on the ground that *The Charkieh* was a public vessel and therefore immune from process. From these pleadings the learned judge observed that the important question was the international status of the Khedive of Egypt. Very scanty evidence was presented at the hearing of the case.

The counsel for the Khedive insisted that it was improper to offer evidence upon such a question. They insisted that the court should take " official cognizance "[56] of his foreign status, and that the court should obtain such information as it considered necessary from the Foreign Office.

At the trial of the case Sir Robert Phillimore, of the Admiralty and Ecclesiastical High Court, with reference to the question before his court, said:

" I have endeavored to inform myself, and have had recourse to the following sources of information:

" 1. The general history of the government of Egypt.

" 2. The firmans which contain the public law of the Ottoman Empire on this subject.

" 3. The European treaties . . .

---

[55] 1873 L. R. 4 A. & E. 59.

[56] Evidently the learned judge meant judicial notice.

"4. The answer which the Foreign Office has furnished to an inquiry which I thought it my duty to make." [57]

Judge Phillimore felt that it was necessary to refer to the past as well as to the then current political history of Egypt in order to determine whether the country had possessed the character of an independent state at any time since the Mohammedan conquest. He entered into a minute examination of the history of the country from the conquest by Amer, General of the Caliphs, in 638 A.D. down to 1873.[58]

On the evidence he felt that the Khedive had failed to establish his immunity from suit as a sovereign prince, "according to the criteria of sovereignty required by the reason of the thing, and by the usage and practice of nations as expounded by accredited writers upon international jurisprudence." The court rendered judgment against the vessel. In this case we find the most elaborate and detailed examination of evidence and historical facts to determine the status of a foreign sovereign that is to be found in all the reported English and American cases.

The case of *The Charkieh* came under the review of the Court of Appeal twenty years later, 1893, and was overruled on all major points, and more particularly on the question of the ability of a court to receive evidence in order to determine the juristic status of a recognized foreign government.[59] The Sultan of Johore had been residing in London under the assumed name of Albert Baker, under which name he had entered into a marriage contract. In an action for breach of promise of marriage the Sultan of Johore, *alias* Albert Baker, set up his sovereign immunity as a bar to the suit. The court held that it had no jurisdiction over an independent foreign sovereign, unless he submitted to the jurisdiction.[60]

---

[57] 1873 L. R. 4 A. & E. 59 at 74.
[58] *Ibid.*, at pp. 75–100.
[59] *Mighell vs. Sultan of Johore*, 1894, L. R. 1 Q. B., p. 149.
[60] Submission cannot take place until the jurisdiction is invoked.

In speaking of the letter from the Colonial (Foreign) Office regarding the status of the Sultan, Lord Esher said that "it was argued that the judge ought not to have been satisfied with that letter, but to have informed himself from historical and other sources as to the status of the Sultan of Johore. It was said that Sir Robert Phillimore did so in the case of *The Charkieh.* I know he did; but I am of opinion that he ought not to have done so."[61] When once there is the authoritative statement of the executive department as to the status of another sovereign, such statement is conclusive on the courts. Lord Justice Kay was of the same opinion.[62]

It thus appears from the attitude taken by the Court of Appeal in *Mighell vs. Sultan of Johore*[63] that the judgment of Sir Robert Phillimore in *The Charkieh*[64] was unwarranted by the facts of the case. A determination had previously been made by the Foreign Office which was ignored, or at least submerged by other evidence, by Judge Phillimore. Sound policy dictates that he should have regarded his court as bound by its decisions: it was before the court in the form of a special communication. Lord Esher was right in saying that "such statement is conclusive on the court."

In overruling *The Charkieh* the Court of Appeal[65] did not deny the right of the court to weigh facts in order to determine the juristic status of a *de facto* situation. Rather, it denies the right of the courts independently to determine

---

[61] *Mighell vs. Sultan of Johore, op. cit.,* p. 158.

[62] "The status of a foreign sovereign is a matter of which the courts of this country take judicial cognizance—that is to say, a matter which the Court is either assumed to know, or to have the means of discovering, without a contentious inquiry as to whether the person cited is or is not in the position of an independent sovereign. Of course the court will take the best means of informing itself on the subject, if there is any kind of doubt, and the matter is not as notorious as the status of some great monarch such as the Emperor of Germany. . . . If Her Majesty condescends to state to one of Her Courts of Justice, that an individual cited before it is an independent sovereign, I think that statement must be taken as conclusive." *Ibid.,* pp. 161–162.

[63] 1894, L. R. 1 Q. B., 149.

[64] 1873, L. R. 4 A. & E. 59.

[65] *Mighell vs. Sultan of Jahore, supra.*

who is the sovereign *de jure* of a particular state when the political departments of the government have already reached a decision. These two cases have been much cited, as well as miscited, in the decisions, and for that reason they have been dwelt upon at length.

It has been said by some of the writers that this third alternative was expressly repudiated by the Supreme Court of the United States in 1821 by its reversal of the decision of the Circuit Court in the case of *La Concepcion*.[66] This is hardly correct, for Mr. Justice Story, who delivered the opinion for the Supreme Court, expressly stated that if the facts had been the same as they were in the Circuit Court, the decision would have been affirmed. On appeal new facts were presented and the decision was reversed on the basis of these new facts and not on the law of the case. The Supreme Court did not address itself to the opinion of the lower court. In fact the opinion is quite short: less than two hundred and fifty words in length.[67]

The alternative has not been overthrown. Rather there appears to be a revival of the principle in recent cases. In 1915 the New Jersey Court of Errors and Appeals said that "in the absence of any government in Mexico . . . the rule by paramount force in any particular district is provable as a matter of fact by evidence, which in this case is neither left in doubt nor subject to possible inference to the contrary." [68] Judge Swaze said that it was open to the courts to decide from evidence whether Huerta or Carranza was in control of a particular territory on a designated date. On the evidence submitted the court decided that the Carranza forces were in control of the Mexican state of Chihuahua and a part of the state of Coahuila " at the time the hides in ques-

[66] 6 Wheaton, 1819, 235 reversing 2 Wheeler Cr. C. 597.

[67] On the new facts the court felt that the case came within the rule laid down a few days earlier in *Bello Corrunes*, 6 Wheaton, 1821, 152, where Justice Johnson delivered a weighty opinion.

[68] *O'Neill vs. Central Leather Co.*, 94 At., 1915, 789 at 791.

tion were there seized and sold." [69] The court held that upon seizure title to the goods passed.

In this case the court attempted to ascertain the policy of the political departments of our government. They had declared that Mexico possessed no government, whereupon the court recognized the *de facto* situation and ascertained for itself whether the Carranza faction was in *firm possession* of the section of Mexico in question before the court.

Two years later, in 1917, Mr. Justic Clarke of the United States Supreme Court, had occasion in two cases to examine the political status of Mexico from February 23, 1913, to October 19, 1915. He gave a detailed recital of the Huerta-Villa-Carranza episode.[70] However, it should be noted that the two cases referred to were decided subsequent to recognition by the United States and that the doctrine of retroactivity was invoked which validated the seizures in question. Therefore, even though Mr. Justice Clarke felt that "a somewhat detailed description of the political conditions in Mexico prior to and at the time of the seizure of the property in controversy" was necessary, such description was *obiter dictum*.

The principle has had its latest affirmation in *Sokoloff vs. The National City Bank*.[71] The action was brought against the National City Bank because of its failure under contract to repay in rubles at its Petrograd branch. Defendants pleaded that the bank had been closed and its assets confiscated by the Soviet government. Sokoloff contended that in the absence of recognition the court could take no cognizance of the Soviet regime or its acts.[72] The court allowed the defense to be sustained by proof of actual conditions prevailing in Russia.

---

[69] *O'Neill vs. Central Leather Co.*, 94 Atl., 1915, 789 at 791.
[70] *Oetjen vs. Central Leather Company*, 246 U. S., 1918, 297; *Ricaud vs. American Metal Company*, 246 U. S., 1918, 304.
[71] 199 N. Y. Supp., 1922, 355, 120 Misc. Rep. (N. Y.), 252.
[72] *Sokoloff vs. National City Bank*, 196 N. Y. Supp., 1922, 364.

Judge Ford implied that there was a distinction between acts performed as attributes of sovereignty, and acts performed as attributes of a government of superforce. He did not make the distinction clear, although without doubt it aided him in coming to a decision in the case. The plaintiff's objection was held applicable to the first type of acts only. On this ground the court allowed the National City Bank to sustain its defense by proof of the *de facto* situation prevailing in Russia.

The following language from Judge Ford is worth noteing. He said: "While this court may not recognize the Soviet Government as sovereign, and therefore possessing power to confiscate property or debts, as must be done in respect of a foreign state which has been recognized either *de facto* or *de jure,* it does not follow that we must assume a state of anarchy in Russia. True, by legal fiction, for some purposes which appertain more particularly to the other, the 'political,' branches of the government than to the judiciary, we must continue to assume that the old Imperial Government is the only sovereign government in Russia.

"I can see no valid objection to permitting the defendants to allege and prove upon the trial the actual conditions prevailing in that great country. Indeed we know as a matter of common knowledge that there is a government there which has been functioning in some fashion for five years or more, and that it is not the Imperial Government of the Czars. Facts are facts, in Russia as elsewhere." [73] This dictum constitutes a beacon light in the maze of superfluous and irrelevant dicta which have issued from the courts in those cases involving the non-recognition of Soviet Russia.[74]

In summary we find that the courts are often urged to acknowledge *de facto* situations in the adjudication of private

[73] *Sokoloff vs. National City Bank,* 199 N. Y. Supp., 1922, 355 at 359.

[74] The majority of these cases have been reserved for treatment in the chapter dealing with recognition and legal capacity.

rights, although incidentally the political question of recognition is involved. If the political departments have taken a fixed attitude toward a *de facto* government or state, the course for the courts is clear. But if the attitude of the political departments is not clear, or if the litigation turns upon the recognition issue, the courts should attempt to determine the attitude of those departments, as a matter of courtesy if for no other reason. In the absence of an attitude, either favorable or unfavorable, some of the courts have regarded "the ancient state of things as remaining unaltered," while others have taken the unusual position of denying outright the existence of state life.

Other courts have taken it upon themselves to determine from the evidence submitted whether a government or a state does in fact exist. They have been able to do it without encroaching upon the functions of the political departments. Yet, lest their ingenious views should tempt the unwary into unwise and fatal practices, the courts in all such cases have deemed it proper to remark that the situations under consideration were *de facto*.

Judged by *O'Neill vs. Central Leather Co., supra, Oetjen vs. Central Leather Co., supra,* and *Sokoloff vs. National City Bank, supra,* the courts are finding it more and more desirable to concede semi-sovereign attributes to unrecognized governments in recognized states. It may well be that the cases will work themselves out along this line. An arbitrary distinction! Well, yes, but no more arbitrary than the distinction between incorporated and unincorporated territories recognized in the *Insular Cases,* or the anemic distinction in the case of individual rights created by the United States Supreme Court in *The Civil Rights Cases.*

Eventually the courts may find it desirable to attribute to an unrecognized *de facto* government the characteristics of internal sovereignty, and perhaps allow it to appear in the courts of non-recognizant states and ask protection for its property and public interests. Certainly, in cases involving only matters of private right it is not only possible, but highly desirable that the courts take cognizance of *de facto* situations, without in any way encroaching upon the functions of the political or policy determining branches of the government.

CHAPTER V

Retroactive Effect of Recognition

In the preceding chapters it has been pointed out that recognition is vested in those departments of our government which, by the constitution and laws, are entrusted with the conduct of foreign affairs. Once a determination has been made, or an attitude has been taken, by those departments it is conclusive and binding upon the courts.

They take judicial notice of such determination. In cases of doubt they may address an independent inquiry to the foreign office of the recognizant state. However, in some cases they have found it necessary to take cognizance of *de facto* situations, and if it involved no determination of policy they have adduced the juristic status of the state in question from history, evidence, and public notoriety.

It has become the well-established rule in England and the United States that the acts of a recognized sovereign over persons or property within its jurisdiction, must be recognized by the courts of the recognizant state as valid and binding upon them as rules of decision. Once a recognized government has acted, the validity of its act cannot be assailed in the courts of recognizant states.

The rule could not well be otherwise, for such acts cannot be wrong under its sovereignty. Such acts of recognized states in dealing with their nationals, or their property, or the property of nationals of other countries within the foreign domain which entail legal consequences elsewhere, such as the nationalisation decrees of Soviet Russia, may or may not be regarded as justiciable by the courts of recognizant states. But, as the courts have frequently said, " every sovereign state is bound to respect the independence of every other sovereign state."[1] The courts of one country should not sit in judgment on the acts of the government of another state done within its own territory, since to do so would doubtless embarrass the diplomatic departments of the government, and "vex the peace of nations."[2] This has been held to be true regardless of whether the authority in question performed the acts as the recognized representative of a *de facto* or a *de jure* government.[3]

This position was taken by Mr. Chief Justice Fuller in *Underhill vs. Hernandez.*[4] In the course of his opinion he said that the principle could not be confined to lawful or recognized governments, or to cases where redress could manifestly be had through public channels. The immunity of individuals from suits brought in foreign tribunals for acts done within their own states, in the exercise of governmental authority, whether as civil officers or military commanders, "must necessarily extend to the agents of governments ruling by paramount force as matter of fact." Where a civil war prevails, that is, where the people of a country are divided into two hostile parties, who take up arms and oppose one another by military force, "generally speaking foreign nations do not assume to judge of the merits of the quarrel. . . . If actual war has been waged, acts of legitimate warfare cannot be made the basis of individual liability."[5]

---

[1] *Underhill vs. Hernandez,* 168 U. S., 1897, 250 at 252.

[2] This attitude appears to have been first assumed in *Hamilton vs. Accessory Transit Company,* 26 Barbour (N. Y.), 1857, 46. See also *Murray vs. Vanderbilt,* 39 Barbour (N. Y.), 1863, 140; dictum in *Williams vs. Bruffy,* 96 U. S., 1878, 176. Perhaps the most important decision, the one most frequently cited, is *American Banana Co., vs. United Fruit Co.,* 213 U. S., 1909, 347 where, in an action for treble damages under the Sherman Act, the Supreme Court refused to pass judgment upon the validity of certain acts of confiscation performed by the then recognized Costa Rican authorities.

[3] *O'Neill vs. Central Leather Co.,* 87 N. J. L. 552, 94 Atlantic, 1915, 789; affirmed, with additional facts in 246 U. S., 1918, 297.

[4] *Op. cit. supra,* pp. 252–253.

[5] In this case, Hernandez was in command of a revolutionary army in

An interesting, yet rather absurd, set of facts was presented to the courts for adjudication in *The American Banana Company vs. The United Fruit Company*[6] in 1909. The American Banana Company alleged that its competitor, the United Fruit Company, in order to monopolize the exportation of bananas to the United States, subsequent to the revolt of Panama, conspired with the officials of Costa Rica, and induced the authorities to seize certain lands and properties which rendered the banana plantation of the American Banana Company in Panama worthless. At a later date a Costa Rican court declared title to be in a person from whom the United Fruit Company took title.

Both businesses being incorporated in the United States, the American Banana Company sued the United Fruit Company for treble damages under the national anti-trust laws. The Supreme Court held that jurisdiction is *prima facie* territorial, and the mere fact that the Sherman Act declared against "every combination" in restraint of interstate and foreign trade did not mean that our courts could exercise jurisdiction over conspiracies in other sovereign countries. Mr. Justice Holmes pointed out that such acts as those in question, performed by a recognized foreign government

Venezuela when an engagement took place with the government forces. It resulted in the defeat of the government forces and the occupation of Bolivar by Hernandez. Underhill was living in Bolivar at the time, where he carried on a machinery repair business. Prior to the occupation by Hernandez, Underhill had constructed a water system for the city. At the time of occupation Underhill applied for a passport to leave the city. It was refused by Hernandez with a view to coerce him to operate the waterworks system and his repair shops for the benefit of the revolutionary forces. The revolutionary forces were unrecognized at the time. Subsequently Underhill was given a passport, and the revolutionary forces acting under Hernandez were recognized by the United States as the legitimate government of Venezuela. Upon coming to the United States Underhill sued Hernandez in the Federal Courts to recover damages caused by the refusal to grant the passport, for alleged confinement, assaults and affronts of Hernandez's soldiers. The Circuit Court, Circuit Court of Appeals, and the Supreme Court, all gave judgment for the defendant. The Supreme Court affirmed the judgment of the Circuit Court of Appeals in saying "that the acts of the defendant were the acts of Venezuela, and as such are not properly the subject of adjudication in the courts of another government."

[6] 213 U. S., 1909, 347.

within its own territory, cannot have their validity assailed in an American court.

Even though the acts complained of were unethical, or even uneconomic as then regarded by the Sherman Act, yet the plantation was within the *de facto* jurisdiction of Costa Rica. That state took and kept possession of it by virtue of its sovereign power, and a seizure by a state is not a thing that can be complained of elsewhere in the courts.

In answer to the plaintiff's contention that the property seized was not within the jurisdiction of Costa Rica, but was within the jurisdiction of Panama, Mr. Justice Holmes said that such a fact, if it was one, did not matter in the least; sovereignty is pure fact. The fact had been recognized by the United States and was assented to by Panama.[7]

Each sovereign in its acts is presumed to be acting lawfully, and it would be a contradiction in terms to say that within its jurisdiction it is unlawful to persuade a sovereign power to bring about a result that it declares by its conduct to be desirable or proper. Foreign courts cannot admit that the influences were improper. "It makes the persuasion lawful by its own acts. The very meaning of sovereignty is that the decree of the sovereign makes law."[8] For these reasons the court refused the relief asked for. If a remedy was to be had, the appeal must be made to the political departments of the government and not to the judiciary.

In a subsequent case the court held that the principle is equally applicable to the property of American nationals, subsequently brought within the jurisdiction of the courts. In *Oetjen vs. Central Leather Company*,[9] wherein it was contended that the ownership of certain confiscated hides within the jurisdiction of the court at the time of the suit should be adjudicated under the law of the recognizant state,

[7] *American Banana Co. vs. United Fruit Co.*, 213 U. S., 1909, 347 at 357–358.

[8] *Kawananokoa vs. Polyblank*, 205 U. S., 1906, 349 at 353.

[9] 246 U. S., 1918, 297.

Mr. Justice Clarke said that "the principle that the conduct of one independent government cannot be successfully questioned in the courts of another is as applicable to a case involving the title to property brought within the jurisdiction of a court, such as we have here, as it was held to be to the cases cited,[10] in which claims for damages were based on acts done in a foreign country; for it rests at last upon the highest considerations of international comity and expediency."[11] The justice gave as his concluding reason that, "to permit the validity of the acts of one sovereign state to be re-examined by the courts of another would certainly 'imperil the amicable relations between governments and vex the peace of nations.'"[12]

The doctrine of exemption from judicial review of acts of a recognized foreign government extends to its legislative and executive acts. The immunity is predicated upon the acts having been confined within the proper limits of the jurisdiction of the recognized government. In the case of judgments of foreign courts, we find that these are not treated as obligatory. Their recognition rests on comity. The judgments of foreign tribunals are always qualified by the universally accepted rule that the court rendering the judgment shall have had jurisdiction of the case.[13]

There is an exception to the general rule that the courts of a recognizant state will not sit in judgment on the acts of a recognized state. The exception extends to cases of prize captures made under the authority of a foreign state,[14] which prize captures were in violation of the neutrality of the recognizant state, into which the prize is carried. The excep-

---

[10] Referring to *American Banana Company vs. United Fruit Company, supra.*

[11] *Oetjen vs. Central Leather Company, supra,* pp. 303–304.

[12] *Ibid.*

[13] In *Rose vs. Himely* Mr. Justice Marshall held that a sale made under a judgment of a court in Santo Domingo did not divest the American owner of title because the court did not have initial jurisdiction.

[14] 7 Wheaton, 1822, 283.

tion was established in *The Santissima Trinidad* in 1822.[15] Since then it has not been seriously questioned.

As a consequence of the doctrine of judicial immunity the English and American courts have held that once recognition is accorded it is to be regarded as retroactive in effect. It follows from this that acts performed by the recognized state within its jurisdiction prior to recognition must be regarded as lawful by the courts of the recognizant states. In the past such acts have included the conversion of the assets of the overthrown government, the levying of forced contributions to perfect military operations or carry out legislative decrees, and the nationalization of private businesses within the jurisdiction of the recognized state.

The doctrine became entrenched in the law by 1878. In that year, Mr. Justice Field in *Williams vs. Bruffy*,[16] in discussing generally the status of a *de facto* state set up by separation from a parent state, said that if such a state fails to establish itself permanently, all its acts perish with it. If it succeeds and becomes recognized, "its acts from the commencement of its existence are upheld as those of an independent nation. Such was the case of the state governments under the old Confederation on their separation from the British crown. Having made good their Declaration of Independence everything they did from that date was as valid as if their independence had been at once acknowledged." [17]

This was the view which had been taken by the Supreme Court in a number of cases involving certain acts passed by

---

[15] Mr. Justice Story, who delivered the court's opinion said: "In each case . . . the illegality of the capture is the same; in each, the duty of the neutral is equally strong to assert its own rights, and to preserve its own good faith, and to take from the wrongdoer the property he has unjustly acquired and reinstate the other party in his title and possession which have been tortiously divested." 7 Wheaton, 1822, 283, at 351.

[16] 96 United States, 1877, 176. The case involved certain confiscatory acts of the government of the Confederate States. The Court held that the acts were void.

[17] *Ibid.*, at 186.

the state legislatures immediately after the Declaration of Independence. As early as 1796, in the course of an opinion [18] concerning confiscation acts of the Virginia legislature, Mr. Justice Chase, had occasion to say that from the 4th of July, 1776, the American states were *de facto,* as well as *de jure,* in the possession and actual exercise of all the rights of independent government, and that he had ever considered it as the established doctrine, that their independence originated from, and commenced with, the Declaration of Congress, on the 4th of July, 1776. He said that no other period could be fixed on for its commencement, and "that all laws made by the legislatures of the several states, after the Declaration of Independence, were the laws of sovereign and independent governments." [19]

His opinion was in accord with the view which the English courts had already taken of the situation. A pronouncement appears in the English cases as early as 1788,[20] wherein the court does not specifically state, but implies, that the recognition of 1783 was retrospective in effect.

The earliest English case arose out of a law enacted by the Georgia legislature shortly after the Declaration of Independence, attainting the former Tory governor of the Georgia colony and confiscating his property. The Georgia law was set up as a defense in the English courts by an English royalist in a suit by one of his American creditors. The Lord Chancellor recognized the defense as valid, inasmuch as the American creditor, under the Georgia law, could have satisfied his debt out of the confiscated property. In touching the validity of the Georgia decree of attainder and confiscation the court said that it might be a question for private speculation whether such a law made in Georgia was a wise or an improvident one, whether a barbarous or civilized in-

[18] *Ware vs. Hylton,* 3 Dallas, 1796, 199.
[19] *Ibid.*
[20] *Wright vs. Nutt,* 1 H. Bl., 1788, 136, 126 English Reprints 83.

stitution. "But here we must take it as the law of an independent country," said the court, "and the laws of every country must be equally regarded in courts of justice here, whether in private speculation they are wise or foolish."[21]

In the United States the issue of retroactivity appears to have been only incidentally involved in the case of *Kennett vs. Chambers*.[22] In this case the appellants insisted that recognition validated a void contract made prior to recognition. The court refused to accept their view. Rather it held that the agreement having been void when it was made, that is, in violation of the neutrality laws of the United States, it could derive no force from subsequent recognition. It is to be noted that *Kennett vs. Chambers*[23] involved an act of parties within and subject to the jurisdiction of the United States. On this ground it is to be distinguished from the case of *The Itata*,[24] which is sometimes cited as contrary to this view.

Such still appears to be the rule. Recognition is not retroactive in that it validates criminal acts committed by persons subject to the jurisdiction of the recognizant state. It is retroactive only as regards acts committed within the jurisdiction of the recognized state.

It will be recalled that in *United States vs. Trumbull*[25] the sole question was whether a vice-consul of Chile who possessed an unrevoked *exequatur* must still be recognized by

---

[21] *Wright vs. Nutt*, 126 English Reprints, 83 at 89. It appears that the case of *Ogden vs. Folliott*, 1790, 3 T. R. 726, 100 English Reprints, 825, affirming judgment in 1 H. Bl. 123, 126 English Reprints, 75, on a similar set of facts wherein the court refused to accord recognition to a bill of attainder which intended a confiscation of the property of certain Tories in New Jersey during the American Revolution, is contra. It is generally cited as such. However, if the Ogden case has not been overruled the doctrine therein enunciated has been confined to its narrowest limits. See *Phillipa vs. Eyre*, 1870, L. R. 6 Q. B. 27, 10 Best & S. 1,004, 40 L. J. Q. B. N. S. 28, and *Huntington vs. Attrill*, 1893, 68 L. T. N. S. 326.

[22] 14 Howard, 1852, 38.

[23] The agreement was entered into at Cincinnati.

[24] 56 Fed., 1893, 505. There was also a substantial difference in the evidence in the two cases.

[25] 48 Fed., 1891, 94.

the courts as the accredited representative of his country, entitled to the usual immunities of his office, notwithstanding that the government which sent him had been overthrown, and an apparently successful revolutionary government inaugurated in its place. Judge Ross of the District Court felt that such an individual was still the accredited representative of the country and entitled to the usual immunities. The revolutionary government of Chile had been recognized by the United States, but prior to the rendition of the decision. This recognition validated the unrevoked *exequatur* in the hands of the Chilean vice-consul.

At the conclusion of his opinion Judge Ross gave an additional reason why he did not think that the vice-consul should be compelled to attend as a witness. The offenses with which the defendants stood charged were violations of the neutrality laws of the United States, and consisted in the giving of aid to those who then constituted the established and recognized government of Chile. Having succeeded and become recognized, the acts of that government from the commencement of its existence must be upheld as those of an independent state. To require the representative of that government to appear and give testimony against those alleged to have aided its establishment would not only be contrary to the principle upon which neutrality laws are based, but " would strongly tend to give grave offense to the government now recognized by the United States," said the court, " and with which this government, happily, is at peace." [26]

However, the reasoning of Judge Ross appears to have been *obiter dictum*. The court had already deemed itself to be bound by the determination of the President, which *ipso facto* disposed of the case, and which was sufficient ground on which to allow the motion of the vice-consul. Furthermore, it appears that Judge Ross himself regarded

[26] *United States vs. Trumbull,* 48 Federal, 1891, 94 at 98.

it as a dictum, for eleven days later in rendering judgment on the initial facts, which had given rise to the decision just referred to, he held that the neutrality laws had not been violated inasmuch as the statute under which Trumbull stood accused prohibited only such military expeditions or enterprises "as originate within the limits of the United States, and are to be carried on from this country." [27] Judge Ross held the evidence insufficient to warrant a conviction, and instructed the jury to find a verdict of not guilty.[28] It thus appears that Judge Ross himself admitted that what he had said in the first case of *United States vs. Trumbull* was *obiter dictum.* These cases do not overrule the previously considered case of *Kennett vs. Chambers,*[29] as has been sometimes stated.

The earliest case in which express reference, at the hands of a court, is made to the doctrine of retroactivity arose in New York in the case of *Murray vs. Vanderbilt,* decided in 1863.[30] The Accessory Transit Company had been created, largely by American capital, under the laws of Nicaragua. It appeared that the Vanderbilt interests furnished a large part of the capital. The purpose of the railway was to facilitate transportation across the country, primarily for the benefit of Americans rushing to the California gold fields. In February, 1856, the Rivas-Walker government, revolutionists in control of the government, annulled the charter of the railway corporation and declared the company abolished. The property of the corporation was to be seized and held subject to a board of inquiry.[31]

The case of *Murray vs. Vanderbilt* [32] involved the title to

[27] *United States vs. Trumbull,* 48 Fed., 1891, 99 at 103.
[28] *Ibid.,* p. 108.
[29] 14 Howard, 1852, 38.
[30] 39 Barbour, 1863, 140.
[31] For a case which was decided six years earlier, which denied a petition by a stockholder to have the company declared insolvent and a receiver appointed, inasmuch as considerable property was situated in the United States, see *Hamilton vs. Accessory Transit Company,* 26 Barbour, 1857, 46.
[32] 39 Barbour, 1863, 140.

certain assets of the corporation. The case rested upon a determination of the validity and effect to be given by the New York courts to the decree of dissolution and seizure recited before. The Rivas-Walker government had been recognized by the United States, but subsequent to the decree which remained in force at the time of the litigation.

The court felt bound to recognize the validity of the Nicaraguan decree, but held that the law did not dissolve the corporation for the purposes of the suit. Mr. Justice Ingraham, speaking for the court, said that from the time of the recognition of the Rivas-Walker government, in May 1856, if not from the time of its inception, the decree must be considered as a valid act of the government of Nicaragua. He was of the opinion "that where the decree was not void at the time of its passage (February 1856), the recognition of the government in May (1856), would have a retroactive effect, so as to give validity in this country to the decrees made previously, so far as to enable the court here to act on it as affecting the charter." [33] The principle was discussed at length by the New York court.

However, strictly speaking, the principle of retroactivity did not become fixed as one of the legal effects of recognition until 1918. From 1917 to 1920 a series of cases involving the success and belated recognition of the Carranza government in Mexico came before the state and the federal courts. In these cases the courts definitely recognized the rule. Prior to this time the principle can be regarded only as a dictum.

The most frequently cited of all these cases are *Oetjen vs. Central Leather Company* [34] and *Ricaud vs. American Metal Company*.[35] These two cases came before the Supreme Court of the United States on appeal in 1918. The former was a

[33] The New York court differentiated the instant case from *Ogden vs. Folliet*, 1790, 3 T. R. 726, 100 English Reprints, 855 and *Kennett vs. Chambers*, 14 Howard, 1852, 38.

[34] 246 U. S., 1918, 297

[35] 246 U. S., 1918, 304.

suit in replevin. It involved the title to a large quantity of hides. The plaintiff claimed as the assignee of the Mexican owner from whom they had been taken by General Villa as a military contribution. General Villa had sold them to the predecessor in title of the defendant.

The Supreme Court refused to sit in judgment on the validity of the acts of Villa, who had acted on instructions from General Carranza, inasmuch as the United States had recognized the Carranza faction as the *de facto* government of Mexico in 1915, and as the *de jure* government in 1917. The court declared that when a government which originates in revolution or revolt is recognized by the political departments of our government as the *de jure* government of the country in which it is established, such recognition is retroactive in effect and validates all the action and conduct of the government so recognized from the commencement of its existence.[36]

In the companion case, *Ricaud vs. American Metal Company*,[37] similar facts were before the same court. The case involved the validity of the seizure of certain lead ore. The ore had been seized as a military contribution by one General Pereyra, a commander of a brigade of the Constitutionalist Army of Mexico of which Carranza was then First Chief, and sold by him to the predecessors in title of the defendant who attempted to ship it into the United States. The plaintiffs, who claimed under purchase from the original American owners, sought to enjoin the collector of customs at El Paso, Texas, from delivering the bullion to the defendants.

The Supreme Court held it to be a lawful seizure, since the recognition of Carranza by the United States was retroactive in effect and validated " all the actions of the Carranza

---

[36] *Williams vs. Bruffy*, 96 U. S., 1877, 176 at 186, and *Underhill vs. Hernandez*, 65 Federal 577, affirmed in 168 U. S., 1897, 250 at 253 cited as being in accord. They are in accord only so far as dicta are concerned.

[37] 246 U. S., 1918, 304.

government from the commencement of its existence . . . and the action of General Pereyra complained of must therefore be regarded as the action, in time of civil war, of a duly commissioned general of the legitimate Government of Mexico." [38]

A similar dispute which arose out of another revolutionary decree of General Villa, acting under General Carranza, was the case of *Terrazas vs. Holmes.*[39] The case involved the seizure of a herd of cattle of a Mexican owner, resident in Mexico. The decree was later affirmed by General Carranza. The Texas court followed the *Oetjen* and *Ricaud* cases in holding that an action of replevin, by the owner at the time confiscation in 1913, would not lie against an American owner who had purchased the cattle in Mexico from the agents of the revolutionary government and subsequently brought them to the United States. The court held that recognition of the Carranza government by the United States subsequent to the confiscation, validated the seizure, and that it was not open to re-examination in the Texas courts. The court found that it had only the power to determine whether General Villa had acted in a certain manner and did not have the power to question the validity of the seizure.[40] The doctrine of retroactivity was expressly recognized and applied by the Texas courts.

Another case before the state courts involved the seizure of a large number of bags of coffee. The coffee was appropriated in 1914 by agents of the Carranza government. It was then sold to an American importing firm at New Orleans. The original owners from whom it was appropriated sequestered and sought to recover it, but the

[38] *Ricaud vs. American Metal Company,* 246 U. S., 1918, 304 at p. 310.

[39] 225 S. W., 1920, 848.

[40] See *Terrazas vs. Holmes,* 227 S. W., 1920, 206, decided the following year by the Texas courts, in which it appears that a part, 350 head, of the same herd was involved and the court reached a like conclusion. An English translation of Villa's decree is reproduced in this companion case; affirmed 275 S. W., 1925, 396.

Louisiana court upheld the title of the American firm, saying that it was precluded from making an independent inquiry as to the validity of the appropriation because of the subsequent retroactive effect of the recognition of the Carranza forces by the United States.[41]

Another case in the state courts involving the validity of certain acts of the recognized Carranza forces was *Molina vs. Commission Reguladora.*[42] The plaintiff, a citizen of the Mexican state of Yucatan, sought to recover for the conversion of certain farm produce. The defendant claimed that he had bought the property in question from the lawful authorities in Mexico who had sequestered and sold it by virtue of confirmed authority from General Carranza prior to the recognition of his government by the United States as the *de jure* government of Mexico. The New Jersey court refused to allow a recovery because of the retroactive effect of recognition. The court cited the *Oetjen* and *Ricaud* cases with approval. It held that these cases governed in the instant case, and that it was unnecessary to inquire whether the action of the Yucatan authorities against the plaintiff's property was legal or not.[43] Recognition validated the acts in question: the courts refused to sit in judgment on the acts of a recognized foreign state.

---

[41] *Monte Blanco Real Estate Corporation vs. Wolvin Line*, 145 La., 1920, 563, 85 Southern 242. The court followed *Ricaud vs. American Metal Co.*, in its decision. But see *De La O vs. Consolidated Kansas City Smelting and Refining Co.*, 202 S. W., 1918, 1,027, where a Texas court gave judgment for the plaintiff in an action for the conversion of the proceeds of certain ores seized by the Mexican authorities. The court held that the defendant was estopped, under the terms of his contract, from asserting his title based on the confiscation in Mexico. The court noted that it could take judicial notice of the fact that General Carranza was the head of the military government of Northern Mexico at the time the ore was imported (prior to recognition by the United States), and that such government could seize and sell the ores for military purposes and that valid title would pass to the purchaser. However, the case can be distinguished because the court felt that the evidence in the case did not show that the officer making the seizure and sale was a duly authorized officer of such a military government.

[42] 104 Atl., 1918, 450.

[43] For the denial of a previous motion in the instant case, see 103 Atlantic, 397.

The rule that our courts will not sit in judgment on the acts of recognized states when they are performed within their jurisdiction did not deprive the American courts of jurisdiction to adjudicate the Mexican confiscation cases just considered. The rule requires only that when it appears that a foreign government has acted in a given manner on the subject matter of the litigation, the details of the action, or the merit of the results cannot be questioned in the courts of a recognizant state. The action of the recognized government must be accepted by the courts as a rule for their decision. "To accept a ruling authority and to decide accordingly is not a surrender or abandonment of jurisdiction but an exercise of it." [44]

In each of the American cases the recognition involved was *de jure* recognition and not *de facto* recognition. In these cases both *de facto* and *de jure* recognition had been accorded and the courts did not differentiate between the two types. The American decisions do not decide the retroactive effect of *de facto* recognition. This question was first presented to the English courts.

The first case in which this issue was presented to the English courts was *Aksionariornoye Obschestvo vs. James Sagor & Company*.[45] The plaintiff was a British corporation, engaged in the manufacture of plywood, doing business under the laws of Russia during the reign of the Czar. In June, 1918, the Soviet government nationalized all private industries of this type and confiscated their assets.

On March 16, 1921, the British government concluded a trade agreement with the Soviets through the agency of M.

[44] *Ricaud vs. American Metal Co., op. cit.*, p. 309; *Molina vs. Comision Reguladora, op. cit.*, pp. 452–453. For a case involving a modification or limitation of the rule enunciated in the *Oetjen* and *Ricaud cases*, see *Cottam & Co., vs. Comision*, 149 La., 1921, 1026, 90 So., 392, where the Mexican authorities did not have absolute authority over the property in question. Another case in point is *Mitchell vs. Banco de Londres y Mexico*, 192 App. Div. N. Y., 1920, 720, 183 N. Y. Supp. 446.

[45] 1921 L. R. 3 K. B. 532, reversing 1921 L. R. 1 K. B. 456 on a slightly different set of facts. This case is commonly cited as *Luther vs. Sagor*.

Krassin. It was by virtue of this agreement that the Krassin delegation continued its operations in London. The Krassin delegation, prior to the consummation of the trade agreement, 1920, had sold a part of the plaintiffs' confiscated plywood to the defendants, an American firm. When the goods began to arrive and the defendants noticed the trade marks of the plaintiffs thereon, they immediately wrote to inquire whether the plaintiffs desired to purchase the goods, and if not, whether they desired that they remove the trade mark before offering them for sale. Upon receipt of this notice the plaintiffs instituted suit for the recovery of the plywood.

The lower court gave judgment for the plaintiffs on the ground that the Soviet regime being unrecognized at the time of the litigation, December, 1920, the acts of the Soviets amounted to pure robbery. On appeal the evidence showed that the seizure and sale of the plywood were the acts of the Soviet government which had been subsequently recognized as the *de facto* government of Russia. The Court of Appeal held that such recognition bound the English courts and that the recognition was retroactive in effect and prohibited any inquiry by the English courts into the confiscatory decree. However, the court felt that the decision below was correct. The Court of Appeal relied strongly on the American precedents.

The counsel for the plaintiffs sought to evade the effect of the decisions of the United States courts on the retroactive issue. They argued that the governments considered by the American courts were recognized by the United States as the governments *de jure* [46] while the Soviet government was recognized only as a *de facto* government. The counsel contended that in the case of *de jure* recognition such recognition might relate back to the acts of a state, committed prior to recognition, and validate them *ab initio,* but that in the

---

[46] As in the *Oetjen* and *Ricaud* cases in the United States which concerned by the recognition of Mexico.

case of *de facto* recognition the rule did not apply. The court refused to accept the purported distinction for the purposes of the instant case. Lord Justice Bankes, admitted that for " some purposes, no doubt, a distinction can be drawn between the effect of the recognition by a sovereign state of the one form of government or the other, but for the present purposes " in his opinion, no distinction could be drawn. The government of England having " recognized the Soviet government as the government really in possession of the powers of sovereignty in Russia, the acts of that government must be treated with all the respect due to the acts of a duly recognized foreign state."[47]

Lord Justices Warrington and Scrutton also read judgments in the case and covered the point in question. The former quoted with approval from *Oetjen vs. Central Leather Company* and said: " It is true that in this case the court is applying the principle to a government recognized as the *de jure* government, but . . . there is no difference for the present purpose between a government recognized as such *de jure* and one recognized *de facto*. In the latter case, as well as in the former, the government in question acquires the right to be treated by the recognizing state as an independent sovereign state, and none the less that our government does not pretend to express an opinion on the legality or otherwise of the means by which its power has been obtained." And after differentiating between *de jure* and *de facto* recognition, he qualified his statements by observing that he expressed " no opinion on the question whether the retroactive effect of recognition is so wide as to cover every act of the recognized government from the commencement of its existence." He considered it unnecessary to express such an opinion because the facts in the instant case did not require it.[48] Lord Justice Scrutton, in his judg-

[47] *Luther vs. Sagor*, 90 L. J. R. K. B. 1921, 1202 at 1212.
[48] *Ibid.*, at 1216.

ment, concurred in the opinions expressed by the other justices, but felt that to have recognition retroactive from "the commencement of its existence" required "very careful consideration" and definition at the hands of the court.[49]

The counsel for the plaintiffs anticipated that the court might deny their contention and follow the American precedents on retroactivity. For this reason, they argued that the nationalization decrees of the Soviet government were so immoral, and so contrary to the principles of justice recognized in England, that the English courts were bound to disregard them. The court labeled the argument "a bold proposition" and denied the point. The court stated that it was "asked to ignore the law of the foreign country under which the vendor acquired his title, and to lend its assistance to prevent the purchaser dealing with the goods." "Even if it was open to the courts of this country to consider the morality or justice of the decree of June, 1918, I do not see how the courts could treat this particular decree otherwise than as the expression by the *de facto* government of a civilized country of a policy which it considered to be in the best interest of that country. It must be quite immaterial for present purposes that the same views are not entertained by the government of this country, are repudiated by the vast majority of its citizens, and are not recognized by our laws," said Lord Justice Bankes.[50]

On the same point of "immorality" Lord Justice Scrutton observed that all individuals must contribute to the welfare of the British state. At that time several British citizens were compelled to contribute to the state more than half of their incomes through an income-tax and super-tax, and a large proportion of their capital in death duties, with the fear of a capital levy over their heads at all times. Under these circumstances the court was not in a position to declare that a foreign state was immoral which considered that to

---

[49] *Luther vs. Sagor, op. cit.*, p. 1219.
[50] *Ibid.*, at 1213.

invest individual property in the State as representing all the citizens was the best form of proprietary right.

When the initial case was first tried in December 1920, Justice Roche, on information received from the Foreign Office, held that the Soviet government had not been recognized by the English government, and that the defendants acquired no title to the property. He accordingly gave judgment for the plaintiff. On appeal it was held that the decision was right according to the information then received from the Foreign Office, but that, inasmuch as after the commencement of the action, further information had been received from the Foreign Office to the effect that England had recognized the Soviet government as the *de facto* government of Russia, the defendants acquired title and were entitled to judgment. The court held that *de facto* recognition was equally as retroactive as *de jure* recognition.

The precedent established in *Luther vs. Sagor* has been followed by the English courts in several subsequent cases. In July, 1924, it was raised in the case of *The Juniper.*[61] A steamship company which had its head office in Paris claimed possession of a vessel, anchored in the English port of Dartmouth, and proceeded *in rem* against the vessel. After the writ had been served on the vessel the representative of the Union of Socialist Soviet Republics put in an appearance and moved to set aside the writ on the ground that the ship was their property, by virtue of a nationalization decree of 1918; that they were a recognized foreign independent state, and that they declined to sanction the institution of the proceedings. Lord Justices Bankes and Scrutton, who rendered judgments in the case of *Luther vs. Sagor,* agreed that *de facto* recognition had been accorded the Soviet Republic, and that under such circumstances, "the court had no jurisdiction to entertain proceedings against the property or to investigate the assertion that the ship was the property of the Russian sovereign."[62]

---

[61] 1924, 40 T. L. R. 815.
[62] *The Juniper, op. cit.*, p. 816.

The case of *White, Child, and Beney vs. Eagle S. & B. Dominions Insurance Company*,[53] involved the decrees of the Soviet government nationalizing banks and their assets. The Court of Appeal held that effect must be given to these decrees. The decision appeared to be a harsh one. The defendant insurance company had guaranteed the plaintiff bankers against loss or damage "directly caused by fire, rioters, civil war, revolutions, rebellions, military or usurped power" but provided that no claim was to attach for "confiscation or destruction by the government of the country in which the property" was situated. In accordance with *Luther vs. Sagor*[54] the learned judges held that the retroactivity rule made the loss fall within the exception clause of the insurance policy, even though the government had been granted *de facto* recognition only.

It appears that if the litigation had been consummated prior to the recognition, recovery would have been allowed. The court created an arbitrary distinction: it did not acknowledge that facts are facts, revolutions are revolutions, in Russia as elsewhere, regardless of recognition. It is this precise, arbitrary distinction into which those courts which follow the retroactivity fiction are driven, to which reference was made in the preceding chapter.

This anomalous situation faced the English Court of Appeal again in 1925, in the much discussed case of *Banque Internationale de Commerce de Petrograd vs. Goukassow*.[55] The plaintiff bank was incorporated in 1869 according to the law of Russia. It had a branch in Paris and a branch in London. The defendant was a customer of the Paris branch. Under the terms of a special agreement made with the Paris branch in 1912, he engaged the bank to purchase shares in other companies for him, he paying only twenty per cent of the value and the bank advancing the other eighty

---

[53] 1922, 127 L. T. N. S. 571, 38 T. L. R. 616.
[54] 1921, L. R. 3 K. B. 532.
[55] 1923, L. R. 2 K. B. 682.

per cent, as security for the repayment of which the shares were deposited with the bank. The net result of these transactions was that prior to the commencement of the Russian revolution the defendant was indebted to the Paris branch to the extent of 44,000 pounds. By the decrees of the Soviet government made in 1917 and 1918 all private banks in Russia, including the plaintiff bank, were extinguished and ceased to exist. Great Britain at the time recognized the Soviets as the *de facto* government of Russia, while France, at the time of the litigation, neither recognized it as the *de facto* nor the *de jure* government.

In 1920 the plaintiff, who continued to carry on the business of the Paris branch, sued the defendant in the English courts. He found his action blocked by the retroactive effect of the *de facto* recognition,[56] while at the same time, the Soviet regime being unrecognized by France, recovery could have been had in the French courts.[57]

---

[56] In commenting on the law applicable to this anomalous situation Lord Justice Bankes said that " if the view of this court is correct that the parent bank in Russia has ceased to have any legal existence, this curious result must follow, namely, that in this country which has recognized the Soviet government, the London branch of the Russian bank has no legal existence and cannot sue, yet in France, which has refused to recognize that government, the Paris branch of that bank has never ceased to have a legal existence and can in France carry on its business and sue and be sued just as it could before the Soviet government was established. The question of law which has to be decided is whether the Paris branch can maintain the present action in this country. From one point of view it may seem absurd to suggest that a plaintiff who, in the eye of the law of this country, has ceased to have any legal existence can maintain an action in this court. On the other hand, it is clear that had the present action been commenced in France it would have been maintainable there. If maintainable there, then why not here? If the question was one merely between capacity to contract and procedure, I should have hesitated long before deciding that the present action was not maintainable, and that the *lex fori* rather than the *lex loci contractus* was the law to be applied. The objection is that the party seeking to maintain the action is, in the eye of our law, no party at all, but a mere name only, with no legal existence. Having decided that this contention is correct, it follows in my opinion, that the action is not maintainable, and the appeal must be dismissed."

[57] Lord Justice Atkin said: "This plaintiff, though alive in France, is dead here. No doubt this case will serve as a solemn warning to the French branches of Russian corporations to beware of allowing assets to pass into a country where, as soon as they reach its territorial limits, they either become the property of the Soviet Government or become *bona vacantia.* With that

It can hardly be said that these two decisions [58] determine the retroactive extraterritorial effect of all nationalization decrees of a recognized *de facto* government. The implication of the cases is that if it appears certain to the courts that the true intent of the decree is to nationalize all corporations, upon recognition, such decrees must be given full effect upon the corporate existence of the corporations outside of Russia.[59] Obviously a nationalization decree by a recognized *de facto* government cannot terminate the existence of a foreign corporation doing business in such state, although the recognized *de facto* government might forbid its doing business within the state.[60] Such a derivative right flows from the fundamental right of independence.

A number of the decisions of the courts deal with the exact time from which the immunity from judicial review of governmental acts dates. No uniform rule has been agreed upon by the courts. The American cases hold that it is retroactive as to all acts from the " commencement of the existence " of the new government. Some of the English judges have questioned whether such a rule is the proper one.

In *Murray vs. Vanderbilt*,[61] the decree annulling the charter in question was made on February 18, 1856, while recognition by the United States was not accorded until the

---

I have nothing to do. We must, as has been said, adhere to principles. On principle the plaintiff is dead, and the action must be dismissed." 1923, L. R. 2 K. B. 682 at 693. The House of Lords set aside the judgment of the Court of Appeal. However, the reversal turned upon a difference of opinion as to the effect intended by the Soviet decrees. 1925, L. R. A. C. 150.

[58] *Banque Internationale de Commerce de Petrograd vs. Goukassow*, 1923, L. R. 2 K. B. 682; *Russian Commercial and Industrial Bank vs. Comptoir de Mulhouse*, 1925, L. R. A. C. 112; same case in Court of Appeal, 1923, L. R. 2 K. B. 630.

[59] See *Canada Southern Railway Co., vs. Gebhord*, 109 U. S., 1883, 527, where Mr. Chief Justice Waite said that wherever a corporation goes for business it carries its charter, as " that is the law of its existence," and whatever disabilities are placed on the corporation at home it retains abroad, and whatever legislative control it is subjected to at home must be recognized and submitted to by those who deal with it elsewhere. To evade the harshness of the rule it appears that the courts have allowed them to continue as *de facto* corporations for a temporary period to wind up their affairs.

[60] *Sokoloff vs. National City Bank*, 239 N. Y., 1924, 158, 145 N. E. 917.

[61] 39 Barbour (N. Y.), 1863, 141 at 146.

following May. Mr. Justice Ingraham was of the opinion that our "recognition of the government in May would have a retroactive effect, so as to give validity" to the decree made the preceding February. However, it was not necessary for the court to make a pronouncement on the precise date of retroactivity inasmuch as, at the time of recognition in May, the decree still remained in force, and was enforced by the Nicaraguan government. Hence it was only necessary that from the time of the recognition of the government in May that the decree should have been considered as a valid act of the Nicaraguan government.

The issue was more complicated in the cases involving the Villa-Carranza revolt in Mexico. It appears from the cases, in fact the courts regarded it as a matter of general history, that General Carranza inaugurated his revolution and proclaimed the organization of his so-called constitutional government under "The Plan of Guadalupe" on the twenty-sixth of March, 1913. Madero, President of the Republic of Mexico, was assassinated on February 23, 1913, whereupon Huerta had declared himself Provisional President of the Republic.[62]

The city of Torreon in the State of Coahuila, in which the hides in question in *Oetjen vs. Central Leather Company* were located, was occupied by Villa, Commander of the North under Carranza, on October 1, 1913. The exact date of the seizure does not appear from the case but it does show that the hides in question were sold in Mexico by order of Villa on January 3, 1914. Mr. Justice Clarke, speaking for the court, held that our recognition of the Carranza government as the *de facto* government of the Republic of Mexico, on October 19, 1915, and as the *de jure* government on August 31, 1917, was sufficiently retroactive to validate the seizure in question which occurred during the latter part of 1913.

---

[62] These facts appear in the cases dealing with the Mexican question.

In *Ricaud vs. American Metal Company* [63] the seizure had been made in September, 1913, although the lead bullion in question had been purchased by an American firm the preceding June. The court in its opinion held that recognition was retroactive and validated "all the acts of the Carranza government from the commencement of its existence." Mr. Justice Clarke intimated that such recognition would not validate acts committed between February 23,[64] and March 26, 1913. The justice prefaced his remarks on the retroactive effects, by stating that the revolution inaugurated by General Carranza against General Huerta proved successful and was recognized. Later in the opinion he regarded the seizure "as the action, in time of civil war, of a duly commissioned general of the legitimate government of Mexico." [65] No case has arisen involving the validity of acts of the Huerta faction from February 23, 1913, to March 26, 1913.[66]

[63] 246 U. S., 1918, 304.

[64] The date of the assassination of Madero.

[65] *Ricaud vs. American Metal Co.,* 246 U. S., 1918, 304 at 309.

[66] Although the chief ground relied upon in the *Oetjen* and *Ricaud* cases was recognition by the United States, yet the court did not decide that the absence of political recognition precluded giving effect to the confiscations. Also it is to be noted that the Supreme Court affirmed the decision of the New Jersey Court of Errors and Appeals which had been handed down prior to political recognition. The decision of the New Jersey court was to the effect that a confiscation or seizure for war purposes by a *de facto* government passes title to the goods. *O'Neill vs. Central Leather Company* 87 N. J. L., 1915, 552, 94 Atl. 789. This rule has been followed even in a court of a country wherein the revolution occurred, *Lemkuhl vs. Kock,* Transvaal L. R., 1903, T. S. 451. For a case contra see, *Cia. Minera Ygnacio Rodriguez Ramos S. A. vs. Bartlesville Zinc Co.* (1925, Texas), 275 S. W. 388, where the court relied on the dictum in *Williams vs. Bruffy,* 96 U. S., 1877, 176 at 186, that the validity of confiscation by an insurgent government depends entirely upon its survival, since the legal effects of "all such acts perish with it." Actually, however, *Williams vs. Bruffy* was not in point because the court in the *Williams* case had in mind a rule only for the courts of the country in which the revolution had occurred and the court based its discussions largely on domestic policy rather than on rules of International Law. The rule laid down by the New Jersey court in the *O'Neill* case recognizes the realities of such situations. Our courts need not give legal effect to all acts of unrecognized *de facto* governments. It should not give effect to those acts which would materially weaken our foreign policy. *Sokoloff vs. National City Bank,* 239 N. Y., 1924, 156, 145 N. E. 917; *Russian Reinsurance Company vs. Stoddard,* 240 N. Y., 1925, 149, 147 N. E. 703.

The problem of retroactivity received its first consideration at the hands of the English courts in the case of *Luther vs. Sagor.*[67] Here the different rules applicable to recognized and unrecognized governments were perspicuously illustrated by the reversal of the judgment of the court of the King's Bench, following recognition of the Soviets, by the Court of Appeal. Also, the doctrine as applied to cases of *de facto* recognition, did not become an undoubted and indisputable principle until the rendition of this case.[68] Each of the Lord Justices of the Court of Appeal treated the subject at length in his judgment.

In the initial case of *Luther vs. Sagor,*[69] the court held, December 21, 1920, on the information from the Foreign Office before it, that His Majesty's Government had not recognized the Soviet government. On appeal the following May two additional letters from the Foreign Office, dated respectively April 20, and 22, 1921, were before the judges. The letter of April twentieth was from the Under-Secretary of State for Foreign Affairs in reply to a letter dated April twelfth from the appellant's solicitors concerning the status of the Soviet regime. In answer to the inquiry the Under-Secretary of State wrote: "I am to inform you that His Majesty's Government recognize the Soviet Government as the *de facto* Government of Russia." [70] The letter of April twenty-second was in reply to a request for information as to whether England recognized the Provisional Government of Russia, and as to the period of duration, and the extent of its jurisdiction. The letter of April 22 contained, *inter alia,* the statement that the Provisional Government came into power on March 14, 1917, that it was recognized by England as the then existing government of

[67] 1921, L. R. 3 K. B. 352.

[68] For a contrary inference see editorial on *Oetjen vs. Central Leather Company* in 86 Central Law Journal, 259.

[69] 1921, L. R. 1 K. B. 456.

[70] 90 L. J. R. K. B. (1921) 1202 at 1211.

Russia, and that the Constituent Assembly remained in session until December 13, 1917, when it was dispersed by the Soviet authorities. With these facts before him Lord Justice Bankes inquired: "What is the effect of the recognition . . . in April 1921, . . . and how far back if at all does that recognition extend?"[71]

The counsel for the respondents insisted that no case had gone so far as to say that the recognition of a *de facto* government was retrospective. In turn, the counsel for the appellants relied upon the implication of the American precedents.[72] Lord Justice Bankes examined these and observed that they were "weighty opinions," but the learned American judges did not cite any authority for their propositions. The American judges treated the matter as one resting on principle.[73]

The Lord Justice considered the views put forward by the learned American judges as sound, but he felt that "there may be cases in which the courts of a country . . . may have to consider at what stage in its development the government so recognized can . . . be said to have 'commenced it's existence.'" This was not such a case. Lord Justice Bankes felt that, relying upon the communications from the Foreign Office, as of April 20, and 22, he should treat the Soviet government, which England had then recognized as the *de facto* government of Russia, "as having commenced its existence at a date anterior to any date material to the dispute" between the parties to the appeal. Judged by the letter of April 22, from the Foreign Office, wherein it appeared that the "Soviet authorities dispersed the then Constituent Assembly on December 13, 1917," he felt "that the Soviet Government assumed the position of the sovereign

---

[71] *Ibid.*, 1211–1212.

[72] *Williams vs. Bruffy, supra; Underhill vs. Hernandez, supra, Oetjen vs. Central Leather Company, supra.*

[73] *Luther vs. Sagor, op. cit.*, p. 1211.

government and purported to act as such."[74] This satisfied the Lord Justice "that the decree of June 20, 1918, the seizure of the plaintiff's goods in January, 1919, and the subsequent sale of them to the defendants in August, 1920, were all acts of the Soviet Government," which then had been recognized, and which must be accepted by the English courts as such.[75]

Lord Justice Warrington, in his judgment, did not enter into as exhaustive an examination as Lord Justice Bankes. He conceded that, " on principle, recognition would be retroactive " although he was not certain as to the extent of the doctrine. On the extent of retroactivity he said that he had not been able to find any authority in English law on the point, but considered it necessary to examine the American precedents. In concluding his judgment on the point he was of the opinion that the Soviet government exercised sovereignty in Russia at the time of the decree of seizure on June 20, 1918. He felt that the court was entitled to infer that the government recognized as the Soviet government existed prior to the date of the decree, and has been the government of Russia ever since.[76]

Lord Justice Scrutton, in speaking of the information before the court from the Foreign Office, said: " We have from the Foreign Office a recognition of the Soviet Republic in 1921, as the *de facto* government, and a statement that in 1917, the Soviet authorities expelled the previous government recognized by His Majesty. It appears to me that this binds us to recognize the decree of 1918, by a department of the Soviet Republic, and the sale in 1920, by the Soviet Republic of property claimed by them to be theirs under that decree, as acts of a sovereign state, the validity of which cannot be questioned by the Courts of this country."[77] In other

[74] *Luther vs. Sagor, op. cit.*, p. 1212.
[75] *Ibid.*, pp. 1212–1213.
[76] *Ibid.*, p. 1216.
[77] *Ibid.*, p. 1218.

words, the Lord Justice considered recognition as retroactive "since the beginning of 1918."[78]

The Lord Justice considered it "unnecessary to express a final opinion whether and to what extent recognition of a *de facto* government is retrospective to previous acts and times." The recognition of a government as a *de facto* government in one year, "does not necessarily recognize that, from the first moment when some of the individuals supporting its cause began to resist or to attack the then established government, it was the *de facto* government." The difficulty of knowing at what time and over what area a struggling faction becomes a government *de facto* may well arise. Lord Justice Scrutton felt that the courts "cannot answer that question by knowing that some years later the Sovereign recognized it as the government *de facto* over a particular area. When that question is to be answered, the court must ask the Sovereign for information."[79] In the instant case the learned justice felt that the information from the Foreign Office was sufficiently definite to enable them to say that *de facto* recognition of the Soviet Republic was retrospective to the beginning of 1918. The learned justice doubted whether recognition validated everything "from the commencement of its existence."[80]

It thus appears that in this particular case, the courts looked to the political departments to stipulate the date to which recognition was to be retrospective. In *Luther vs. Sagor*,[81] the English courts interpreted the communications from the Foreign Office in this light. The implication of Lord Justice Scrutton's judgment is that the date should be fixed by the political departments for the Foreign Office, through its diplomatic and consular records, by its correspondence and state papers, is in a much better position to

[78] *Luther vs. Sagor., op. cit.*, p. 1219.
[79] *Ibid.*
[80] *Ibid.*
[81] 1921, L. R. 3 K. B. 532.

ascertain the commencement of the existence of a government than the courts.

It would not be advisable to have the political departments specify the date of origin of a stipulated government.[82] If the courts are in doubt they should make inquiry of the Foreign Office. The Foreign Office should present all the data to the court. In all cases the courts must interpret the communications from the Foreign Office and decide whether the recognized government was in existence at the time the acts in question were performed.

The courts created the fiction of retroactivity to evade the necessity of sitting in judgment on the acts of recognized foreign governments. Yet, by the creation of the fiction they have put the judiciary at variance with the political departments. Recognition is a political function. The courts regard it as retroactive in effect. This means that the English courts regarded all acts of the Soviet Republic as valid from "the beginning of 1918" while more than a year later,[82a] Mr. Lloyd George, the official spokesman for the political departments, had said: "The Bolshevist government has committed crimes against the allied subjects, and has made it impossible to recognize it even as a civilized government."[83] Two years later, in 1921, the English courts, through the fiction of retroactivity, expressly repudiated the statements of the ex-Prime Minister. The courts of the United States did exactly the same thing with reference to Mexico, by regarding as legal all the acts of the Caranza government "from the commencement of its existence," in spite of the vehement protests of President Wilson during its formative period.[84]

---

[82] Lord Justice Bankes in *Luther vs. Sagor* felt that the Foreign Office should specify the date of origin. Later he reversed his judgment on this point. See the interesting case of *White, Child and Beney, Ltd. vs. Simmons,* 1922, 127 L. T. R. 571.

[82a] April 16, 1919.

[83] Speech delivered before the House of Commons.

[84] "Annual Message to Congress," *New York Times,* December 3, 1913.

The legal effects of the withdrawal of diplomatic relations upon the doctrine of retroactivity do not appear from the cases. Although England has severed relations with the Soviet Republic it does not appear that the question has been raised in any of the reported cases.[85] In time the issue may prove to be a very potent one.

[85] See comment, *Legal Consequences of the Break with Russia,* 71 Sol. Jl., 1927, 504.

CHAPTER VI

Recognition and Legal Capacity

One of the most baffling problems which has been presented to the English and American courts has been that of the inability of the representatives and creatures of foreign states to protect themselves through the courts of non-recognizant states. This issue has been pushed into the limelight in the United States in recent years by a number of decisions denying the ability of the unrecognized Soviet Republic to sue or to protect itself from suit in the American courts.

By their decisions the courts have rendered it impossible for unrecognized *de facto* governments to protect their representatives or property through the courts of a non-recognizant state. In the absence of recognition an unrecognized government cannot sue. Likewise it may not claim immunity from suit. Recently the New York courts have shifted their position and held that immunity attaches in the absence of recognition. At the same time they hold that such *de facto* governments may not sue in their courts. In a few instances where the suit has been brought in the name of the state, rather than in the name of the government of the state, pending suits have been entertained or continued.

At the present time it is well settled that a foreign sovereign may sue in the courts of a foreign recognizant state. The issue was raised in the English courts early in the nineteenth century,[1] although no positive language on the issue was forthcoming from the courts: it is there by implication

[1] *City of Berne vs. Bank of England,* 9 Vesey Jr., 1804, 347, 32 English Reprints, 636; *Dolder vs. Bank of England,* 10 Vesey Jr., 1805, 353, 32 English Reprints, 881; *Dolder vs. Huntingfield,* 11 Vesey Jr., 1805, 284, 32 English Reprints, 1097.

only. The question was raised, seemingly, for the first time, in the reported cases in the United States in 1810, in *The King of Spain vs. Oliver.*[2] In that year Mr. Justice Washington refused to inquire, upon a motion, whether Ferdinand VII, King of Spain, could institute a suit, the government of the United States, at the time, not having acknowledged him as king. The case did not settle the issue. The court referred to English cases which had been cited but the report does not disclose the names of the cases.[3]

The first case in which the courts enunciated the principle as a positive rule of law was *Hullett and Company vs. King of Spain.*[4] The King of Spain sought to compel the defendants in England to deliver up certain moneys which belonged to certain Spanish nationals. The defendants objected that the recognized King of Spain could not sue in the English Courts.[5] The House of Lords held that the suit could be prosecuted and gave judgment for the King of Spain. The Lords held that a foreign sovereign could sue in both law and equity. Lord Redesdale in his judgment, said there was no doubt on the point.[6] Changing the tone of his judgment somewhat he observed that " there is no ground for the notion, that a foreign sovereign cannot sue in the

---

[2] 2 Washington C. C. 429.

[3] *Ibid.*, at 432.

[4] 1 Dow & Clark, 169, 6 English Reprints, 488. For the same case in the lower courts see *King of Spain vs. Machado,* 1827, 4 Russ. 225, 560. The case has been cited with approval in *United States of America vs. Wagner,* 1867, L. R. 3 Eq. 724, L. R. 2 Ch. 582; *Duke of Brunswick vs. King of Hanover,* 1844, 6 Beav. 13, 21, 37; *Mighell vs. Sultan of Johore,* 1894, 1 Q. B. 149; and *South African Republic vs. La Compaignie France Belge du Chemin du Fer du Nord,* 1897, 2 Ch. 487.

[5] Machado had received the money as the agent of the King of Spain from the French government and had deposited it with Hullett and Company of London. Machado refused to deliver up the money. Machado having left England the King of Spain instituted this suit to compel Hullet and Company to pay the money into court. They demurred that the foreign sovereign could not sue in the English equity courts. The court overruled the demurrer and allowed a recovery by the King of Spain. This was affirmed by the House of Lords in the instant case.

[6] Lord Redesdale said " I have no doubt but a foreign sovereign may sue in this country, otherwise there would be a right without a remedy. He sues here on behalf of his subjects, and if foreign sovereigns were not allowed to do that, the refusal might be a cause of war." 1 Dow & Clarke 169 at 175.

courts of this country. It appears to me clear that he can sue, and it would be monstrous injustice if he could not."[7] Subsequent cases have reaffirmed the point so that today in English law the statement that a foreign sovereign may sue in the courts of a recognizant state is accepted as commonplace.[8] The same principle is accepted as law in the United States,[9] the outstanding case being that of *The Sapphire*.[10] This case was before the Supreme Court of the United States in 1871.

The importance of *The Sapphire* has been revived in recent years in those cases involving the right of the Soviet Republic to maintain actions for state property in this country. For this reason, it is necessary to note carefully the facts of the case and words of the court.

It appears that in December, 1867, the French transport *Euryale* was damaged in a collision in the harbor of San Francisco. Thereupon a libel was filed in the American courts in the name of Napoleon III. The lower courts gave judgment in favor of the libellant, but an appeal was taken to the Supreme Court of the United States Meanwhile Napoleon III had been deposed, and at the trial before the Supreme Court in February, 1871, it was urged that the deposition of Napoleon III, in whose name the suit had been instituted, had abated the action. The court unanimously upheld the right to continue the suit although it found it necessary to reverse the decree of the lower courts on the facts.

Mr. Justice Bradley, who wrote the opinion of the court,

---

[7] 1 Dow & Clarke 169 at 176.

[8] See also *Emperor of Brazil*, 5 Dowling, 1837, 522; *Emperor of Austria vs. Day & Kossuth*, 1861, 3 De Gex, Fisher & Jones, 174; *Queen of Portugal*, 7 Clarke & Finelly, 1840, 466; *King of Greece*, 6 Dowling's Practice Cases, 12; *De Haber vs. Queen of Portugal*, 1851, 17 Q. B. 169.

[9] *King of Prussia vs. Kuepper's Administrator*, 22 Mo., 1856, 550, where the court held that the King of Prussia, who had become subrogated to rights of the owners of embezzled property against the embezzling officer, could maintain an action against such an absconded officer in the Missouri courts.

[10] 11 Wallace, 1870, 164.

said that "a foreign sovereign, as well as any other foreign person, who has a demand of a civil nature against any person here, may prosecute it in our courts. To deny him this privilege would manifest a want of comity and friendly feeling."[11] It should be noted that the justice felt that the right flowed from comity or courtesy. He did not regard capacity to sue as a matter of absolute right.[12] A change in the representative of the national sovereignty worked no change in the rights of the national sovereignty. "The next successor recognized by our government is competent to carry on a suit already commenced and receive the fruits of it."[13]

There has been no difficulty as regards the capacity of a recognized state to sue. But a state cannot in and of itself institute a suit. It can act only through authorized agents: government. Here lies the crux of the difficulty for the courts. Granted that a recognized government within a recognized state may sue, may an unrecognized government within a recognized state institute an action in the court of a non-recognizant state? The early decisions evade the issue. They register a doubt on the point.[14] There are dicta denying the right in a number of the cases. The courts have said that the power to sue depends upon recognition, which

---

[11] *The Sapphire,* 11 Wallace, 1871, 164 at 167.

[12] *Republic of Mexico vs. De Arrangois* (N. Y., 1855) 11 How. Pr. 1, affirmed the following year in 5 Duer 634; *Republic of Honduras vs. Soto,* 112 N. Y., 1889, 310, 19 N. E. 854; *United States of America vs. Wagner,* 1867, L. R. 2 Ch. App. 582, for similar views. *Columbia Government vs. Rothschild,* 1826, 1 Sim. 94, raised the question as to whether a suit could be maintained in the name of a government, and apparently answered it in the negative. More recently the federal courts allowed a suit to be instituted in the name of the Imperial Russian Government, although the pleadings were later amended and the name of the plaintiff changed to the State of Russia. *State of Russia vs. Lehigh Valley Railway Co.,* 293 Federal, 1919, 133; *Ibid.,* 293 Federal 135; *Ibid.,* 21 Federal 2d., 1927, 396. There are some cases which hold that a suit may be brought by an individual agent if he is duly authorized to sue by his own government. *The President of the United States of America vs. Drummond,* 33 Beav., 1864, 449; *Peel vs. Elliott,* 16 How. Pr. (N. Y. 1858), 481; *Yzuierdo vs. Clydebank,* etc., 1902, L. R. A. C. 524.

[13] 11 Wallace, 1871, 164 at 168.

[14] *King of Spain vs. Oliver,* 1819, Federal Case No. 7, 814; *The Hornet,* 1870, Federal Case No. 6,705; *City of Berne vs. Bank of England,* 1804, 9 Vex. Jr. 348; *Taylor vs. Barclay,* 1828, 2 Sim. 213.

implies that in the absence of recognition no action can be brought.[15] The courts have followed this implication: only one case being contra.

There is no doubt on the point in the New York courts. Whenever the question has been raised in that state the courts have uniformily held that " the test of a foreign sovereignty to sue " is its recognition by our own government.[16]

The outstanding case of recent years is *Russian Socialist Federated Soviet Republic vs. Cibrario.*[17] In 1918, the Cinematographic Committee of the Commissariat of Public Instruction of the Soviet government paid over to one Dr. William C. Huntington, the United States commercial attaché in Petrograd, one million dollars which was to be deposited in the National City Bank of New York. The defendant[18] entered into an agreement with the Soviet Republic to supply the plaintiff government with films for educational purposes. Defendant had the privilege of drawing on the account at the National City Bank.

It was rumored that through the creation of dummy corporations the defendant had converted approximately half of the initial deposit to his personal account Thereupon the Soviet government brought an action for an accounting in the New York court.[19] The court dismissed the action.

[15] *The Sapphire,* 11 Wallace, 1871, 164; *Republic of Honduras vs. Soto.,* 19 N. E. 845; *Republic of Mexico vs. De Arrangois,* 11 How. Pr. (N. Y.), 1855, 1; *Emperor of Austria vs. Day,* 3 De G. F. J. 217.

[16] *Republic of Mexico vs. De Arrangois,* 12 N. Y. Sup. Ct. 1855, 634 at 637; *Republic of Honduras vs. Soto,* 112 N. Y., 1889, 310, 19 N. E. 845; *Waldes vs. Basch,* 179 N. Y. Supp. 713. Affirmed in 181 N. Y. Supp., 1920, 918. In *Yucatan vs. Argumedo,* 157 N. Y. Supp., 1915, 219 the authorities are discussed at length.

[17] 191 N. Y. Supp., 1921, 543.

[18] Defendant was the purchasing agent of Cinematographic Committee of the Commissariat of Public Instruction of the Soviet Government.

[19] The case was finally disposed of in 1923, 235 N. Y. Supp. 255, by the Court of Appeals. Judge Andrews wrote an opinion holding that the right to sue depended upon comity and that in the absence of comity there was no such right. "We reach the decision, therefore, that a foreign power brings an action in our courts not as a matter of right. Its power to do so is the creature of comity. Until such government is recognized by the United States, no such comity exists. The plaintiff concededly has not been so recognized. There is, therefore, no proper party before us." *Ibid.,* p. 262.

This dismissal was affirmed by the appellate division of the Supreme Court on the ground that the plaintiff government had not been recognized by the United States government. The court proceeded on the theory that the power to sue depended on recognition; without it the court could not know that the plaintiff was a government.[20]

The court proceeded to examine the attitude of the political departments. It found that the Committee on Foreign Relations of the United States Senate on April 14, 1920, had referred to the Soviet Republic as " a regime which has never been recognized by the government of the United States, and which in International Law has no standing as a constituted authority." [21] It found that the State Department had issued an official public statement to the effect that" the United States has not recognized the Bolshevist regime at Moscow as a government " and warned the public that " extreme caution should be exercised as to representations made by any one purporting to represent the Bolshevist government." [22] The court also noted that one Ludwig C. A. K. Martens, who purported to represent the Soviet Republic in the United States, had been deported. " All these facts appearing without contradiction," said the court, " it follows that the plaintiff, never having been recognized as a sovereignty by the executive or legislative branches of the United States government," had no capacity to sue in the courts of New York State.[23]

The court cited *The Penza and Tobolsk et al*[24] and *The*

---

[20] The Court said: "In the case at bar, while plaintiff claims to be a *de-facto* government, and its title and right to sue alike rest on that claim, it is unable to show any acts of recognition by the government of this country. On the contrary, the record proves that, so far as this country is concerned, the plaintiff is non-existent as a sovereign." 191 N. Y. Supp., 1921, 543 at 549 and 550.

[21] 277 Federal, 1921, 91.

[22] 191 N. Y. Supp., 1921, 543 at 550.

[23] *Ibid.*

[24] 277 Federal, 1921, 91.

Rogdai [25] as being in accord. At first glance they appear to support the general principle. Actually, however, the cases may be distinguished. In the cases of *The Penza* and *The Rogdai,* the chief issue decided by the court was whether the court should hand over property which admittedly belonged to the Russian nation to the unrecognized Soviet faction, while the State Department continued to recognize the Provisional Government. The instant case involved the right of an unrecognized faction to protect its own property brought within the jurisdiction of a non-recognizant state.

Furthermore, in the instant case the money was brought to the United States with full cognizance by the American government. Thus one may argue that in such a case, where only property rights are involved, the foreign government, though unrecognized, should be allowed to sue. In support of the rule it must be said that such a denial of the right to sue, gives the State Department additional power in its negotiations with the unrecognized nation. Certainly that much can be said in favor of the rule enunciated by the court.[26] The allegation that the Soviet Republic was a sovereign government was not conclusive on the court.[27]

In *Taylor vs. Barclay* [28] a bill in equity was based on an agreement which it alleged had been made in 1825 by agents of "the government of the Federated Republic of Central America, which was a sovereign and independent state, recognized and treated as such by His Majesty, the King of these realms." On demurrer, Vice Chancellor Shadwell dismissed the bill, saying that he had communicated with the Foreign Office, and was "authorized to state that the Fed-

[25] 277 Federal, 1920, 133. In these two cases the Soviet government requested the federal courts to attach Russian vessels which were in the ports of the United States at the time and to decree that these vessels belonged to the Soviet rather than to the Provisional authorities.

[26] The court refused to allow an action for the same moneys to be brought by an agent of the Soviet Republic in his individual name. *Preobazhenski et al. vs. Cibrario,* 192 N. Y. Supp., 1922, 275, 199 App. Div. 899.

[27] 191 N. Y. Supp. 543 at 545.

[28] 2 Sim. 213.

eral Republic of Central America " had not been recognized as an independent government by the government of his country.[29] In the absence of recognition the right to sue was disallowed.

In some instances cases have been pending at the time of the overthrow of a recognized government. In these cases the courts have recognized the distinction between a state and a government and have held that a state, once recognized, is a continuing personality, and that suits instituted on behalf of the state remain unaffected by a change in the person of the sovereign or the form of government.

This point was before the Supreme Court of the United States for the first time in the case of *The Sapphire*. The court said that the reigning sovereign represents the national sovereignty. Sovereignty is continuous and perpetual, and resides in the proper successors of the sovereign for the time being. Napoleon was the owner of the vessel *Euryale*, not as an individual, but as sovereign of France. On his deposition the sovereignty did not change, but merely the person or persons in whom it resided. The foreign state was the true and real owner of its public vessels of war. The reigning emperor, or national assembly or other actual person or party in power was but the agent and representative of the national sovereignty or its rights. "The next successor recognized by our government is competent to carry on a suit already commenced and receive the fruits of it."[30] The vessel always belonged to the French nation For this reason the court allowed the suit to be continued.

This language was recently quoted with definite approval by Judge Goddard of the Federal District Court for the Southern District of New York in *Russian Government vs.*

[29] This doctrine was quoted with approval by the Supreme Court of the United States in *Jones vs. United States*, 137 U. S., 1890, 202 at 215. This method is the usual one followed by the courts in determining the exact attitude of the political departments of the government.

[30] *The Sapphire*, 11 Wallace, 1871, 164 at 168.

Lehigh Valley Railway Company.[31] The learned judge stated that the importance of recognizing governmental continuity, irrespective of considerations as to the existing form of a foreign government, or as to the human being in control at any particular time, is mentioned in many of the cases and text-books.

Suit had been instituted in 1918 by the then Provisional Government to recover alleged damages to the extent of $1,675,000, occasioned by the Black Tom explosion of 1916. The State Department in a communication before the court had stated that the Provisional Government had been recognized on March 22, 1927. One Bakhmeteff served as its ambassador to the United States from July 5, 1917, until June 30, 1922, after which date the State Department considered the custody of all property of the Russian Government in this country to have vested in Mr. Serge Ughet, the financial attaché of the Russian embassy. The State Department further advised that the Soviet regime had not been recognized.

The defendants moved for a dismissal of the suit, on the ground that the Provisional Government had been overthrown and was thereby deprived of authority to continue with the prosecution. The court said that the answer was that the Provisional Government had fallen when Mr. Bakhmeteff began the suits, and they were held to have been properly begun for the reason that at that time, 1918, our government recognized him as such ambassador. The court was bound by the action of the executive department. Regardless of whether the government had fallen, if the State Department considered the "financial attaché of the Russian embassy, whose diplomatic status with this government, was

[31] 293 Federal, 1923, 135 at p. 137. This case was before the federal courts for more than nine years. It was finally disposed of in August, 1927: 21 Federal, 2d, 1927, 396. See comments in 41 *Harv. Law Rev.*, 1927, 102; 20 *Law and Banking*, 1927, 284; 13 *Cornell L. Q.*, 1928, 297; 37 *Yale L. J.*, 1928, 360.

not considered to be altered," as vested with the custody of the property of the Russian government after Mr Bakhmeteff's retirement, such determination was conclusive and binding upon the court.

No precedent for such a situation was presented to the court and after diligent research Judge Goddard confessed that he was unable to find one. He felt, however, that our government may have adopted this attitude for the express purpose of preventing what otherwise would have been a loss of right to Russia, " because of its refusal to recognize the present regime now functioning in Russia." He granted the motion to entitle the plaintiff *The State of Russia.* The case was originally styled Imperial Russian Government.

The court judicially recognized that the State of Russia survived,[32] regardless of the name or form of the government. The court said that the real party in interest was the State of Russia, and that Russia, the state, still lived and was a continuing entity in the contemplation of the law. An attempt was next made in 1924 to secure a writ of prohibition from the Supreme Court of the United States to prevent further proceedings in the action.[33] This attempt failed by a denial of the writ.

The trial was held in the spring of 1925 It resulted in a verdict for the plaintiff, whereupon an appeal was taken to the Circuit Court of Appeals for the Second District. At the beginning of the trial a motion was made on behalf of the Soviet government for the appointment of a receiver to conserve the proceeds of the action. The motion was denied by Judge Mack as prematurely made, without prejudice to its renewal at a later date. A similar motion after verdict was similarly disposed of because of the projected appeal.

At the trial before Circuit Judges Manton, L. Hand, and Swan, the same objections were urged against a continuation

---

[32] The change in the name of the plaintiff was consistent with Mr. Justice Bradley's opinion in *The Sapphire,* 11 Wallace, 164.

[33] 265 U. S., 1924, 573.

of the suit. Judge Manton, who delivered the opinion, said that "the right to recover damages for breach of this carrier's obligation became the property of the State of Russia on July 30, 1916, when the loss occurred. The government was then the Russian Imperial Government." [34]

The court created the important distinction between a state and its government. The court defined a state as a community or assemblage of men, and a government as the political agency through which the state acts in international relations.[35] The foreign state is the true or real owner of its property, and the agency the representative of the national sovereignty.[36]

The Circuit Court of Appeals held that the various preliminary motions to dismiss the complaint had been properly rejected because there had been no change recognized in the government or agency for Russia by the political branches of our government. Judicially the State of Russia continued.[37]

The distinction between the state and its government was important. Abatement of the action could be sustained only by reason of the non-existence of the state, or the renunciation by our government of the agency once accredited and recognized. The agency thus employed was obliged to institute and continue [38] the suit until some other government was recognized by the political departments of our government.

The state and the government are distinct legal entities. The granting or refusal of recognition to a government within a state has nothing to do with the recognition of the

[34] *Lehigh Valley Railway Co., vs. State of Russia,* 21 Federal 2d, 1927, 396, at 399.

[35] *State of Texas vs. White,* 7 Wallace, 1868, 700; *Cherokee Nation vs. Georgia* 5 Peters, 1861, 52; and *Foulke, International Law,* Vol. 1, pp. 62, 82, 102, and 192 cited as in accord.

[36] *The Sapphire vs. Napolean* III, 11 Wallace, 1871, 164; *The Rogdai,* 278 Federal 294.

[37] *Lehigh Valley Railway Company vs. State of Russia,* 21 Federal (2d), 1927, 396 at 400.

[38] *Republic of Mexico vs. De Arangois,* 12 N. Y. Sup. Ct. 643.

state itself.[39] If a foreign state refuses to recognize a change in the form of government of an old state, the state does not thereby lose its recognition as an international person.[40] Therefore, said the Circuit Court of Appeals, the instant suit " did not abate by the change in the form of government in Russia; the state is perpetual and survives the form of its government. *The Sapphire, supra.* The recognized government may carry on the suit, at least until the new government becomes accredited " in the United States by recognition.[41] The court affirmed the award of the lower court. It allowed damages to the State of Russia to the extent of $556,166.58 plus $297,734.50 interest.

An appeal was taken to the Supreme Court of the United States. On December 12, 1927, the Supreme Court refused to review the petition for a *writ of certiorari* to the Circuit Court of Appeals, Second District.[42] Thereupon the Lehigh Valley Railway Company asked that the payment be made to the court, which would have the power to turn it over to the proper Russian representative. This course was adopted. It was thought to be the best way to protect the judgment debtor against possible suits by the Soviet government.

---

[39] " Changes in the government or the internal polity of a state do not as a rule affect its position in International Law. Monarchy may be transformed into a republic, or a republic into a Monarchy; absolute principles may be substituted for constitutional, or the reverse; but, though the government changes, the nation remains, with rights and obligations unimpaired." Moore, *Digest,* Vol. 1, p. 249.

[40] Oppenheim, *International Law,* Vol. 1, p. 141; Moore, Digest, Vol. 1, p. 298. "Recognition of a new state must not be confounded with other recognitions." Recognition of changes in government is important. But the grating or refusing of such recognition " has nothing to do with recognition of the State itself. If a foreign State refuses the recognition of . . . a change in the form of the Government of an old State, the latter does not thereby lose its recognition as an International Person, although no official intercourse is henceforth possible between the two States as long as recognition is not given either expressly or tacitly. And if recognition of a new title of an old State is refused, the only consequence is that such State cannot claim any privileges connected with the new title." I Oppenheim, p. 139.

[41] *Lehigh Valley Railway Company vs. State of Russia,* 21 Federal (2d), 1927, 396 at 401.

[42] Memorandum decision, October term, 1927, 48 *Supreme Court Rep. . . . , advance sheets,* West Pub. Company, January 15, 1928, p. 159.

Thereupon, the Lehigh Valley Railway Company tendered its check to the Federal District Court for $984,104.62. On December 22, 1927, the money was paid by the clerk of the court to Mr. Serge Ughet, the financial attaché of the Russian embassy.[43]

Mr. Charles Recht, representative for the Soviet government in the United States, announced that he would file a protest. The writer is not aware of any protest having been filed. But it should be remarked, that based upon both reason and precedent, such an action would not be entertained.[44]

---

[43] *New York Times*, December 23, 1927.

[44] *The Rogdai*, 278 Federal, 1920, 294, at 296 where District Judge Dietrich in speaking of a controversy over Russian property, the vessel ***Rogdai***, said: "It will be noted that fundamentally there is no controversy touching the real ownership of the transport; she belongs to Russia; no adverse claim, either public or private is involved. By Russia, of course, I do not refer to any particular political group or organization, but to the National entity or sovereignty." Did Martens or Bakhmetieff represent the National Sovereignty of Russia? "Plainly, consideration of such an issue upon the merits would of necessity draw us into the realm of international diplomacy; and it is equally plain that no useful purpose could be subserved by such an investigation. If the court assumes the right to make an original inquiry, it logically follows that it must exercise its own independent judgment upon the facts thus disclosed and reach an independent conclusion. In that view it might recognize Martens, while Washington recognizes Bakhmeteff. To state the proposition is to discredit it. True, the Russian sovereignty may speak through different representatives, and it may have business agents as well as diplomatic agents; but all must derive their authority from a single source. The National Will must be expressed through a single political organization; two conflicting governments cannot function at the same time. By the same token, discordant voices cannot express the sovereign will of the American Nation. Either the executive or the judiciary must be supreme in a given sphere.

"The question at issue is one of state: It involves international relations, and is primarily for the State Department. If, as contended . . . it be granted that a revolution has taken place in Russia, and that the Soviet Republic is in actual control, the question when, if at all, such *de facto* government shall be recognized, is a political one. It involves considerations of national policy, which are not justiciable, and touching it the voice of the Chief Executive is the voice, not of a branch of the government, but of the national sovereignty, equally binding upon all departments. . . . It is to be reiterated that we are not here concerned with the claim of a third party, either public or private, to the property in controversy, nor have we a case where the Department of State has failed to act, or where it is sought only to protect a party in actual possession. The case is one where the court is asked to take property conceded to be that of the Russian Nation from the actual possession of those whom the State Department unmistakably recognizes as the accredited agent of the Russian government, and turn it over to other persons whom that department has declined to recognize as having

The instant case differs from that of *The Sapphire* in that in the instant case the Provisional Government had ceased to function in Russia, whereas the governmental successor of Napoleon III was admittedly functioning in France. This acknowledged difference in facts did not disturb the court because in both cases the political departments had assumed an attitude. In the instant case it was negative, while in *The Sapphire* it was positive The court took judicial notice of each determination. Both were binding on the court in its decisions.

This case establishes the doctrine that the rights and liabilities of a state are unaffected by a recognized change either in the form or personnel of its government, howsoever accomplished, whether by revolution or otherwise. "No other doctrine is thinkable, at least among nations which have any conception of international honor." [45] The principle applies

any official standing whatsoever." See also 21 Fed. (2d), 1927, 396 at 400. The only case contra is *United States of Mexico vs. National Bank of Haverhill* reported in 17 A. J., 1923, 743. Two Mexican officials fled to the United States with 140,000 pesos, which they deposited with the National Bank of Haverhill, Mass. The "Government of Mexico" secured a temporary injunction forbidding the withdrawal of the money. At the trial in May, 1923, the district attorney presented on behalf of the Attorney-General of the United States a statement from the State Department to the effect that "the Government of the United States, has not accorded recognition to the administration now functioning in Mexico, and therefore has at present no official relations with that administration. This fact, however, does not affect the recognition of the Mexican state itself, which for years has been recognized by the United States as an "international person" as that term is understood in international practice." The plaintiff moved to amend the pleadings: to substitute "United States of Mexico" for "Government of Mexico." In the absence of recognition the defendant questioned the capacity of the plaintiff to sue. Thereupon evidence was presented which showed that the Obregon government was in effective control of Mexico, that negotiations were being carried on between the states, that it had a chargé d'affaires at the Mexican Embassy building at Washington. On this evidence the court continued the injunction. Recognition was accorded the Obregon government on August 31, 1923. See *State of Yucatan vs. Argumedo,* 157 N. Y. Supp., 1915, 219, where the New York Supreme Court held that recognition was sufficiently retroactive to validate a similar suit.

[45] *Agency of Canadian Car and Foundry Company, Limited et al vs. American Can Company,* 253 Federal, 1918, 152 at 157. District Judge Mayer also said that "the change in the form of Russian government and the fact that in the original papers that government was described as the "Imperial Russian Government," while the settlement papers are executed on behalf of the "Russian Government" are matters of no significance."

only to cases entertained by foreign states to enforce demands of a strictly civil nature.[46]

Turning to the second phase of this chapter we find that it is firmly settled, both in English and American jurisprudence, that a sovereign state is not, without its consent, subject to suit either in its own courts or in those of a foreign state.[47] The basis of immunity from suits in its own courts was stated by Mr. Justice Holmes in *Kawananakoa vs. Polyblank.*[48] The learned justice said that " a sovereign is exempt from suit not because of any formal conception or obsolete theory, but on the logical and practical ground that there can be no legal right as against the authority that makes the law on which the right depends." [49] In recent years the doctrine of immunity of a sovereign from suit in its own courts has been subjected to much criticism.[50]

See also *United States vs. McRea,* 1869, L. R. 8 Eq. 69; Moore, *Digest,* Vol. 1, p. 249 and 251; *Comanche County vs. Lewis,* 133 U. S., 1889, 198 at 205 where Mr. Justice Brewer said a change in form does not destroy responsibility.

[46] *Wisconsin vs. Pelican Insurance Company,* 127 U. S., 1887, 265 at 290; *Russian Government vs. Lehigh Valley Railway,* 293 Federal 1923, 135.

[47] This point is so thoroughly entrenched in the law that citations are unnecessary. On the first point one of the most interesting cases in *The Queen vs. McCleod,* 8 Canada Supreme Court Reports, 1882, 1, which involved the legal status of the Intercolonial Railway of Canada. In the initial suit the evidence showed that the railway in question was in such a poor state of repair that for a mile on each side of the curve at which the accident in question occurred, many of the ties could be kicked to pieces and that spikes could be picked from the rotten ties. The Supreme Court reversed a $36,000 judgment on the sole ground that a sovereign could not be sued in the courts of his own country. In a fifty page opinion the court discusses the authorities at length. See also *Kansas vs. Colorado,* 206 U. S., 1906, 46; *Oregon vs. Hitchcock,* 202 U. S., 1906, 60; *United States vs. Lee,* 106 U. S., 1882, 196; *The Davis,* 10 Wallace, 1869, 15; *The Siren vs. United States,* 7 Wallace, 1868, 152; *Beers vs. Arkansas,* 20 Howard, 1857, 527; *United States vs. Clarke,* 8 Peters, 1834, 436; *Brown vs. United States,* 6 Ct. of Cl., 1870, 171; *Brunswick vs. Hanover,* 6 Beav. 1, 49 English Reprints, 724; *The Athol.,* 1 Wm. Rob. 374. The best and most exhaustive historical discussion will be found in *Briggs vs. The Lightboats,* 93 Mass., 1863, 157 beginning at 166. On the second point, immunity from suit in a foreign state, see *The Exchange* 7 Cranch, 1812, 116; *Roumania vs. Guaranty Trust Co.,* 250 Federal, 1918, 341, same case 246 U. S., 1918, 663; *De Simone vs. Transportes Maritimos Do Estado,* 199 N. Y. Supp., 1922, 864; *Compania Mercantil Argentian vs. United States Shipping Board,* 1924, 4 T. L. R. 601.

[48] 205 United States, 1906, 349.

[49] *Ibid.,* 349 at 353.

[50] Laski, *Responsibility of the State in England,* 32 Harvard Law Rev.,

The basis of the immunity of a foreign sovereign from suit is different. Immunity from suit in its own courts flows, as was stated by Mr. Justice Holmes, from the historical belief that the sovereign is above the law The immunity of a foreign sovereign flows from considerations of practical expediency in friendly international intercourse.[51] The basis of the immunity was early given by Mr. Chief Justice Marshall in *The Exchange*.[52] Discussing the non-jurisdiction of the United States courts over a French war vessel, he declared that the vessel was exempt from process.[53] Resort was had to analogy rather than to precedent. The basis of Mr. Chief Justice Marshall's declaration was that to permit process to issue would " vex the peace of nations."

Recently the question has been raised as to whether the immunity from suit extends to unrecognized governments within recognized states. The issue appears to have been raised for the first time in *Wulfsohn vs. Russian Socialist Federated Soviet Republic*.[54] Wulfsohn and Company were

---

1918, 20; Duguit, *Law in the Modern State*, 1919, *Passim;* Borchard, *Government Responsibility in Tort—A Proposed Statutory Reform*, A. B. A. J., August 1925, p. 495.

[51] Weston, *Actions against the Property of Sovereigns*, 32 Harvard Law Rev., 1919, 266.

[52] 7 Cranch, 1812, 116.

[53] "This full and absolute territorial jurisdiction being alike the attribute of every sovereign, and being incapable of conferring extraterritorial power, would not seem to contemplate foreign sovereigns, nor their sovereign rights, as its objects. One sovereign being in no respect amenable to another; and being bound by obligations of the highest character not to degrade the dignity of his nation, by placing himself or its sovereign rights within the jurisdiction of another, can be supposed to enter a foreign territory only under an express license, or in the confidence that the immunities belonging to his independent sovereign station, though not expressly stipulated, are reserved by implication, and will be extended to him.

"This perfect equality and absolute independence of sovereigns, and their common interest impelling them to mutual intercourse, and an interchange of good offices with each other, have given rise to a class of cases in which every sovereign is understood to waive the exercise of a part of that exclusive territorial jurisdiction, which has been stated to be the attribute of every nation.

"One of these is admitted to be the exemption of the person of the sovereign from arrest or detention within a foreign terrritory." *The Exchange*, 7 Cranch, 1812, 116 at 137.

[54] 234 N. Y., 1923, 372. Same case in 202 App. Div., 1922, 421. Reargument denied, 235 N. Y., 1923, 579. See also 266 U. S., 1924, 580.

importers of furs. On June 25, 1920, a large quantity of their furs, valued at $127,935.75, was seized at Yakutsk. Wulfsohn brought an action in the New York courts for conversion and secured an attachment on certain properties of the defendant which were within the jurisdiction of the court at that date.

On December 16, 1921, an appellate division of the New York Supreme Court had held that the Soviet Republic could not sue in the New York Courts.[55] On analogy the defendants reasoned that it could not be sued. Thereupon the defendants moved to set aside service of summons and dismiss the complaint. The defendant argued that it could not be sued because it was a foreign government and immune from process. The Supreme Court held that the immunity of a foreign government from suit is not based upon any absolute right by virtue of its sovereignty, but upon international comity. In the absence of any international comity existing between the United States and the Soviet Republic, the court held that it had no valid claim to the immunity. The inability to sue did not create any immunity from suit. The court allowed the recovery against the Soviet Republic as a public corporation.

This determination was affirmed by the appellate division of the second department of the Supreme Court.[56] The appellate division concluded that immunity from suit is based on international comity rather than upon absolute right and that the Soviet Republic, being unrecognized and unacknowledged was " not entitled to the immunities accorded to recognized governments." The appellate division relied heavily upon *Luther vs. Sagor*,[57] where, in the initial case, Judge Roche had said that the Soviet government was not " able

[55] *Russian Socialist Federated Soviet Republic vs. Cibrario*, 198 App. Div., 1921, 869; affirmed in 235 N. Y., 1923, 255.

[56] 202 App. Div., 1922, 421. Both the ability to sue and the immunity from suit are based on international comity, said the court.

[57] 1921, L. R. 1 K. B. 456; 1921, L. R. 3 K. B. 532.

by decree to deprive the plaintiff of its property." Lord Justice Scrutton, in the same case on appeal, after recognition, in explaining the immunities and privileges accorded on recognition, had said that should there be any government which appropriates other peoples property without compensation, the remedy would appear to be to refuse to recognize it as a sovereign state. "Then the courts could investigate the title without infringing the comity of nations." [58] The appellate division held that the Soviet Republic was " a foreign corporation aggregate " and liable to suit.

Thereafter the question was certified to the Court of Appeals whether an unrecognized government could be sued. The Court of Appeals answered the question in the negative, reversed the order of attachment and granted the motion to vacate the judgment and dismiss the complaint.[59]

The opinion, written by Judge Andrews, was based upon the ground that a *de facto* government is immune from suit regardless of recognition because the immunity does not rest upon comity but upon fundamental considerations of international relations. The court said: " They may not bring a foreign sovereign before our bar, not because of comity, but because he has not submitted himself to our laws. Without his consent he is not subject to them. Concededly that is so as to a foreign government that has received recognition.[60]

" But, whether recognized or not, the evil of such an at-

[58] Equally strong language was used by Mr. Chief Justice Marshall in *United States vs. Percheman,* 7 Peters 1833, 51. " It may not be unworthy to remark," said he, " that it is very unusual, even in cases of conquest, for the conqueror to do more than to displace the sovereign and assume dominion over the country. The modern usage of nations, which has become law, would be violated; that sense of justice and of right which is acknowledged and felt by the whole civilized world would be outraged, if private property should be generally confiscated, and private rights annulled," p. 86.

[59] 234 N. Y., 1923, 372.

[60] A number of cases are cited, among which are, *Porto Rico vs. Rosaly y Castillo,* 227, U. S., 1913, 270; *Hassard vs. United States of Mexico,* 29. Misc. Rep., 1903, 511, 61, N. Y. Supp. 939, affirmed in 173 N. Y. 645, 66 N. E. 1110; *Mason vs. Intercolonial Railway of Costa Rica,* 44 L. T. 199.

tempt would be the same. 'To cite a foreign potentate into a municipal court for any complaint against him in a public capacity is contrary to the law of nations and an insult which he is entitled to resent.' [61] In either case to do so would 'vex the peace of nations.' In either case the hands of the State Department would be tied. Unwillingly it would find itself involved in disputes it might think unwise. Such is not the proper method of redress if a citizen of the United States is wronged. The question is a political one, not confided to the courts but to another department of government. Whenever an act done by a sovereign in his sovereign character is questioned it becomes a matter of negotiation, or of reprisals or of war." [62]

Immediately a motion for a reargument was made. This was denied,[63] but a *writ of error* was granted to the Supreme Court of the United States. On motion this writ was dismissed by the Supreme Court on the ground that no question of jurisdiction was involved.[64]

The instant case is a notable departure from former decisions. It is at variance with the law laid down by the English Court of Appeal in *Luther vs. Sagor.*[65] The case implies that the sovereign immunity attaches to a recognized state, and as such may be claimed by any government which professes to represent the national sovereignty.

It appears that the Court of Appeals, in the *Cibrario case,* by holding that an unrecognized government may not sue, thereby implied that such unrecognized governments were liable to suit. This implication was confirmed by the initial decisions in the *Wulfsohn case.* Yet, this view was put at

[61] *De Haber vs. Queen of Portugal,* 17 Q. B. 169, 1851, 117 English Reprints 1246.

[62] 234 N. Y., 1923, 372 at 376.

[63] 235 N. Y., 1923, 579.

[64] 266 U. S., 1924, 580.

[65] 1921, L. R. 1 K. B. 456; 1921, L. R. 3 K. B. 1921, 532. The English Court of Appeal did not hold that the Soviet Republic was liable to suit. It held that in the absence of recognition no validity would be given to its confiscation decrees once the property is brought within the jurisdiction of the English courts. They were regarded as a nullity.

rest by the reversal of the *Wulfsohn* case at the hands of the Court of Appeals. This court held that the Soviet Republic was immune from process.

Wulfsohn weakened his case by an admission that the Soviet Republic was the existing *de facto* government of Russia, and this was pointed out by the Court of Appeals. Yet, regardless of the admission, the decision seems to be thoroughly sound. The *de facto* character of the Soviet Republic was a matter of common knowledge. It was being sued for an exercise of authority within its own jurisdiction. If the Court of Appeals had insisted upon making recognition the criterion of immunity, the court would have blundered into the very sort of political question which it is the rule in regard to recognition to avoid. The distinction is a new one which the writer regards as sound.

Subsequent decisions show that the courts regard the Wulfsohn case as good law. In *Nankivel vs. Omsk All-Russian Government,*[66] the Court of Appeals reaffirmed this new principle of immunity from suit of an unrecognized government within a recognized state

In the *Nankivel case* a default judgment for $96,392.38 had been obtained. The plaintiff attempted to enforce this default judgment against certain banks which they claimed held property of the defendant government. The banks, against which the proceedings had been brought, contended that the default judgment which formed the basis of the proceedings was void because the defendant was either a foreign *de facto* government immune from suit, or else totally defunct and out of existence at the time of the commencement of the action. Both contentions were denied by the Supreme Court and its appellate division.[67] Thereafter the question whether the defendant had, prior to the commencement of the action, so totally ceased to exist as to render the

[66] 237 N. Y., 1923, 150.
[67] 203 App. Div., 1921, 740.

default judgment void, was certified to the Court of Appeals. This court unanimously answered the question in the affirmative, Judge Pound writing the decision.

The Court of Appeals held that the proof was conclusive that, prior to the commencement of the action, the defendant had ceased to exist because it ceased to govern. The Soviet government had defeated its armies and driven its commander into exile. The default judgment therefore was void and subject to attack by third parties.[68] So long as the Omsk Government maintained an independent existence it was immune from suit for its governmental acts. "Lack of recognition by the United States Government," said the court, "does not permit an individual suitor to bring a *de facto* government before the bar.[69] To sue a sovereign state is to insult it in a manner which it may treat with silent contempt. It is not bound to come into our courts and plead its immunity. It is liable to suit only when its consent is duly given.[70] When defendant was extinguished by conquest, it became, so far as its continued corporate existence is concerned, as if it had never existed." [71]

---

[68] "It is a matter of common knowledge and the moving papers establish the fact that if the Omsk All-Russian Government was at any time even a *de facto* government in the international sense," it was created as such with Admiral Kolchak at its head at Omsk in November 1918, and recognized by General Simionoff and his forces at Vladivostok, and thereafter driven out of all regional control by the Bolshevik government, not later than March, 1920. "During its ephemeral and disastrous career, it asserted its authority over a portion of the inhabitants of the former Russian Empire who had, after the debacle, separated themselves from the central government and established an independent sovereign government over a limited territory in Siberian Russia. It was not a subordinate state nor a civil division of the Soviet Republic. It was either what plaintiffs choose to call it, a *de facto* government, and therefore sovereign in character, or it was a mere aggregation of robbers and murderers, outside the protection of the laws of war. When its leaders failed in their endeavors to establish themselves permanently; when the armed forces of the Soviet Government defeated its armies, overran its territory, executed Kolchak and drove Seminoff into exile, its sovereignty ceased and the Omsk All-Russian Government utterly perished. Whether alive or dead, no valid judgment could be obtained against it." 237 N. Y. 150 at 156.

[69] *Wulfsohn vs. Russian Socialist Federated Soviet Republic,* 234 N. Y. 372.

[70] *Porto Rico vs. Rosaly,* 227 U S., 1913, 270.

[71] *Nankival vs. Omsk All-Russian Government,* 237 N. Y., 1923, 150 at 156 and 157.

The respondents then contended that even though the objections did exist, they could not be raised by third parties. The court thought the necessities of the case compelled an opposite conclusion. The defendant was not called upon to plead its immunity. The dead government could not plead its own demise in abatement of the action. It could not by default admit its own existence. "The fact of such existence could not be litigated in the action. Acquiesence will not be inferred from the silence of the dead. The judgment was void," said the court. The appellants were affected by it and had a right to ask that its nullity be officially declared.[72] The Omsk All-Russian Government was immune from suit, said the court.

We conclude that the immunity from suit of a recognized state with a recognized government has become well settled. There appears to be only one exception. This refers to the immunity of state property used for commercial purposes. The judges have not agreed on this point.

With the deposition of kings and the passing of the divine right theory, sovereign immunity has gradually weakened. With the increased socialization of the state and the expansion of governmental activities, the distinction between public and commercial functions has become more obscure. Still greater obscurity is to be expected in the future. If the immunity is left to the courts to be decided upon principle confusion may be the result.

Although Mr. Justice Holmes has stated that there can be no remedy as against the authority which makes the law, yet the writer defends the position that such should not be the rule. Those charged with the dispension of justice, should be held to account in order that justice may be done. Slowly, but surely, this view is working its way into the law. Legislatures, both state and national, have shown a desirable tendency to cancel the immunities of the government in cer-

[72] 237 N. Y., 1923, 150 at 158.

tain of its activities. The courts in the United States have demonstrated less reverence for the immunity than in former times.

As early as 1882, the cases were reviewed, a dissent was expressed and the modern tendency was explained by Mr. Justice Gray of the Supreme Court.[73] More recently the courts have held that Congress did not intend that the Emergency Fleet Corporation of the United States Shipping Board should be immune.[74] The Supreme Court unanimously agreed upon this point, although the court was divided as to whether such suits should be instituted in the Court of Claims or in the Federal District Courts. It appears that the immunity of similarly engaged domestic vessels has been canceled by Italy.[75]

In the United States the problem of the immunity of foreign government owned and government operated merchant vessels was presented to the Supreme Court for the first time in 1926. The sole question before the court was whether a ship owned by Italy and operated by it in the

---

[73] *United States vs. Lee,* 106 U. S., 1882, 196, from 223 to 251.

[74] *Sloan Shipyards vs. United States Emergency Fleet Corporation,* and two other cases considered together, 258 U. S., 1921, 249, where the sole issue was whether the Emergency Fleet Corporation was liable to suit. It involved an interpretation of the will of Congress. Mr. Justice Holmes, who delivered the opinion of the court, held that it was not immune. Mr. Chief Justice Taft delivered an instructive dissenting opinion in which Mr. Justice Van Devanter and Mr. Justice Clarke concurred, in which they did not disagree as to liability but only as to the court in which such suits should be instituted. Other cases involving liability of the Emergency Fleet Corporation are *Stewart vs. U. S. Shipping Board Emergency Fleet Corporation,* 7 Federal 2d, 1925, 676; *Mallory S. S. Co. vs. Garfield,* 10 Federal 2d, 1926, 664; *United States Shipping Board Emergency Fleet Corporation vs. Texas Star Flour Mills,* 12 Federal 2d, 1926, 9; *Ibid. vs. Rosenberg Brothers & Company,* 12 Federal 2d, 1926, 721; *Marshall Hall Grain Company vs. United States Shipping Board Emergency Fleet Corporation,* 14 Federal 2d, 1926, 141; *Fidelity Trust Company of New York vs. United States Shipping Board Emergency Fleet Corporation,* 15 Federal 2d, 1926, 600; *Cohn vs. United States Shipping Board,* 20 Federal 2d, 1927, 398.

[75] 277 Federal, 1921, 473. It was this non-immunity from suit in Italy which served as the basis of Judge Mack's decision. *United States vs. Sisal Sales Corporation,* 274 U. S., 1927, 268, reversing the decision of the trial court which had regarded *American Banana Company vs. United Fruit Company,* 213 U. S., 1909, 359 as controlling. Mr. Justice McReynolds delivered the opinion of the court. No cases are cited in accord.

carriage of merchandise for hire, was immune from arrest under process based on a libel *in rem* by a private suitor in a Federal District Court exercising admiralty jurisdiction.[76] The court quoted at length from The *Exchange* [77] and *The Parlement Belge* [78] and concluded that the Italian vessel was was immune from process "as an instrument of sovereignty." [79]

In a recent case, 1927, the Federal District Court for the Southern District of New York, held that a corporation which was sponsored and favored by a foreign government was liable for breach of contract and that the property of such a corporation was not exempt from execution as the property of a foreign government.[80]

On May 17, 1919, the Swiss Department of Commerce, acting under a delegation of authority from the Federal Council, organized the Société Cooperative Suisse des Charbons to purchase and import coal into Switzerland. Certain Swiss coal importers were eligible to membership and 6 per

---

[76] *Berizzi Bros. Co. vs. S. S. Pesaro,* 271 U. S., 1926, 562. Mr. Van Devanter said that "this precise question has never been considered by this court before," p. 570.

[77] 7 Cranch, 116.

[78] 1880, L. R. 5 P. D. 197.

[79] As early as 1918 the district courts had affirmed the immunity of such vessels. See *The Maipo,* 252 Federal, 1918, 627, for denial of a libel for cargo damages against a Chilean vessel, by District Judge Mayer "on authority and in consideration of existing conditions." The best reasoning is to be found in *The Maipo,* 259 Federal, 1919, 367, where Circuit Judge Hough sitting in admiralty said: . . . "I do not think the enormous extension of sovereign privilege demanded by vessels in all kinds of business of late months and years indicates any advance or change in the law at all. The law remains the same. What has changed is the view which the governments of the world assume toward public duties or public enterprises." The reason back of the exemption of war vessels is that it is a part of the exercise or manifestation of sovereign power: not because it is a public vessel as such.

"Now, it may be the opinion of counsel, as it assuredly is my opinion, that when a sovereign republic, empire or whatnot, goes into business and engages in the carrying trade, it ought to be subject to the liabilities of carriers just as much as any private person; but I think it must be plain that if I, in my official capacity, were to assert that view and enforce it, I would be assuming (in this case), as one of the humbler officers of the government of the United States, to define for the Republic of Chile what that republic should consider to be governmental function."

[80] *Coale et al. vs. Société* etc., 21 Fed. (2d), 1927, 180.

cent was to be paid upon the capital invested. Profits above 6 per cent went to the government. The government appointed seven of the seventeen directors. The charter and amendments and rules were subject to the approval of the government. These facts were set up by the corporation in answer to a suit for breach of contract. The plaintiff demurred and the court sustained the demurrer. The court said that "if the Swiss government chose to do its business by means of the Société, the latter as a corporate entity, was liable for its corporate obligations. . . . If the Société had contracted as the agent of the Swiss government, the case might have been different; but in this instance the Swiss minister signed the contract for the corporation."

Two cases were cited by the court in support of the doctrine.[81] Examination reveals that neither of the cases are strictly applicable inasmuch as they did not involve the suit of foreign government favored corporations. The cases involved the suit of domestic government owned corporations.

In the instant case the court proceeded on the theory that the corporation is a separate entity, distinct from the government or the stockholders. The court followed the doctrine stated in innumerable cases that a corporation is distinct from its stockholders.[82]

In the light of this decision the following paragraph from Circuit Judge Hough's opinion in *The Maipo*,[83] is provocative of much thought: "If the Republic of Chile considers it a governmental function to go into the carrying trade, as would appears to be the case here, that is the business of the Republic of Chile: and if we do not approve of it, if we do not like it, if we do not wish any longer to accord that respect to the property so engaged, which has hitherto been accorded

---

[81] *Commercial Pacific Cable Co., vs. Philippine National Bank,* 263 Fed., 1920, 218, affirmed 269 Fed., 1921, 1022; and *U. S. vs. Strang.* 254 U. S., 1921, 491.

[82] *Donnell vs. Herring-Hall-Marvin Safe Co.,* 208 U. S. 267; *Continental Tyre and Rubber Co., Ltd., vs. Daimler Co., Ltd.,* 1 K. B., 1915, 893.

[83] 259 Fed., 1919, 367 at 368.

to government property, then we must say so through diplomatic channels, and not through the judiciary. Otherwise, the judiciary are really contributing to what might become, under conceivable circumstances, a *casus belli.*" [84]

In summary it may be said that a recognized government in a recognized state may sue in the courts of a recognizant state. An unrecognized government in a recognized state may not sue. This is the law and the writer regards it as eminently sound. However, a recognized government whose non-existence is a matter of world notoriety may continue suits previously instituted provided they are continued in the name of the state, and not in the name of the government. A number of the cases imply that an unrecognized state may be sued; that it may be made a party defendant as a *de facto* public corporation, while at the same time it is incapable of being a party plaintiff. Recently, however, some of the courts have disallowed suits against unrecognized *de facto* governments on the theory that the immunity attaches to the state and may be claimed by the *de facto* as well as by the *de jure* agents of such state.

There has been much discussion by the courts as to the basis of the immunity from suit. The initial basis was comity, or courtesy between nations, rather than absolute right.[85] The immunity was allowed in order to preserve the peace and harmony of nations: to regulate state intercourse

---

[84] A similar case is *The Carlo Poma,* 259 Federal, 1919, 369. See *The Pesaro,* 13 Fed. 2d, 1926, 468. The leading case contra is *The Pesaro,* 277 Federal 473, which was reversed in 271 U. S., 1926, 562. The *Gul Djmal* is sometimes cited as contra. 264 U. S. 90. However the *Gul Djmal* was not a government operated vessel, so that the cases can be squared by the essential difference in their facts. On the probable decision of the Supreme Court see, *The United States vs. Sisal Sales Corporation,* 274 U. S., 1927, 268, seemingly holding a Mexican public corporation liable for violation of the anti-trust laws. No cases are cited in accord. The Department of Justice has given it as its opinion that immunity from process would not attach.

[85] "The right of immunity of a foreign government from suit is not based upon absolute right by virtue of its absolute sovereignty, but upon international comity." *Wulfsohn vs. Russian Socialist Federated Soviet* Republic, 195 N. Y. Supp., 1922, 472 at 474. This basis was first given by Mr. Chief Justice Marshall in *The Exchange vs. McFaddon,* 7 Cranch, 1812, 116.

in a manner commensurate with its dignity and rights.[86] It was originally considered to be the legal consequence of the absolute independence of every sovereign authority.[87] More recently, however, the courts have placed the immunity of foreign sovereigns upon the same basis as the domestic sovereign.[88]

Questions have been raised as to the method by which a foreign sovereignty should raise the question of its sovereign immunity. Suffices to say that the government may appear and set up its jurisdictional claims, or its accredited representatives may appear and take the same steps. If there is any objection to such an appearance the government may present its asserted public status through the usual diplomatic channels. If the asserted claim is recognized by the executive department of our government, it may be set forth in appropriate suggestion to the court by the Attorney-General of the United States, or by some law officer acting under his direction.[89]

---

[86] *The Santissima Trinidad,* 7 Wheaton, 1822, 282 at 352 and 355.

[87] The *Parlement Belge,* L. R., 1880, 5 P. D. 197. "We are of the opinion," said Lord Justice Brett of the Court of Appeal, "that the proposition deduced from the earlier cases (referring especially to *The Exchange,* supra) . . . is the correct exposition of the law or nations, viz., that as a consequence of the absolute independence of every sovereign authority and of the international comity which induces every sovereign state to respect the independence of every other sovereign state, each and every one declines to exercise by means of any of its courts, any of its territorial jurisdiction over the person of any sovereign or ambassador of any other state, or over the public property of any state which is destined to its public use, or over the property of any ambassador, though such sovereign, ambassador or property be within its territory, and therefore, but for the common agreement, subject to its jurisdiction," p. 217.

[88] Mr. Justice Holmes in *Kawananakoa vs. Polyblank,* 205 United States 349 at 353 declares that "some doubts have been expressed as to the source of the immunity . . . but the answer has been public property since before the days of Hobbes., Leviathan, Ch. 26, 2. . . . '*Car on peut bien recevoir loy d' autruy, mais il est impossible por nature de se donner loy.*' Bodin, *Republique,* 1, c. 8. Ed. 1629, p. 132."

[89] The method is discussed by the court in *De Simone vs. Transportes Maritimos Do Estado,* 199 App. Div. N. Y. 602, 191 N. Y. Supp. 864. See also, *Attestation by Foreign Government through Amici Curiae,* Univ. of Penna. Law Review, 1921, v. 69, pp. 385–386.

CHAPTER VII

Extraterritorial Operation of Acts of Recognized and Unrecognized Governments

After coming into power in November 1917, the Russian Socialist Federated Soviet Republic proceeded to " relieve the working man from the exploitation of capital," and provide for " the proper organization of national economic life." It did this through a series of nationalization decrees.[1] The decrees covered such businesses as shipping, manufacturing, woodworking, banking[2] and insurance.[3] They declared these businesses to be monopolies of the state, confiscated their properties and proceeded to dissolve the companies engaged therein. The decrees were signed by Lenin as Chairman of the Council of the People's Commissaries.

They had scarcely been signed before the courts of non-recognizant states were compelled to consider their extra-territorial effects. Modern financial and commercial relations between states have become so intimately interwoven that the decrees of the Soviet Republic entailed repercussions throughout the globe. It became incumbent upon the English and American courts to determine the legality of such decrees, and their task has been neither pleasant nor easy.[4]

---

[1] Translations of some of the decrees may be found in the judgment of Viscount Cave in the case of *Russian Commercial and Industrial Bank vs. Comptoir d'Escompte de Muhouse,* 93 L. J. B. N. S., 1098 at 1099 to 1107, 40 T. L. R. 837; 1925, A. C. 112 before House of Lords.

[2] *Gurdus vs. Philadelphia National Bank,* 273 Penna., 1922, 110, 116 Atl. 672; Sokoloff vs. National City Bank, 239 N. Y. 158, 145 N. E. 917.

[3] *Hennenlotter vs. Norwich Union Fire Insurance Company,* 124, Misc., (N. Y.), 1924, 626, 207 N. Y. Supp. 588. Other cases are covered in later notes. See P. Wohl, *Nationalisation of Joint Stock Banking Corporations in Soviet Russia and its Bearing on Their Legal Status Abroad,* 75 U. of Pa. L. Rev., 1927, 385, 527, 622.

[4] Anarchical legislation produces results " difficult to fit in with the leg-

If recognition has been accorded by the political departments of the government, no difficulty is involved.[5] In such cases the laws, acts and decrees of the government are accepted as valid and binding upon the courts as a rule for their decisions, unless such laws, acts or decrees are contrary to law or the public policy of the recognizant state.[6] Legal effect must be given to such acts regardless of what the courts may think of the wisdom or justice of the acts in question. Furthermore, it is immaterial whether the foreign power has been recognized as a *de jure* or only as a *de facto* government. These issues were considered at length in a preceding chapter and will not be reconsidered here.

The cases of gravest concern to the courts have been those arising out of *de facto* situations to which recognition at the time remained unaccorded. The cases in point have centered chiefly around the *de facto* situation in Russia, and in most instances the issue has been raised in the form of a defense. In each instance the important issue before the court has been the exact extraterritorial effect to be given to the acts, laws and decrees of the unrecognized government.

In two classes of cases the law is well settled. In the first place, the courts have uniformily held that individuals who

---

islation of orderly States. The judges can only endeavor to apply settled principles; legislation, or abstention by the Sovereign from recognition of anarchical States, must do the rest." Lord Justice Scrutton, *Banque Internationale de Commerce vs. Goukassow,* 1923, L. R. 2 K. B. 693.

[5] "It is not an agreeable task for a British court of justice to consider the effect of a series of decrees and orders providing for the compulsory acquisition by a foreign state of the assets of private persons 'on the basis of complete confiscation.' But the Soviet government has been recognized by Great Britain as the lawful government of Russia; and this being so its decrees must . . . be treated by the courts of this country as binding so far as the jurisdiction of the Russian government extends. . . ." Viscount Cave, *Russian Commercial & Industrial Bank vs. Comptoir d'Escompte de Mulhouse,* supra.

[6] *Oetjen vs. Central Leather Co.,* 246 U. S., 1918, 397. See also Max Habicht, *The Application of Soviet Laws and the Exception of Public Order,* 21 A. J., 1927, 238; O. K. Fraenkel, *Juristic Status of Foreign States,* 25 Colum. Law Rev., 1925, 668; E. D. Dickinson, *Unrecognized Government or State in English and American Law,* 22 Mich. Law Rev., 1923, 29 and 118; L. Connick, *Effect of Soviet decrees in American Courts,* 34 Yale Law Jl., 1925, 499.

have submitted to the *de facto* situation are protected against subsequent prosecution in the courts of the recognizant state. In the second place the courts will not give extraterritorial effect to confiscation by unrecognized factions where the confiscated property is carried within the jurisdiction of the adjudicating court.

Cases of the first type were originally presented to the Supreme Court of the United States in 1819. The first case was *United States vs. Rice.*[7] The Supreme Court held that goods which had been brought into the United States through a port which was under the control of the British during the War of 1812 could not be held for further import duties.[8] The sovereignty of the United States was suspended during its occupation by the British forces, and for all practical purposes the port was during such occupation a foreign port. The court recognized the validity of the demands of the faction in *de facto* control and held that importers were protected from the payment of further duties.[9]

A more recent case also involved the payment of import duties to a military faction.[10] An action was brought against

---

[7] 4 Wheaton, 1819, 246.

[8] A similar issue was raised in *Fleming vs. Page,* 9 Howard, 1850, 603 where an action was brought to recover customs duties which had been paid upon goods imported into Philadelphia from Tampico, Mexico. The issue before the court was whether Tampico, at the time, was under the dominion of the United States to such an extent that no duties were payable. The Supreme Court denied the contention; it held that Tampico was a foreign port and that the goods were liable to duty. However, the case turned upon the construction of an act of Congress. Yet the court did say that "other nations were bound to regard the country, while our possession continued, as the territory of the United States, and to respect it as such." Mr. Chief Justice Taney, at p. 615.

[9] Protection for individual acts was also raised in *Underhill vs. Hernandez.* A suit for damages arose out of alleged unlawful detention in time of civil war. Judgment was given for the defendant by the district, circuit and supreme courts. The courts held that judicially no relief could be had by reason of the acts of a government: that where acts occur in the course of a political revolt as the result of actual war, no liability can be based thereon, even when the revolt fails. The court said: "Redress of grievances by reason of such acts must be obtained through the means open to be availed of by sovereign powers as between themselves." 168 U. S., 1897, 250 at 252. The *American Banana Company vs. United Fruit Company* is sometimes cited in point, but a doubt may be expressed as to whether this case is in accord with the others. 213 U. S., 1909, 347.

[10] *MacLeod vs. United States,* 229 U. S., 1913, 416.

the United States, to recover for duties paid during the military occupation of the Philippine Islands, for imports to the Island of Cebu which was then in the control of certain Philippine insurgents. The duties had been paid to the rebel authorities. The Supreme Court remanded the case to the Court of Claims with instructions to enter judgment for the claimants, holding that the claimants having acted in compliance with the orders of the *de facto* government were protected from further exactions. The court felt that such duties, collected on cargoes imported at ports which had not been reduced to possession by the United States but were in possession of the *de facto* government of insurgents, were an illegal and unwarranted exaction.[11] The government was one of paramount force comparable to that discussed in *Thorington vs. Smith*.[12] The claimants were entitled to protection for their past acts.

A case somewhat analogous to *MacLeod vs. United States* had arisen in 1899.[13] An insurrectionary movement of Bluefields, headed by one General Heyes, had acquired undisputed control of the Mosquito Territory in Nicaragua. His control continued from February 3, to February 25, 1899. Then subsequent to the reestablishment of Nicaraguan authority over the territory, the government demanded of American merchants the payment to it of certain duties which, during the interregnum, they had been compelled to pay to the insurgent authorities in *de facto* control. The United States government remonstrated. The duties were, by agreement, deposited in the British Consulate pending a settlement of the controversy.[14] The United States in-

[11] "The statement of the facts shows that the insurgent government was in actual possession of the Custom house at Cebu, with power to enforce the collection of duties there, as it did." 229 U. S., 1913, 416 at 428.

[12] 8 Wallace, 1869, 1 at pp. 8–10.

[13] *The Bluefields case*, 1 Moore, *Digest*, p. 49.

[14] The Department of State received the sworn statements of the American merchants that they were not accomplices of General Reyes, that the money actually exacted was the amount due on bonds which then matured for duties levied the preceding December, that payment was made to the

sisted that her nationals should be protected: that to demand a second payment would be "an act of international injustice."[15]

The money was returned to the American merchants with the assent of the Government of Nicaragua. An attempt was made to compel the American merchants to establish their defense in the Nicaraguan courts. The United States objected that the question had become a diplomatic one, and the attempt failed.

The State Department insisted that individuals subject to the jurisdiction of a *de facto* government, who had paid import duties in pursuance of its orders must be protected against penalties for obedience to such commands.[16] Likewise the courts hold that individuals must be protected for similar acts done in obedience to *de facto* governments.

Let us now turn to the second class of cases; those which involve title to property found within the non-recognizant state, where the property has formerly been seized by *de facto* authorities. There are only two cases on the point.

titular head who was continued in office by General Reyes, that payment was demanded under threat of suspension of importations, and that from February 3, to February 25, 1899, General Reyes was in full control of the civil and military agencies of the Mosquito Territory. On these facts the United States expressed the opinion that to exact the second payment would be "an act of international injustice."

[15] Moore, *Digest,* Vol. 1, p. 51.

[16] A similar case had arisen a quarter of a century before in which the United States was requested by Great Britain to use its good offices to prevent the exaction by the Mexican Government of certain duties of Mazatlan, which duties had been previously paid to insurgents. Mr. Fish, Secretary of State, in his instructions to Mr. Nelson, our Minister to Mexico, said that it was difficult to understand upon what ground of equity or public law such duties could be claimed. The United States felt that "the obligation of obedience to a government at a particular place in a country may be regarded as suspended, at least, when its authority is usurped, and is due to the usurpers if they choose to exercise it. To require a repayment of duties in such cases is tantamount to the exaction of a penalty on the misfortune, if it may be so called, of remaining and carrying on business in a part where the authority of the government had been annulled. . . ." He referred to *United States vs. Rice* and to the cases which arouse out of the Civil War. With reference to the latter he said: "Since the close of the Civil War in this country, suits have been brought against importers for duties on merchandise paid to insurgent authorities. Those suits, however, have been discontinued." Moore, *Digest,* Vol. 1, p. 49.

One is an early American case. The other is a recent English decision.

The first case, *The Nueva Anna and Liebre,* was before the Supreme Court of the United States in 1821.[17] The Spanish owners of two vessels, which had been captured and condemned under the authority of the Mexican Republic, libelled them in the American courts. In the absence of any kind of recognition of the Mexican Republic on the part of the United States, the Supreme Court stated that it "could not consider as legal, any acts done under the flag and commission of such republic or state."[18] The Supreme Court regarded the capture, under such purported authority, as a nullity. No cases or authorities were cited in the decision.[19]

The other case in point came before the English courts in 1921.[20] The court held that in the absence of any recognition by the political departments, the seizure in Russia of plywood subsequently brought to England, was to be regarded as void. The court implied that validity to acts of seizure would be given effect only as a matter of comity. The case was reversed on appeal because of the retroactive effect of subsequent *de facto* recognition.[21] Nevertheless, the Court of Appeal approved the determination of the court below on the facts as they then stood. A dictum to the same effect was expressed by the first department of the supreme court of New York on an appeal in *Bourne vs. Bourne* in 1924.[22]

---

[17] 6 Wheaton 193.

[18] *Ibid.*, pp. 193–194.

[19] A dictum to the same effect by the same court may be found in *Williams vs. Bruffy,* 96 U. S., 1877, 176.

[20] *Luther vs. Sagor,* 1921, L. R. 3 K. B. 532.

[21] *Ibid.*

[22] 209 App. Div., (N. Y.), 419 at 427, referring to the Singer Sewing Machine Company. "The Company had been doing business in all parts of the world. Subsidiary companies had been organized throughout Europe. . . . Prior to December 31, 1918, the revolution in Russia had taken place and certain alleged decrees or edicts pronounced by means of which the confiscation of much property was intended to be brought about. This government has never recognized the revolutionary government of Russia and such decrees have no force or effect and are of no importance except as

In numerous recent cases the courts, more especially the New York Court of Appeals, have implied that effect would be given to other decrees, laws and acts of unrecognized *de facto* governments in so far as justice would thereby be accomplished. Some of the justices, especially Judge Cardozo, have felt that " justice and common sense " require the court to give some effect to the factual situation in Russia.[23]

The germ of the " justice and common sense view " is found in the cases of the nineteenth century.[24] It found expression in numerous cases which turned upon the validity of decrees of the Confederate States. The Supreme Court of the United States sustained numerous acts relating to the creation of domestic corporations,[25] the sale of property,[26] and payment of debts in the specie of the regime.[27] It generally upheld all laws which were necessary to the peace and good order of the realm, such as sanctioning and protecting marriage, determining laws of descent, regulating the transfer of property and providing legal redress for injuries.[28] The Civil War cases involve the rule in its positive form: in each instance the acts, decrees or laws are recognized as valid by the Supreme Court unless public policy and justice required otherwise.

The genesis of the inverted exception of justice and public policy in recent years is to be found in Judge Cardozo's dictum in *Sokoloff vs. National City Bank*.[29] In June, 1917,

---

interesting facts tending to fix dates." (*Russian Commercial and Industrial Bank vs. Comptoir d'Escompte de Mulhouse,* 1923 L. R. 2 K. B. 630.) The Singer Sewing Machine Company lost approximately $75,000,000 under the nationalization decrees.

23 *Sokoloff vs. National City Bank,* 239 N. Y., 1924, 158, 145 N. E. 910. The same doctrine was reaffirmed the following year, 1924, in *James vs. Second Russian Insurance Company,* 239 N. Y. 248, 146 N. E. 369.

24 *United States vs. Rice,* 4 Wheaton, 1819, 246. The same idea runs through *MacLeod vs. United States,* 229 U. S. 1913, 416.

25 *United States vs. Insurance Companies,* 22 Wallace, 1874, 99.

26 *Thorington vs. Smith,* 8 Wallace, 1868.

27 *Delmas vs. Merchants National Insurance Company,* 14 Wallace, 1871, 661.

28 *Texas vs. White,* 7 Wallace, 1868, 700; *Williams vs. Bruffy,* 96 U. S., 1877, 176; *Baldy vs. Hunter,* 171 U. S., 1897, 388.

29 239 N. Y., 1924, 158.

one Sokoloff paid over $30,225 to the National City Bank of New York, in New York, to be repaid in rubles at its branch bank at Petrograd. A contract to that effect was entered into by the parties. In November 1917, and February 1918, certain checks of the plaintiff were dishonored at the Petrograd branch although the plaintiff's books showed a balance of $28,365. Thereupon Sokoloff brought an action in the New York courts against the National City Bank to rescind the contract.

The National City Bank defended that the Soviet government had nationalized all private banks, that Sokoloff's deposit at Petrograd had been seized and his title divested, and that therefore the bank's liability had been discharged. Sokoloff contended that the Soviet Republic was not recognized by the United States, and that in the absence of recognition, either *de jure* or *de facto,* the laws and decrees of the Soviets should be accorded no force. The court decided that the decrees, even though of an unrecognized government, might be given quasi-governmental validity by the court if justice and public policy demanded it. However, the court held that public policy did not require recognition of the decrees in the case before the court. Judge Cardozo wrote the opinion.

The court acknowledged that other courts of high repute had held that confiscation by a government to which recognition has been refused has no more effect in law than seizure by lawless bodies.[30] "It would be hazardous," said Judge Cardozo, "none the less, to say that a rule so comprehensive and so drastic is not subject to exception under pressure or some insistent claim of policy or justice.

"Juridically, a government that is unrecognized may be viewed as no government at all, if the power withholding

[30] *Russian Commercial and Industrial Bank vs. Comptoir d'Escompte de Mulhouse,* 1923, L. R. 2 K. B. 630 at 638; *Banque Internationale de Commerce vs. Goukassow,* 1923, L. R. 2 K. B. 682; *Luther vs. Sagor,* 1921, L. R. 1 K. B. 456; *Child & Beney vs. Simmons,* 1922, 127 L. T. N. S. 571.

recognition chooses thus to view it. In practice, however, since juridicial conceptions are seldom, if ever, carried to the limit of their logic, the equivalence is not absolute, but is subject to self-imposed limitations of common sense and fairness, as we learned in litigations following our Civil War." [31]

Violence to our own fundamental principles of justice in the instant case did not require that the courts give validity to the acts in question. The defendant was not a bailee: the *res* was not a physical object committed to the plaintiffs keeping, but a *chose in action,* a right to receive rubles in the future under an executory contract. The Soviet government could not terminate the charter of the National City Bank which had been formed under the laws of New York rather than of Russia, so that the defense fell to the ground. " Everything in Russia might have been destroyed by fire or flood, by war or revolution," said the court, and still the " defendant would have remained bound by its engagements." The court gave judgment for the plaintiff. The case is im-

[31] " In those litigations acts or decrees of the rebellious governments, which, of course, had not been recognized as governments *de facto,* were held to be nullities when they worked injustice to citizens of the Union or were in conflict with its public policy. . . . On the other hand acts or decrees that were just in operation and consistent with public policy were sustained not infrequently to the same extent as if the governments were lawful. . . . These analogies suggest the thought that, subject to like restrictions, effect may at times be due to the ordinances of foreign governments which, though formally unrecognized, have notoriously an existence as governments *de facto.* Consequences appropriate enough when recognition is withheld on the ground that rival factions are still contending for the mastery may be in need of readjustment before they can be fitted to the practice, now a growing one, of withholding recognition whenever it is thought that a government, functioning unhampered, is unworthy of a place in the Society of Nations. Limitations upon the general rule may be appropriate for the protection of one who has been the victum of spoliation, though they would be refused to the spoliator or to others claiming under him. We leave these questions open. At the utmost, they suggest the possibility that a body or group which has vindicated by the course of events its pretensions to sovereign power, but which has forfeited by its conduct the privileges or immunities of sovereignty, may gain for its acts and decrees a validity quasi-governmental if violence to fundamental principles of justice or to our own public policy might otherwise be done.

"We think the defendant, though we were to assume the existence of such exceptions to the need of recognition, has not brought itself within them." *Sokoloff vs. National City Bank,* 239 N. Y. 158, 145 N. E. 917 at 918 and 919.

portant because it holds that no extraterritorial effect will be given to the decrees of an unrecognized government unless justice and public policy require it. They did not require it in the instant case.

Two months later the same court had occasion to examine the extraterritorial effects of similar decrees in the case of *James and Company vs. Second Russian Insurance Company.*[32] A Russian corporation doing business in New York, contracted to pay a marine insurance policy issued to the plaintiff's assignor. Losses were sustained, and in a suit by the plaintiff on the contract the defendant denied its existence as a corporation. It argued that inasmuch as it was a Russian corporation its corporate life had been termined by a decree of the Soviet government nationalizing the business of insurance companies in Russia. The defendant moved that the plaintiff be directed to reply to their defense. Thereupon, four questions relating to the essence of the defense were certified to the Court of Appeals. Judge Cardozo, speaking for the Court of Appeals, said that the confiscation decrees of Russia were obviously not a defense at all.[33]

Following *Sokoloff vs. National City Bank,*[34] he held that the decree had no effect in the United States, "unless it may be, to such extent as justice and public policy require that effect be given." Justice and public policy did not require that the defendant in the instant case should be pronounced immune from suit. The defendant had complied with the provisions of the New York statutes prescribing the terms under which foreign insurance companies might do business in the state. It had written policies of insurance covering millions of dollars worth of property risks and had

[32] 239 N. Y., 1925, 248, 146 N. E. 369.

[33] "A corporation with vitality sufficient to answer a complaint has, by the very terms of the hypothesis, vitality sufficient to permit it to be sued. The shades of dead defendants do not appear and plead." 239 N. Y. 248 at 251.

[34] 239 N. Y., 1924, 158, 145 N. E. 917.

collected the premiums on the same. Such facts showed conclusively that its corporate life had not been terminated.

The court declared that the case was not governed by any technical rules regarding recognition or non-recognition. It was governed by the largest considerations of public policy and justice. Neither exacted an exception in the instant case. Russia might terminate the liability of Russian corporations in Russian courts or under Russian law. But, "its fiat to that effect could not constrain the courts of other sovereignties, if assets of the debtor were available for seizure in the jurisdiction of the forum." [35]

A subsequent case came before the New York courts the same year. It was an action by the Russian Reinsurance Company against Stoddard and the Bankers Trust Company, to recover certain securities which had been deposited in accordance with the New York law to guarantee the performance of insurance contracts. The action was opposed upon the ground that the plaintiff corporation had been dissolved by Soviet decrees: that it was incapable of maintaining a suit in the New York courts.

The directors of the Russian Reinsurance Company had met in Paris after the Soviet Revolution. There they took steps looking to the termination of the trust agreement in New York and the recovery of the deposited securities. The Supreme Court held that the attempted revocation of the trust agreement was invalid: that the corporation had been dissolved by the Soviet decrees. This decision was reversed by an appellate division of the Supreme Court.[36] The Court

---

[35] *Fred S. James & Co. vs. Second Russian Insurance Co.*, 239 N. Y., 1925, 248 at 252. Same case before the appellate division of the supreme court in 208 App. Div., 1924, 141 and 210 App. Div., 1924, 82. "One government does not . . . help another in enforcing a penalty or forfeiture. . . . If this is so where the foreign statute or decree is that of a recognized government *de jure*, it is still more clearly so where the decree is that of a government to which recognition has been denied. Neither comity nor public policy requires us to enforce a mandate of confiscation at the behest of such a government to the prejudice either of our own citizens or of those of a friendly power seeking justice in our courts," Judge Cardozo, p. 257.

[36] 240 N. Y., 1925, 149.

of Appeals in turn reversed this determination and reinstated the opinion of the trial court.[37]

The Court of Appeals based its decision almost entirely on the possibility that subsequent recovery might be had by the Soviet government against the Bankers Trust Company. True, such recovery could not be had in the courts of the United States, because it would not be supposed that the State Department would recognize a government without requiring the recognized government to abide by any decisions which had been rendered by the courts of the United States, but that did not preclude a recovery against the Bankers Trust Company in some other country which had recognized the Soviet regime.

The court felt that it was repulsive to common sense and justice to declare that the Soviet decrees were of no force in the instant case.[38] Both required that the court give effect

[37] 211 App. Div. N. Y., 131.

[38] "For us the law of Russia, in its strict sense, may still be the law as it existed when the czar ruled, for other nations the law of Russia is the law sanctioned by the Soviet Republic. Our view of what is the law of Russia rests upon a juridical conception not always in consonance with fact; in other nations recognition has brought juridical conceptions and facts into harmony. Do these juridical conceptions require us to hold that the law of Russia has remained unchanged since December, 1917; that the Soviet Republic does not exist, and therefore cannot act; that the plaintiff corporation still lives and is domiciled in Russia, and is under the management of its former directors; though we know that its property in Russia has been sequestrated, its directors driven into exile, its business monopolized by an agency which enforces its decrees as if it were a government and is recognized as a government by most of the countries of Europe? Shall we recognize the right of the corporate directors to revoke the deed of trust and to receive property deposited thereunder though their authority is no longer recognized in the country of the corporate domicile, or in the country where the directors reside; though they might probably urge the non-existence of the corporation as a defense to any action brought by policyholders, creditors or stockholders in any forum which gives effect to the decree of nationalization made by the Soviet Republic, and the corporation will be immune from suit here after it withdraws from this jurisdiction? If the logical application of juridical conceptions leads to this result, then we should consider its practical consequences to determine whether we have not been carried beyond the "self-imposed limits of common sense and fairness." We shall not attempt to collate the authorities in order to deduce from them a new general rule which will define these limits. The very nature of the problem shows that general definitions must hamper rather than promote its solution. The facts of each case, the result of each possible decision determines whether that decision accords with common sense and justice.

to the conditions existing in Russia, even though those conditions were created by a force which the court was not ready to acknowledge as entitled to recognition as a government.

On denial of a motion for reargument,[39] the court said that it did not hold that it could not take jurisdiction of some other action in which some measure of relief might be granted which would be fair to the plaintiff and yet afford adequate protection to the defendant. The motion for a reargument was denied " without prejudice to the commencement of a new action for such relief." The court held only that considerations of justice and fairness to the defendant required that the instant case be dismissed.

A slightly different approach was made in *Andre vs. Beha*.[40] A stockholder of a Russian insurance corporation attempted to recover certain assets which had been deposited with the New York Superintendent of Insurance and a trustee prior to the deposition of the czar. The case differed from *Russian Reinsurance vs. Stoddard*,[41] in that the company had done no business in New York since 1917. The plaintiff was not only a stockholder, but also manager of the company under a broad power of attorney issued to him in 1918. The Supreme Court directed the Superintendent of Insurance and the trustee to deliver the securities to the plaintiff upon his receipt.

There can be no true precedent in the books when the facts are unprecedented. It remains for us to determine whether the result of the present judgment is contrary to common sense and justice. . . .

"We grant admission to the courts of this state to foreign corporations because of comity. We have not admitted to our comity the Soviet Republic, and the plaintiff denies allegiance to it. The claims based upon comity with a government of the czar, which may exist as a juridical concept, but is in fact not functioning and is without representative here is tenuous. It should not prevail where injustice follows to one of our own nationals. . . .

"To the extent that until that time the courts should not take jurisdiction of this equitable cause of action, both justice and common sense require us to give effect to the conditions existing in Russia, though those conditions are created by a force which we are not ready to acknowledge as entitled to recognition as a state or government." 240 N. Y., 1925, 149, *passim*.

39 240 N. Y., 682 memorandum decision.

40 211 App. Div. (N. Y.), 1924, 380.

41 240 N. Y., 1925, 149. See also *First Russian Insurance Co. vs. Beha*, 240 N. Y., 1925, 601, for a similar case.

An appellate division of the Supreme Court reversed this decision and dismissed the complaint. This court held that the proper proceeding was for a liquidation in accordance with the insurance law of the state, or else the appointment of a receiver as provided by the general corporation laws. It declared that one of the methods suggested should be resorted to in order to protect the creditors, policyholders and stockholders.[42] This decision was affirmed by the Court of Appeals. It held that the plaintiff had no capacity to sue. The court did not discuss the questions relating to Russia, yet, in view of its silence, it may be inferred that the Court of Appeals acquiesced in the opinion of the lower court that to allow the instant suit " would seem to be a travesty on justice." [43]

It has been alleged that one decision of the Court of Appeals of New York in *contra* to the dicta in the Sokoloff and subsequent cases. This is the *Joint Stock Company of Volgakama Oil and Chemical Factory vs. National City Bank.*[44] Plaintiff was a Russian corporation. It sought to recover a deposit made in 1918. The defendant claimed that the plaintiff's entity had been destroyed by the Soviet decrees. The defense was disallowed and judgment given and affirmed in favor of the plaintiff.[45] The courts held that

[42] "The undisputed evidence in this case, according to Andre himself," said the court, " is that the company's property was destroyed and sequestered by the Soviet government in 1918. Whether we can regard such seizure as legal or illegal, the fact remains that the company was destroyed by a *de facto* government then and still in power in the country which gave this corporation its birth. It never had birth or legal sanction to exist in this country at all. It did have a license to carry on business here, as a foreign corporation, upon compliance with our laws applicable to such situation. These laws require that the very cash and securities which Andre now seeks should be deposited here as a protection to creditors and policyholders; and these deposits are now here, safely on deposit in accordance with the law. To allow them to be taken out by the plaintiff in the peculiar action sought to be maintained here, without any security or protection to the owners of the property, whether they be policyholders, creditors, or stockholders, would seem to be a travesty on justice." 211 App. Div., N. Y., 380 at 394.

[43] 240 N. Y., 1925, 149.

[44] 240 N. Y., 1925, 368.

[45] 210 App. Div., 1924, 665.

the decrees of the Soviet government would not be considered because of non-recognition. Also the defendant was estopped from raising the defense because it had dealt with the plaintiff as a corporate entity.[46]

This decision was unanimously affirmed by the Court of Appeals, which held that the defendant's corporate entity had not been destroyed by the Soviet decrees.[47] Judge Crane wrote the opinion. He said that unless the "alleged decrees, as stated by the defendant, show that the plaintiff has ceased to exist as a corporation in the land of its creation, the defendant's answer is insufficient and it must pay back the deposit according to its agreement. No matter what has happened to the plaintiff's property or to its method and means of conducting business, if it be a fact that it still exists as a corporation, it is entitled to its property, and may maintain this action." [48] The court examined the decrees relied upon by the defendant. It found that there was "nothing to show that 'nationalization' terminated the plaintiff's corporate existence, or that all its rights to exist in some form had ceased."

But Judge Crane, who wrote the opinion of the Court of Appeals, said that even if the defendant's contention was correct and the facts showed that the Soviet government had actually and effectually terminated the plaintiff's corporate existence so that for all purposes it had ceased to be a corporation in the state of its creation, he personally would be of the opinion that the courts of the United States should not recognize the Soviet decrees in an action at law such as the instant case. Numerous cases, chiefly from the New York

[46] Judge McAvoy, who delivered the opinion of the court, said: "Having dealt with the plaintiff as a corporate entity, received the money it holds from plaintiff in its apparent guise, and assumed the obligation to pay out the fund according to its contract as a depository, it cannot equitably be heard now to deny the corporate existence of its depositor to escape liability on its obligation." 210 App. Div., 1924, 665 at 570.

[47] 240 N. Y., 1925, 368.

[48] *Ibid.*, at 374.

Court of Appeals, are cited in support of his position.[49] An examination reveals that these are the very cases in which that court enunciated the exception in favor of justice and public policy, so that the instant case reaffirms rather than denies the exception. In fact it may well be argued that the appellate division of the Supreme Court had recognized the exception inasmuch as Judge McAvoy held that the defendant could not equitably be heard to deny the corporate existence of its depositor in order to escape liability.[50]

In the above cases the courts allowed the suits to be prosecuted by the Russian corporations, or their assignees, despite the contention that the corporations had been destroyed. The courts did not feel that justice and public policy required that the suits be disallowed, although such considerations prevent the Soviet Republic as such from instituting any suits in our courts.

There is a latent danger in such decisions, in that all of the parties in interest may not be before the court. In case of recognition of the Soviet regime by the United States these results would be further complicated by the retroactive effect of such recognition. Some means should be devised whereby the proceeds of such litigations can be protected from dissipation by irresponsible persons and until the rights of all parties in interest are satisfied.

---

[49] *Sokoloff vs. National City Bank*, 239 N. Y. 158; *James & Co. vs. Second Russian Insurance Co.*, 239 N. Y., 248; *Wulfsohn vs. Russian Socialist Federated Soviet Republic*, 234 N. Y. 372; R. S. F. S. R. 235 N. Y. 255; *Gibbs vs. Societe Industrielle des Metaux*, 1890, 25 Q. B. D. 399.

[50] This view has received its latest affirmation in *James & Co., vs. Rossia Insurance Co.*, 247 N. Y., 1928, 262 at 269 where Mr. Justice O'Brien said: "In normal times under a government recognized by our own as a sovereign even *de facto*, the question of authority to effect the transfer *of title to property located in New York* might become the subject of serious doubt. If the decrees of the Soviet Republic were for all purposes accorded full credit by our government . . . the Russian corporation on April 1, 1919, might be regarded as dead, its assets confiscated by the Republic, its liabilities obliterated and its directors mere fugitives and refugees shorn of all power even to conserve its property amid the chaos of revolution. We have never recognized that government. Its decrees are treated as a nullity except in so far as there is need to recognize them for the purpose of promoting justice and equity as we regard justice and equity." Italics ours.

The dictum of Judge Cardozo in the Sokoloff case has served as a basis on which the courts have gradually evolved the new rule. The refusal of the political departments to hold official intercourse with the Soviet Republic should not be allowed to affect private rights dependent upon provable existing conditions in Russia. Reason and justice demand that effect should be given in the courts of non-recognizant states to those acts in Russia upon which rights and obligations depend, provided that in so doing the courts neither encroach upon nor dictate a policy to the political departments of the government.

If rights and obligations are to be adjudicated in the American courts, to that extent, at least, effect should be given to the Soviet decrees. This seems all the more necessary where recognition is withheld for a considerable length of time. It is inexpedient for the courts to close their eyes to the present regime in Russia and to presume a continuation of the old order which is inconsonant with the facts and the ends of justice. Judge Cardozo and his associates of the New York Court of Appeals have indicated the legal avenue of escape. The decisions of this court are founded upon both reason and precedent and it is to be hoped that the federal courts will bring their decisions in accord therewith.

CHAPTER VIII

Conclusions

The writer submits that the cases discussed justify the following conclusions. First: Recognition is the admission of the facts of state life. It does not create the state: rather, state life is a condition requisite to recognition. Yet, recognition is necessary before a state or government can assert its fundamental rights of independence, existence and intercourse through diplomatic channels or through the courts of foreign states.

Second: The recognition function is vested in the political departments of the government and may be exercised at their discretion. The judicial branch must act in unison with the political departments in the conduct of foreign relations. Once those departments have acted, whether favorably or unfavorably, the courts are bound thereby. The courts cannot entertain evidence as to the competency or incompetency of a recognized foreign government. They take judicial notice of the acts and decisions of the political departments.

Third: In the absence of a definite attitude, either favorable or unfavorable, on the part of the political departments of the government the courts have a choice of three alternatives. They may regard "the ancient state of things as remaining unaltered," or deny completely the existence of state life, or evaluate the governmental competency as a matter of fact. The first alternative arose from the cases involving the recognition of new states although it has since been applied to new governments in old states. The last two emerged with the shift of governments within recognized states. The majority of the courts have adopted the first alternative: they regard the acts of unrecognized *de facto* governments as of no effect. Some of them even refuse to asknowledge governmental existence in the absence of recognition. When the question of injustice has been raised the courts have replied that the proper remedy is an appeal to the political departments and not to the judiciary. The third alternative is in the ascendency at the present time. Subject to fixed limits, the writer regards it as the best of the three and it may well be that the new problems arising out of the continued non-recognition of the Soviet Republic will be worked out by this method.

Fourth: Recognition is retroactive in its effects. It validates all the official acts of the recognized government, or state, which have been performed within it's jurisdiction since the "commencement of it's existence." The writer concludes that this is too ambiguous and that it would be advisable for the political departments to present their "diary of events" with reference to a government in question to the courts and allow the courts on the basis of these facts to decide in each case before them whether the government in question had "commenced its existence" at the time the acts in litigation were committed.

Fifth: A recognized state with a recognized government may sue in the courts of a recognizant state. Recognized states with unrecognized governments should not be permitted to sue where the political departments of the non-recognizant government have declared against the *de facto* situation. However, in the absence of an adverse determination recognized states with unrecognized governments, subject to two limitations, should be permitted to sue. In the first place the right to sue should depend upon the nature of the action. If it is in any way political it should not be entertained: the suit should be in accord with the public policy of the government of which the court is an instrumentality. In the second place the suit should be brought in the name of the state: not in the name of the government. State property belongs to the national sovereignty. It does not belong to the faction which happens to be in power at a designated moment. If this be true, then the state should be able to protect its property in the courts of foreign states.

The writer is conscious that such a proposal is open to objection in that in case an unrecognized government never achieves recognition a subsequent recognized government might hold the recognizant state to account for all properties which it had turned over to the usurping factions. Also, in so far as non-recognition is an instrument of policy of the political departments it is thereby rendered less effective. Admit that it is open to these objections, nevertheless it seems inequitable that the national sovereignty should be unwillingly deprived of state property.

In order to avoid such injustice and at the same time overcome the objections to such a proposal, the writer concludes that Congress should provide that such properties or the moneys derived therefrom should be held in trust by the United States for the benefit of the recognized state, pending recognition of the government by the political departments. In the absence of such legislation the courts should administer the properties until such time as the political departments deem it expedient to act. The right to suceed to state property located in foreign states should depend upon recognition.

Sixth: A recognized government within a recognized state, together with its diplomatic representatives and governmental property, is immune from process in the courts of a recognizant state. However, there has been confusion among the courts concerning the immunity of state owned property used for commercial purposes. This point remains unsettled in the United States: it should be handled by the political departments of the government. The judicial code should be revised, either to include or to exclude, the new governmental activities.

It may prove expedient to clarify, if not to incorporate, restrictions as to the immunities of commercially-used property through international conventions. Resolutions looking to this end were adopted by the Institute of International Law as early as 1891. The principle was to some extent written into the recent Treaty of Peace with Germany.[1] Further steps in this direction may be looked for in the future as the socialization of the state advances.

Seventh: Where a *de facto* government functions without question, the courts of non-recognizant states should admit this fact and give effect to its acts and decrees in so far as they affect individual rights, where equity and public policy require it to do so, and where such acts are not contrary to the law of the forum. Courts of recognizant states should give effect to the facts which flow from the acts of such governments as fairness requires that it be done. Acting on this principle the courts have held that American corporations doing business in Russia at the time of the confiscatory decrees were not dissolved by the decrees and cannot escape liability on their contracts executed in foreign states to be performed in Russia by setting up the Russian decrees as a defense. Under the same rule Russian corporations doing business in the United States cannot set up their dissolution as a defense in order to escape liability where they have complied with the American laws and have property within the jurisdiction of the court.

The Court of Appeals of New York has repeatedly held that effect should be given to the factual results which flow from the Soviet decrees in so far as it will promote justice. It may be argued that the refusal of the courts to give full effect to such decrees appears to conflict with the rule which holds that the courts of one state will not sit in judgment on the acts of another state, but the latter rule is based on comity

[1] This provision is recited by Judge Mack in his opinion in the initial *Pesaro* decision. See also A. K. Kuhn, *Competence of the Courts in Regard to Foreign States*, 21 A. J., 1927, 742.

and is therefore not applicable to unrecognized governments. Moreover, the law is more than logic.

In saying that effect would be given to the acts of unrecognized governments within recognized states so far as justice and public policy require, the courts have inverted a well established rule which holds that effect will be given to all acts of recognized governments so long as they are not in conflict with public policy or the laws of the forum. The exception of justice and public policy furnishes the legal avenue of escape from the Russian dilemma. It is to be hoped that the federal courts will look with more approval on the doctrine. It evades the encroachment upon the province of the political departments and at the same time reduces the possibilities of international complications. Although the doctrine is unsustained by precedents, in fact is opposed by judicial utterances, yet it is sustained by both reason and analogy. It marks an advance in the law: it demonstrates that the courts have not allowed their eyes to be filled by the dust of obsolete theories or to be blinded to the realities of international life in which the United States stands destined to play a dominant rôle.

FINIS

BIBLIOGRAPHY

Periodicals

American Journal of International Law

Concerning the Recognition of New Governments by the United States, C. C. Hyde, v. 13, 1919, p. 306.

Power of Recognition, C. A. Berdahl, v. 14, 1920, p. 519.

Recognition of New Governments, A. S. Hershey, v. 15, 1921, p. 59.

Suits brought by Foreign States with Unrecognized Governments, Q. Wright, v. 17, 1923, p. 742.

Award of Mr. Chief Justice Taft as the Sole Arbitrator in the Controversy Between Great Britain and Costa Rica, v. 18, 1924, p. 147.

Recent Recognition Cases, comments, v. 19, 1925, p. 263.

Editorial on Difference in Recognition of Government, etc., v. 20, 1926, p. 541.

Application of Soviet Laws and Exception of Public Order, M. Habicht, v. 21, 1927, p. 238.

Competence of the Courts in regard to Foreign States, A. K. Kuhn, v. 21, 1927, p. 742.

American Law Review

Recognition of a New State: Is It an Executive Function?, W. L. Penfield, v. 32, 1898, p. 390.

Recognition in International Law, N. D. Houghton, v. 62, 1928, p. 228.

American Political Science Review

Recognition of the Czechoslovak Nation, comment, v. 12, 1918, p. 715.

Bi-Monthly Law Review

Can the United States Recognize Ireland Without Committing a Breach of International Law in Reference to Great Britain?, L. J. Ward, v. 5, 1922, p. 129.

Boston University Law Review

Recognition of Soviet Russia, E. A. Harriman, v. 5, 1925, p. 15.

Central Law Journal

Recognition of New Governments, C. Pergler, v. 98, 1925, p. 61.

Columbia Law Review

Juristic Status of Foreign States, O. K. Fraenkel, v. 25, 1925, p. 544.

The Constitutional Review
No Recognition of Soviet Russia, comment, v. 7, 1923, 248.
The Question of Recognizing the Soviet, comment, v. 10, 1926, p. 125.
Big Business Refuses Russian Recognition, comment, v. 11, 1927, p. 248.
Cornell Law Quarterly
Actions Against a Foreign Sovereign, F. B. Wettig, v. 10, 1924-1925, p. 390.
The Russian Government in Our Courts, Boardman Wright, v. 11, 1925-1926, p. 49.
Effect in American Courts of the Decree of an Unrecognized Government, Alexander Pirnie, v. 11 1925-1926, p. 99.
Harvard Law Review
Responsibility of the State in England, Harold J. Laski, v. 32, 1918, p. 447.
Actions Against the Property of Sovereigns, Charles H. Weston, v. 32, 1919, p. 266.
Judicial Determination of the Status of Foreign Governments, comment, v. 35, 1919, p. 607.
Michigan Law Review
The Executive, Legislative and Judicial Recognition of International Law in the United States, Charles G. Fenwick, v. 11, 1912, p. 296.
International Recognition and The National Courts, notes, v. 18, 1920, p. 531.
The Unrecognized Government or State in English and American Law, Edwin D. Dickinson, v. 22, 1923, p. 29 and p. 118.
Minnesota Law Review
Recognition of De Facto Governments and the Responsibility of States, J. W. Stinson, v. 9, 1924-1925, p. 1.
North Carolina Law Journal
Extraterritorial Operation of Confiscatory Decrees of the Soviet Government, J. P. Trotter, v. 3, 1924-1925, p. 88.
Saint Louis Law Review
Recognition of Changes in Government, S. McKittrick, v. 2, 1917, p. 37.
Recognition in International Law, O. H. Thormodsgard and R. D. Moore, v. 12, 1927, p. 108.
Solicitor's Journal and Weekly Reporter
Recognition of Governments, comment, v. 62, 1917-1918, p. 359.
Legal Consequences of the Break with Russia, comment, v. 71, 1927, p. 504.
Confiscatory Decrees of Foreign Governments, comment, v. 72, 1928, p. 5.

Texas Law Review
The Effect Upon Private Property Rights of the Acts and Decrees of Revolutionary Governments, W. L. Matthews, v. 4, 1925–1926, p. 226.
Yale Law Journal
A Foreign Sovereign in an American Court: a Novel Case in International Practice, J. W. Foster, v. 9, 1899, p. 283.
Legal Aspects of the Panama Situation, Edwin Maxey, v. 13, 1903, p. 85.
Rights of States under International Law, P. M. Brown, v. 26, 1916, p. 85.
So-called De Facto Recognition, Thomas Baty, v. 31, 1921, p. 469.
Effect of Soviet Decrees in American Courts, Louis Connick, v. v. 34, 1924, p. 499.
Sovereign Immunity, E. Angell, v. 35, 1925, p. 150.
University of Pennsylvania Law Review
Nationalisation of Joint Stock Banking Corporations in Soviet Russia and its bearing on their legal Status abroad, P. Wohl, v. 75, 1927, pp. 385, 527, 622.

Texts and Special Studies

British Yearbook of International Law
1921–1922, 1922–1923, 1923–1924, 1924–1925, 1925–1926.
Brown, Philip Marshall
International Society, New York, 1923.
International Realities, New York, 1917.
Brunet, Rene
New German Constitution, New York, 1922.
Corbett, Pitt
Leading Cases on International Law, London, 1922, vol. 1.
Corpus Juris
Volume 33.
Corwin, E. S.
President's Control of Foreign Relations, Princeton, 1917.
Crandall, S. B.
Treaties: their Making and Enforcement, 2d ed., Washington, 1916.
Davis, G. B.
Elements of International Law, 3d ed., New York, 1908.
Dickinson, E. D.
Equality of States in International Law, Cambridge, 1920.
Duguit, Leon
Law in the Modern State, New York, 1919.

Edmunds, Sterling
Lawless Law of Nations, Washington, 1925.
Foulke, Roland R.
International Law, 2 volumes, Philadelphia, 1920.
Fraenkel, Osmond K.
A Digest of Cases on International Law Relating to Recognition of Governments, American Office of Institute of Soviet Laws of University of Moscow, 1925.
Goebel, Julius, Jr.
Recognition Policy of the United States, New York, 1915.
Hall, W. E.
International Law, Oxford, 1909.
Halleck, H. W.
International Law, 2 volumes, London, 1908.
Hershey, A. S.
Essentials of International Public Law and Organization, New York, 1927.
Houghton, N. D.
De Facto Governments, unpublished manuscript, 1927.
Hyde, C. C.
International Law, 2 volumes, Boston, 1922.
Kent, James
Commentary on International Law, Cambridge (Eng.), 1878.
La Garde, Ernest
La Raconnaissance du Gouvernement des Soviets, Paris, 1924.
Lawrence, T. J.
Principles of International Law, London, 1911.
McBain, H. L. and Rogers, L.
New Constitutions of Europe, Garden City, 1922.
Mathews, John M.
Conduct of American Foreign Relations, New York, 1922.
Moore, John B.
Digest of International Law, 8 volumes, Washington, 1906.
Moyer, G. S.
Attitude of the United States toward the Recognition of the Soviet Republic, Philadelphia, 1926.
Opinions of the Attorney General
Volume 7.
Oppenheim, Lassa Francis Lawrence
International Law, 2 volumes, 3d ed., London, 1920.
United States
Senate Document No. 40, 52d Congress, 2d session.
Ruling Case Law
Volume 15.

Wharton, Francis
Digest of International Law of the United States, 3 volumes. Washington, 1886.
Wheaton, Henry
International Law, 5th English edition, London, 1916.
Wilson, G. G. and Tucker, G. F.
International Law, New York, 1922.
Woolsey, Th. D.
Introduction to the Study of International Law, New York, 1899.

Newspapers

New York Times
December 3, 1913, address of President Wilson.
January 23, 1917, address of President Wilson.
United States Daily
December 13, 1927, report on case of State of Russia vs. Lehigh Valley Railway Company.

INDEX